T0214095

Lecture Notes in Artificial Intelligence   12589

Subseries of Lecture Notes in Computer Science

Series Editors

Randy Goebel
University of Alberta, Edmonton, Canada
Yuzuru Tanaka
Hokkaido University, Sapporo, Japan
Wolfgang Wahlster
DFKI and Saarland University, Saarbrücken, Germany

Founding Editor

Jörg Siekmann
DFKI and Saarland University, Saarbrücken, Germany

More information about this subseries at http://www.springer.com/series/1244

Cristina Baroglio · Jomi F. Hubner ·
Michael Winikoff (Eds.)

Engineering Multi-Agent Systems

8th International Workshop, EMAS 2020
Auckland, New Zealand, May 8–9, 2020
Revised Selected Papers

 Springer

Editors
Cristina Baroglio
Dipartimento di Informatica
Università di Torino
Torino, Torino, Italy

Jomi F. Hubner
Federal University of Santa Catarina
Florianopolis, Santa Catarina, Brazil

Michael Winikoff
School of Information Management
Victoria University of Wellington
Wellington, New Zealand

ISSN 0302-9743   ISSN 1611-3349 (electronic)
Lecture Notes in Artificial Intelligence
ISBN 978-3-030-66533-3   ISBN 978-3-030-66534-0 (eBook)
https://doi.org/10.1007/978-3-030-66534-0

LNCS Sublibrary: SL7 – Artificial Intelligence

This Springer imprint is published by the registered company Springer Nature Switzerland AG
The registered company address is: Gewerbestrasse 11, 6330 Cham, Switzerland

Preface

The International Workshop on Engineering Multi-Agent Systems (EMAS) was formed in 2013 as a merger of three long-running workshops: Agent-Oriented Software Engineering (AOSE), Programming Multi-Agent Systems (ProMAS), and Declarative Agent Languages and Technologies (DALT). This merger established EMAS as a reference venue for work concerned broadly with engineering of agents and multi-agent systems.

The three parent events had a long history of association with the International Conference on Autonomous Agents and Multi-Agent Systems (AAMAS), and since its inception EMAS has been co-located at AAMAS: EMAS 2013 at St. Paul (with post-proceedings published as Springer LNCS/LNAI volume 8245), EMAS 2014 in Paris (LNCS/LNAI 8758, and a special issue in the International Journal of Agent-Oriented Software Engineering (IJAOSE) Vol. 5 No. 2/3, 2016), EMAS 2015 in Istanbul (LNCS/LNAI 9318), EMAS 2016 in Singapore (LNCS/LNAI 10093), EMAS 2017 in São Paulo (LNCS/LNAI 10738), EMAS 2018 in Stockholm (LNAI 11375, and a report in Software Engineering Notes[1]), and EMAS 2019 in Montreal (LNAI 12058).

EMAS 2020 aimed to build on this history by gathering researchers and practitioners in the domains of agent-oriented software engineering, programming multi-agent systems, declarative agent languages and technologies, artificial intelligence, and machine learning to present and discuss their research and emerging results in MAS engineering. The overall purpose of this workshop is to facilitate the cross-fertilisation of ideas and experiences in the various fields to:

1. Enhance our knowledge and expertise in MAS engineering and improve the state of the art
2. Define new directions for MAS engineering that are useful to practitioners, relying on results and recommendations coming from different but contiguous research areas
3. Investigate how practitioners can use or need to adapt established methodologies for the engineering of large-scale and open MAS
4. Encourage masters and PhD students to become involved in and contribute to the area

Like previous editions, this edition of the EMAS workshop was planned to be co-located with AAMAS, which was planned to be held in May, in Auckland, New Zealand. Then Covid-19 happened and borders closed.[2]

---

[1] SIGSOFT Softw. Eng. Notes, 44(1): 18-28. https://doi.org/10.1145/3310013.3322175

[2] On the 19th of March, New Zealand prime minister the Rt Hon Jacinda Ardern announced the closure of the border to all but New Zealand residents and citizens. At the time of writing entry to New Zealand is still very limited, and all arrivals are subject to a two-week isolation/quarantine.

EMAS 2020 was held as a virtual (online) event, spanning two days. It received 14 submissions, each of which was reviewed (single blind) by three reviewers. EMAS 2020 accepted 12 papers (7 full papers, 3 short papers, 1 doctoral paper, and 1 demonstration). In addition to these 12 papers, the chairs also invited presentations from authors of recently published IJAOSE papers, and of relevant AAMAS 2020 Extended Abstracts. The chairs also invited talks from two relevant competitions (see the last two papers in this volume). Finally, we also had an invited talk titled "*Explainable artificial intelligence: beware the inmates running the asylum (or How I learnt to stop worrying and love the social and behavioural sciences)*" by Professor Tim Miller.[3]

The keynote was delivered synchronously over Zoom, but all other talks were pre-recorded. Presentations were kept short (10 minutes for full papers, 5 minutes for short). Participants were provided with a schedule[4] that each followed in their own time zone. This was carefully designed to encourage commitment and engagement, and also to allow people in the same time zone to synchronise and engage both professionally and socially (using Jitsi for video conferencing). Slack was used to discuss the papers, and authors were expected to regularly check for questions, and respond.

Given this novel approach to running EMAS, and that many events are moving online, we feel it might be useful to share lessons learned. A survey of participants after the event found that:

– The approach of having a schedule interpreted in each participant's local time zone was seen very positively (52.2% of respondents said it was a good idea, and 43.5% said it was a very good idea)
– Having short talks was seen very positively (91.3% said it was just right, with 8.7% [two people] indicating they felt it was too short)
– Using Slack for questions and answers was seen as being very effective. On a 1-5 scale (1 = strongly disagree; 5 = strongly agree) no one responded with a 1, 1 person indicated 2, 6 people said 3, 6 said 4, and 10 said 5. The mean of the responses was around 4.1 and the median was 4
– On the other hand, only 1 person used Jitsi
– Overall, participants indicated that, compared with a traditional face-to-face event, they found the experience of:

   • watching pre-recorded presentations better in this online format (1 = much worse, 5 = much better; 3 people responded with 2, 6 with 3, 9 with 4, and 5 with 5; mean = approx. 3.7)
   • discussing papers better in this online format (5 people responded with 2, 7 with 3, 4 with 4, and 5 with 5; mean = approx. 3.6)
   • interacting socially with people worse in this online format (7 people responded with 1, 9 with 2, 5 with 3, and 1 each with 4 and with 5; mean = approx. 2.6)

– All respondents (100%) indicated that EMAS 2020 was useful and enjoyable

---

[3] The talk and slides are available from the EMAS website at: https://emas2020.in.tu-clausthal.de/invited-talk-tim-miller.html.

[4] https://emas2020.in.tu-clausthal.de/schedule.html.

- When asked whether they would prefer to have EMAS 2021 virtual or face-to-face opinions were split between the four options: 17.4% indicated they would prefer returning to face-to-face, 26.1% indicated that they would prefer retaining the online model, 26.1% indicated that they would prefer something else, e.g. some sort of hybrid model, and 30.4% indicated that it depended on details and circumstances

Overall, while the online format was not as successful in facilitating social interaction (hindered also by time zones), the presentations and professional interactions were seen as very effective. We would recommend the model that we used as being highly effective for a similar event.

This volume contains revised selected papers from the workshop, as well as two additional papers about two relevant competitions: the agent programming competition, and the intention progression competition (both papers were submitted for the post-proceedings, and were peer reviewed).

The first paper, by O'Neill *et al.* is the winner of the best paper award at the workshop.

We would like to thank:

- the authors for their work in writing papers, in recording talks, and in engaging on Slack;
- the members of the Program Committee for their reviewing;
- the members of the EMAS Steering Committee for their valuable suggestions and support;
- Associate Professor Matteo Baldoni for designing the EMAS 2020 logo;
- Tim Miller for his fantastic keynote; and
- The AAMAS workshop chairs, Jaime and Mehdi, for all their work and support.

November 2020

Cristina Baroglio
Jomi Fred Hübner
Michael Winikoff

Organization

Program Committee Chairs

Cristina Baroglio   Università degli Studi di Torino, Italy
Jomi Fred Hübner   Federal University of Santa Catarina, Brazil
Michael Winikoff   Victoria University of Wellington, New Zealand

Steering Committee

Matteo Baldoni   Università degli Studi di Torino, Italy
Rafael H. Bordini   PUCRS, Brazil
Mehdi Dastani   Utrecht University, The Netherlands
Juergen Dix   Clausthal University of Technology, Germany
Amal El Fallah Seghrouchni   LIP6 - Pierre and Marie Curie University, France
Brian Logan   University of Nottingham, UK
Jörg P. Müller   TU Clausthal, Germany
Ingrid Nunes   Universidade Federal do Rio Grande do Sul (UFRGS),
                                   Brazil
Alessandro Ricci   University of Bologna, Italy
M. Birna Van Riemsdijk   University of Twente, The Netherlands
Rym Zalila-Wenkstern   The University of Texas at Dallas, USA
Danny Weyns   Katholieke Universiteit Leuven, Belgium
Michael Winikoff   Victoria University of Wellington, New Zealand

Program Committee

Matteo Baldoni   Università degli Studi di Torino, Italy
Luciano Baresi   Politecnico di Milano, Italy
Olivier Boissier   Mines Saint-Étienne, France
Rafael H. Bordini   PUCRS, Brazil
Daniela Briola   University of Milano-Bicocca, Italy
Rafael C. Cardoso   The University of Manchester, UK
Moharram Challenger   University of Antwerp, Belgium
Amit K. Chopra   Lancaster University, UK
Andrei Ciortea   University of St. Gallen, Switzerland
Stefania Costantini   Università degli Studi dell'Aquila, Italy
Mehdi Dastani   Utrecht University, The Netherlands
Maiquel de Brito   Federal University of Santa Catarina, Brazil
Lavindra de Silva   University of Cambridge, UK
Louise Dennis   The University of Manchester, UK
Juergen Dix   TU Clausthal, Germany
Amal El Fallah Seghrouchni LIP6 - Pierre and Marie Curie University, France

Contents

Delivering Multi-agent MicroServices Using CArtAgO 1
   Eoin O'Neill, David Lillis, Gregory M. P. O'Hare, and Rem W. Collier

Aplib: Tactical Agents for Testing Computer Games 21
   I. S. W. B. Prasetya, Mehdi Dastani, Rui Prada, Tanja E. J. Vos,
   Frank Dignum, and Fitsum Kifetew

Exploiting Simulation for MAS Development and Execution—The
JaCaMo-Sim Approach 42
   Alessandro Ricci, Angelo Croatti, Rafael H. Bordini, Jomi F. Hübner,
   and Olivier Boissier

Fragility and Robustness in Multiagent Systems 61
   Matteo Baldoni, Cristina Baroglio, and Roberto Micalizio

Fault Tolerance in Multiagent Systems. 78
   Samuel H. Christie V and Amit K. Chopra

Multi-agent Control of Industrial Robot Vacuum Cleaners 87
   Joe Collenette and Brian Logan

Orthos: A Trustworthy AI Framework for Data Acquisition 100
   Moin Hussain Moti, Dimitris Chatzopoulos, Pan Hui, Boi Faltings,
   and Sujit Gujar

Simulating Vehicular IoT Applications by Combining a Multi-agent System
and Big Data 119
   Ryo Neyama, Sylvain Lefebvre, Masanori Itoh, Yuji Yazawa,
   Akira Yoshioka, Jun Koreishi, Akihisa Yokoyama, Masahiro Tanaka,
   and Hiroko Okuyama

Accept a Challenge: The Multi-Agent Programming Contest: Challenging
Tasks and How to Deal with Them 129
   Tobias Ahlbrecht, Jürgen Dix, Niklas Fiekas, and Tabajara Krausburg

The Intention Progression Competition 144
   Simon Castle-Green, Alexi Dewfall, and Brian Logan

Author Index 153

Delivering Multi-agent MicroServices Using CArtAgO

Eoin O'Neill, David Lillis⊙, Gregory M. P. O'Hare⊙,
and Rem W. Collier(✉)⊙

School of Computer Science, University College Dublin, Dublin, Ireland
eoin.o-neill.3@ucdconnect.ie,
{david.lillis,gregory.ohare,rem.collier}@ucd.ie

Abstract. This paper describes an agent programming language agnostic implementation of the Multi-Agent MicroServices (MAMS) model - an approach to integrating agents within microservices-based architectures. In this model, agents, deployed within microservices, expose aspects of their state as virtual resources that are externally accessible using REpresentational State Transfer (REST). Virtual resources are implemented as CArtAgO artifacts, exposing their state to the agent as a set of observable properties. Coupled with a set of artifact operations, this enables the agent to monitor and manage its own resources. In the paper, we formally model our approach, defining *passive* and *active* resource management strategies, and illustrate its use within a worked example.

Keywords: Multi agent systems · Microservices · CArtAgo

1 Introduction

This paper builds on previous work that has introduced the *Multi-Agent MicroServices (MAMS)* model [24,34]: a model that promotes a view of agents as hypermedia entities whose body includes a set of virtual resources that can be interacted with using REpresentational State Transfer (REST) [10] and can be deployed as microservices. Overall, the work has three main objectives: to facilitate the seamless deployment of Multi-Agent Systems (MAS) within microservices ecosystems; to exploit modern industry tools to enhance the deployment of MAS; and ultimately, to enable the development of an emerging class of systems known as *Hypermedia MAS* [4,5].

The specific focus of this paper is to improve on the approach described in [34] by proposing an agent-programming language independent approach based on CArtAgO [28] and to introduce support for hypermedia links through the use the Hypertext Application Language (HAL) [16] as described in [24]. To achieve this, Sect. 3 describes the refined MAMS model; Sect. 4 introduces the suite of CArtAgO artifacts developed to implement the model; Sect. 5 describes the integration with the ASTRA agent programming language; and Sect. 6 illustrates its use through a worked example. Finally, Sects. 7 and 8 present discussion and concluding remarks.

© Springer Nature Switzerland AG 2020
C. Baroglio et al. (Eds.): EMAS 2020, LNAI 12589, pp. 1–20, 2020.
https://doi.org/10.1007/978-3-030-66534-0_1

2   Related Work

There has been a significant amount of research into the integration of agents and services. A good historical perspective on this can be found in [5]. An excellent overview of agent-based service-oriented computing is provided in [12], with a focus on Web Services technologies. [25] is an excellent recent survey of agent-based cloud computing applications that is heavily focused on agent-based service-oriented computing (in the cloud). Much of it tackles the relationship between agents and services from a more traditional perspective. In this paper, the objective is to focus more closely on the relationship between agents and microservices - an architecture style linked to service-oriented computing that promotes a more decentralised approach to software development.

Microservices are increasingly seen as an important innovator in software design. They champion the decomposition of monolithic systems into loosely-coupled networks of services [33] that are necessary to deliver internet-scale applications [9]. This has the effect of reducing the complexity of many of the components, but comes at the cost of increasing the complexity of deployment [32]. However, this challenge has been met through the rise of DevOps [3] and Continuous Software Engineering methods [23].

The rise of microservices presents an opportunity for Multi-Agent Systems (MAS) research. As is illustrated in [34], there is a strong affinity between the principles of microservices and MAS that can be exploited to deliver innovations, both in terms of the use of MAS technologies with microservices and the use of microservices technologies with MAS. This affinity is reinforced in [30], which argues that microservices can be used to facilitate agility of development for agent-based Internet of Things (IoT) systems. This view is further reinforced in [18], which argues that microservices-based IoT systems can be modelled as agents, and in [17], which presents a multi-agent trust model for IoT.

While not directly referencing microservices, [21] argues for a new "Agents as a Service" paradigm that would enable a new generation of agile services founded on the MAS models and techniques. Similarly, [34] argued for the emergence of an "Organisation as a Service" paradigm in which MAS implementations of organisational models are implemented and deployed as microservices that can be utilised by other non-agent-based microservices.

Key to realising this vision of agents and microservices is the need for dedicated programming tools and frameworks that help to simplify the development process. To date, there have been two main attempts to achieve this. Firstly, [35] introduces CAOPLE: a Caste-centric Agent-Oriented Programming Language and Environment for programming microservices. Conversely, [34] presents an extension to ASTRA [6] (a variant of AgentSpeak(L) [26]) that supports the implementation of microservices.

3   Multi-agent Micro-Services

The concept of Multi-Agent Micro-Services (MAMS) was originally introduced in [34]. The paper argues that microservices share many common traits with

Multi-Agent Systems (MAS), to the extent that both approaches can be broadly characterised as being concerned with the creation of loosely-coupled distributed systems comprised of small independent (autonomous) components with internal state. Of course, there are also many differences between the two approaches, not least the incorporation of practical reasoning, but this commonality suggests that we are beginning to see the emergence of approaches within industry that are, at least, compatible with the MAS perspective.

As mentioned in the introduction, the ultimate goal of MAMS is to allow agents to be deployed as entities that co-exist with other agents and resources in a *hypermedia space*. This space encompass all resources that can be: addressed using a Uniform Resource Identifier (URI); accessed using the HyperText Transfer Protocol (HTTP); and connected through a network of hyperlinks. Through these aspects, agents become not only identifiable and discoverable, but also observable. That is, the body of an agent can be directly observed and interacted with through the use of appropriate HTTP requests.

This notion of observability can lead to direct benefits in terms of enabling emergent behaviour. To illustrate this, consider a scenario in which a person overhears a conversation between other people in a public space. By listening to the conversation, the person is able to build not only models of the beliefs and goals of the other people, but also the protocols/rules that underpin the conversation. At some point the person may interject into the conversation simply by applying the learnt protocols/rules. With MAMS, this type of behaviour could be replicated by modelling inboxes as virtual resources that return a filtered view of the agents conversation history upon receipt of a GET request. Performing the GET request is the agent equivalent of listening in to the conversation of the other agent. Upon receipt of the conversation history, it could mine the messages to not only understand: what beliefs the other agent has, what services it provides, and what protocols it uses for that interaction; but also the URIs of the other agents that it has interacted with. This approach would also facilitate integration with a model of agent conversation reasoning (e.g. [1,19]).

3.1 Basic MAMS Model

At its core, MAMS adopts the view of a microservice as a container for one or more agents. Agents may be internal (private) to the container or external (public). Public agents are associated with a Uniform Resource Identifier (URI) based on a combination of the host name and port of the service plus the name of the agent. They are also associated with a hypermedia body that is constructed from a set of virtual resources. Private agents have standard string-based identifiers and no hypermedia body. Both types of agent should be implemented using a common agent programming language or framework. A microservice is not considered a MAMS service if there are no public agents.

Figure 1 presents a sketch of a standard layered microservices architecture, access to which is mediated by an API Gateway, a common microservices design

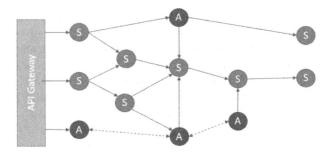

Fig. 1. Agent/Service integration

pattern[1] that employs a front-facing service that acts as a single point of entry to the layered architecture. In the context of this architecture, one of the goals of MAMS is to facilitate interaction between agent-based (A) and non agent-based (S) microservices (i.e. agent-agent, agent-service, service-agent and service-service). Agent-service interaction is achieved by giving agents the ability to submit HTTP requests and process HTTP Responses. Service-agent interaction is achieved by exposing the virtual resources through REST using URIs - based on the associated agent's URI - providing a HTTP-based interface that does not require knowledge of agent concepts.

Agent-agent interaction, using an Agent Communication Language (ACL) or equivalent, can also be realised through virtual resources. Specifically, each agent's inbox can be modelled as a virtual resource. Sending a message to an agent is reduced to submitting a HTTP POST request to the receiver agent's inbox URI, with the content of the request being the message. This approach is demonstrated later in Sect. 4.4. It is useful to note that FIPA's HTTP message transport service specification [22] works in a similar, if more convoluted, way: the sender agent passes the message to a message transport service which wraps the message in an envelope. It then POSTS the wrapped message to an Agent Communication Channel hosted on the receiver agents platform which unwraps the message and delivers it to the relevant agent.

Another form of agent-agent communication that is supported by MAMS is through non-ACL-based virtual resources. Each agent is also able to interact with other agents using the same model that is used for agent-service interaction. While this can be used in place of ACL-based interaction, the more interesting scenario is where the virtual resources represent abstractions of the agent state, such as public beliefs and goals, lists of acquaintances, or services offered. Such resources would be publicly accessible and, as such, discoverable by other agents. This posits a view where agents could directly observe the behaviour of other agents, explore the acquaintance networks of their own acquaintances, and potentially seek out other agents that provide the services that they need access to. Hyperlinks are essential to achieving this vision. While hyperlinks could be

---

[1] https://microservices.io/patterns/apigateway.html.

used externally to identify virtual resources, relevant links were not included in the resource representations returned by HTTP requests. [24] extended the basic MAMS model to include such hyperlinks based on the Hypertext Application Language (HAL). This extended model is described briefly in the next section.

3.2 Extending MAMS with HAL

The introduction of a resource representation that includes hyperlinks is a key step in achieving the vision of agents as hypermedia entities. There are many potential technologies for use in this area, and [20] presents a good summary of those in the context of the Web of Things. In [24], we selected Hypertext Application Language (HAL) [16] for adoption with MAMS. While HAL is not an IEFT standard, it is one of the simplest linked data models to have been proposed, it is relatively easy to implement, and it is currently in use in multiple projects[2].

```
{
    "_links": {
        "self": { "href": "/api/books/1234" }
    }
    "id": 1234,
    "title": "Hitchhiker's Guide to the Galaxy",
    "author": "Adams, Douglas"
}
```

Fig. 2. Example HAL resource representation (from [11])

HAL augments JSON representations with additional keys prefixed by an underscore (_). The _links key is used to define a set of named hypermedia links relevant to the resource being represented. For example, the JSON in Fig. 2 represents a book resource. The self link, is the URI of the representation itself. Additional links can added that define operations specific to the resource (e.g. a library system may add a link to the loan resource for that book).

A weakness of HAL is that the semantics associated with the links is application dependent. Using HAL requires the definition of what valid links can be used for each resource. In response to this, best practice for the use of REST in industry was reviewed. This highlighted that many REST APIs focus on two styles of resource: individual items and lists of items [29] that were manipulated through the mapping of HTTP verbs to Create/Read/Update/Delete (CRUD) operations. Based on this, it was decided that a generalised implementation of these resource types would be developed based on this best practice.

---

[2] https://github.com/mikekelly/hal_specification/wiki/APIs.

Table 1. Core resource types and key HTTP verb mappings

Resource type	URI	POST	GET	PUT/ PATCH	DELETE
Item	/id	n/a	Get the item	Update the item	n/a
List	/list_name	Add to the list	Get entire list of items	n/a	n/a
ListItem	/list_name/id	n/a	Get the item	Update the item	Remove item from list

Table 1 contains a summary of the standard set of HTTP verbs that are associated with these resource types and their associated behaviours. For example, as can be seen in this table, it is increasingly common for individual items (singleton resources) to support retrieval of their state using a GET request and a partial/full update using PATCH/PUT. POST operations are typically not permitted because they are creation-oriented (which does not apply to a singleton). Similarly, DELETE operations are typically not supported because there is no way to recreate the resource once it is deleted.

The choices described above represent just one possible resource implementation strategy for MAMS. It was made in an effort to facilitate exploration of the MAMS model. Our long-term goal is to explore the use of JSON-LD [31] due to its use of the Resource Definition Framework (RDF) as a schema [7].

4   An Artifact-Based Framework for Building MAMS Agents

To illustrate the MAMS model, a prototype implementation has been developed. When designing the prototype, two potential approaches were discussed: creating a bespoke implementation from first principles, or adapting an existing framework. In this paper, the latter approach was preferred because our goal is to provide an implementation that is agnostic to agent programming language. To this end, the CArtAgO framework [28] was chose because it was felt that virtual resources can be modelled as artifacts and because CArtAgO is an established and tested technology that is integrated with multiple established agent programming languages. This has allowed us to focus on the model rather than lower-level integration issues.

A key difference between MAMS and the CArtAgO approach is that artifacts combine observable properties (state) and operations (behaviour) while virtual resources support only state. In our implementation, the state of a virtual resource is modelled as observable properties. Operations are provided to enable the agent to manipulate the resource (e.g. updating an observable property, linking the artifact, etc.) in a way that is compliant with the MAMS model. A limitation of using CArtAgO is that virtual resources are private, but artifacts are designed to be shared. This means that it is possible to misuse our implementation and an agent within the same microservice could gain access to another agent's virtual resources. As the aim of this study is to demonstrate a prototype concept, rather than provide an industry standard deployable system, we have not attempted to address this issue at this stage.

To implement the MAMS model, a number of artifacts have been developed that represent key concepts. A high-level view of our approach is illustrated in Fig. 3, where each agent is associated with a hypermedia body, consisting of a set of CArtAgO artifacts that model the virtual resources of the agent. A `base` artifact is provided as a shared base to which each `resource` artifact is linked and this in turn is linked to a shared `webserver` artifact that exposes the resources over HTTP. The `webserver` artifact is implemented using Netty: an asynchronous Java-based event-driven network application framework for high performance protocol servers[3].

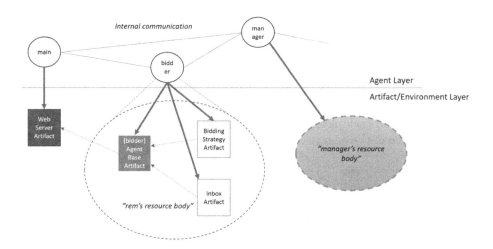

Fig. 3. Modelling a RESTful agent body as artifacts

The `base` artifact acts as the root of a resource tree that implements our model of a MAMS agent. To be clear, we are using CArtAgO to implement our model rather than attempting to extend CArtAgO to support the model. As a result, we do not make use of underlying concepts such as the CArtAgO agent body in this work.

Modelling resources explicitly as artifacts allows for clearly-defined semantics that includes a description of how each HTTP verb will affect the state of the artifact modelling the associated resource. It also specifies the interface between the agent and the resource, which is defined in terms of the operation, observable property, and signal concepts of CArtAgO. This paper describes two approaches to implementing virtual resources as artifacts: a passive resource management

---

[3] https://netty.io/.

model (Sect. 4.2), and an active resource management model (Sect. 4.3). However, before discussing these approaches, Sect. 4.1 describes how artifacts are used to implement virtual resources.

Two additional artifacts are created when a MAMS microservice is started. The `restclient` artifact implements a REST client that can be used to perform REST API calls. For example, the `postRequest` operation takes a URI and string representation of a JSON body as input and generates a response code and string content. Similar operations exist for GET, PUT and DELETE. The `comms` artifact provides support for sending FIPA-ACL style messages to other MAMS agents. More information on this is provided in Sect. 4.4.

4.1   Implementing Virtual Resources as Artifacts

Figure 4 illustrates how MAMS exposes artifact-based virtual resources on the web and the relationship between an agent and the associated set of artifacts that implement those resources. Each artifact created by the agent is linked to another artifact, creating a back channel through which incoming HTTP requests are routed to the relevant artifact. The back channel consists of a set of *handlers* that implement the routing behaviour. Collectively, the set of handlers form a tree structure rooted at the `base` artifact. Each handler is associated with a single artifact and each path from the root to a handler represents the URI of a virtual resource of the agent.

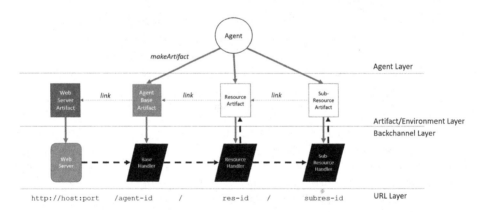

Fig. 4. Use of CArtAgO artifacts for linking RESTful resources to agents

Listing 1 contains some pseudocode for creating the body of an agent. As can be seen, the agent starts by retrieving a reference to the `webserver` artifact. Once it has this, a `base` artifact is created. This artifact is given a name of the form `base-<aid>` (where "`<aid>`" is the agent's unique identifier) and is then linked to the `webserver` artifact. The agent focuses on the newly created artifact so that it will receive updates on observable properties and signals. Finally, a createRoute() operation is executed on the newly created `base` which creates the associated handler and links it to the `webserver` artifact's handler.

```
1   lookupArtifact("webserver", id)
2   makeArtifact("base-<aid>", "mams.BaseArtifact",[<aid>], id2)
3   linkArtifacts(id2, "out-1", id)
4   focus(id2)
5   createRoute()[id2]
```

Listing 1: Pseudo Code for Creating the body of a MAMS Agent

To support the model described in Table 1, three additional types of artifact are required: `item`, `list` and `listitem`. However, the exact form that each of these artifacts takes depends on whether a passive or active management model is being used.

Section 4 defined the representation of an `item` resource as the set of observable properties associated with it. Receipt of a request for a representation of that resource involves transforming the observable properties into that relevant representation format. For the model described in Sect. 3.2, we use a Java object and an intermediary format that is transformed to/from JSON using the Jackson API[4]. For GET requests, the _links field is appended to the resulting JSON object based on the linkages that exist between artifacts (those that are used to form the backchannel). For POST, PUT and PATCH requests, the JSON is transformed into a Java object whose fields correspond to the observable properties of the artifact and whose values are used to update those propertied. To facilitate this, each `item` or `list` artifact is associated (at creation time) with a Java class that defines what type of object is to be used for the intermediary format. On creation, either default values are used to initialise observable properties or an instance of the class is passed to provide the initial values.

4.2 Passive Resource Management

In the passive model, agents are not responsible for enforcing the changes associated with any HTTP requests received. They simply act in response to resource changes. How the resource is updated depends on an associated set of semantics which is loosely described in Table 1.

As the artifact receives each request, depending on the HTTP verb used, the agent receives a CArtAgO signal indicating the nature of the update that was applied. This allows the agent to act in response to expected changes in the resources, but does not affect the speed by which the response is returned to the system making the request. Additionally, the agent is also able to make changes to the state of the resources through a suite of internal operations. The passive model is illustrated in Fig. 5.

---

[4] https://github.com/FasterXML/jackson.

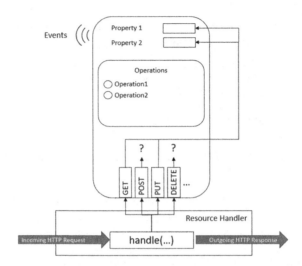

Fig. 5. Schematic of a passively managed resource

This idea allows rapid interaction between the resource and the entity making the request, while maintaining that the agent is still informed about the state of each resource. A key factor of this method is the fact that although the agent may have control over the resource, the resource is open to the world as an endpoint. This permits any service (or agent) to make a request and receive a timely response from this entity, something that may not be possible when the mentalistic aspect of deliberation that is associated with agents is introduced. In terms of usage, this type of resource model seems suited either to closed systems where trust is not an issue and all resource changes follow expected patterns of behaviour, or to open systems where the manipulation of resources is a desirable aspect.

4.3   Active Resource Management

For active management, each artifact also has a set of HTTP verbs that it can handle based on Table 1. In contrast, however, the agent is now placed in control of the response given by any artifacts under its stewardship. This is illustrated in Fig. 6.

Once a valid HTTP request is made of an artifact, a CArtAgO signal is generated based on the type of HTTP verb passed to the agent. For GET and DELETE requests, the request body is ignored. Conversely, the body is included for POST, PUT and PATCH requests. This event is passed to the agent which then deliberates to decide on the correct response.

If deemed acceptable, the agent executes the "accept" operation on the artifact. The request is then be removed from the event queue and processed. A response detailing that the request made was handled correctly would be issued. In the case where the request was rejected by the agent, the "refuse" operation would be invoked, issuing a response that the request was denied.

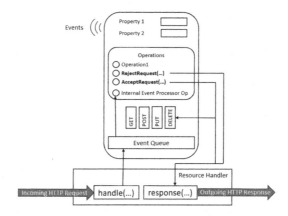

Fig. 6. Schematic of an actively managed resource

With regard to a use case, this scenario can be utilised when dealing with a resource that is highly constrained and only wants to accept requests of a given standard/type. This then lends itself to Quality of Service (QoS) based systems, as it allows the system to guarantee certain criteria with regard to the manipulation of resources.

4.4 FIPA-ACL Based Interaction

ACL-based communication between MAMS services is supported through the creation of a custom `inbox` virtual resource. This resource is somewhat similar to a standard `list` resource, with the exception that it only accepts POST requests. This resource is designed to be used in tandem with the `comms` artifact, which includes an operation for sending messages to MAMS agents via a POST request. The content of the message is submitted in the form of a JSON string. It is left to the developer to decide how to generate this content.

In its current form, the FIPA Message class that models messages only includes the: sender, receiver, performative, language and content fields. The content itself is converted into a JSON string that is transmitted as the body of the POST. A signal is generated by the `inbox` resource for each message received. The content of this signal the performative, the sender URI, and a string representation of transmitted content. Again, conversion of this JSON into a more useful form is left to the developer. The current prototype is currently released as part of the ASTRA-MAMS integration, which is described in more detail next in Sect. 5 and comes with built-in support for converting functional terms into JSON and vice versa. It should be noted that the artifacts described here do not map onto the model defined in Sect. 3.2 but are purpose-built to facilitate FIPA-based interaction.

5   Integration with ASTRA

To further explore our MAMS model, we have integrated our CArtAgO based solution with the ASTRA agent programming language [6,8]. ASTRA is an implementation of AgentSpeak(ER)[27] a recent evolution of AgentSpeaK(L)[26].

All of the source code for MAMS and for the ASTRA integration with MAMS is open source and available to download from Gitlab[5]. This includes:

- `mams-cartago-core` package: webserver, restclient, and base artifacts; support for handlers and a basic web server.
- `mams-cartago-hal` package: implementation of item, list and itemlist artifacts together with support for Java classes as schema.
- `mams-astra-hal` package: integration of ASTRA and also the MAMS +HAL model and the prototype FIPA-ACL based communication model.
- `examples`: a set of sample programs (implemented as Maven projects).

```
1   agent MAMSAgent {
2     rule +!setup() {
3       cartago.startService();cartago.link();
4       cartago.makeArtifact("webserver", "mams.artifacts.WebServerArtifact",
5             cartago.params([9000]), cartago.ArtifactId id);
6       +artifact("webserver", "webserver", id);
7       cartago.makeArtifact("restclient", "mams.artifacts.RESTArtifact",
8             cartago.params([]), cartago.ArtifactId id2);
9       +artifact("restclient", "restclient", id2);
10      cartago.makeArtifact("comms", "fipa.artifact.Comms",
11            cartago.params([]), cartago.ArtifactId id3);
12      +artifact("comms", "comms", id3);
13    }
14    inference have(string name) :-
15                 artifact(name, string qname, ArtifactId id);
16    rule +!init() {
17      cartago.link();!have("webserver");!have("restclient");
18    }
19    rule +!have(string name) : ~have(name) {
20      cartago.lookupArtifact(name, cartago.ArtifactId id);
21      +artifact(name, name, id);
22    }
23    rule +!created("base") : ~created("base") &
24          artifact("webserver", string qualifiedName, ArtifactId id2) {
25      string baseName = S.name()+"-base";
26      cartago.makeArtifact(baseName, "mams.artifacts.BaseArtifact",
27          cartago.params([S.name()]), cartago.ArtifactId id);
28      cartago.linkArtifacts(id, "out-1", id2);
29      cartago.focus(id);cartago.operation(id, createRoute());
30      +artifact("base", baseName, id);
31    }
32  }
```

Listing 2: Part of the mams.MAMSAgent program

---

[5] https://gitlab.com/mams-ucd.

The main ASTRA code for creating a MAMS Agent is implemented in the
MAMSAgent class. Partial code for this class is shown in Listing 2. The +!setup()
rule on lines 2–13 is invoked only once by the first agent to be created. This plan
configures the MAMS service, creating all the default artifacts. In contrast, the
+!init() rule on lines 16–18 are to be used by all other MAMS agents. The
associated goal is used to link the agent to the already created artifacts. Once
the !init() goal has been achieved, the agent is able to create the base artifact
using the rule on lines 23–31.

```
1   agent MAMSAgent {
2     module mams.HALConverter hal;
3
4     rule $cartago.signal(string sa,
5             message(string perf, string sender, string content)) {
6       !signal_message(perf, sender, hal.toRawFunct("content", content));
7     }
8     rule +!signal_message(string performative,
9             string sender, content(funct content)) {
10      !message(performative, sender, content);
11    }
12    rule +!transmit(string perf, string receiver, funct content)
13          : artifact("comms", string qname, ArtifactId id) {
14      !itemProperty("base", "uri", funct agentUri);
15      cartago.operation(id, transmit(perf, F.valueAsString(agentUri, 0),
16            receiver, hal.toJsonString(content(content))));
17    }
18  }
```

Listing 3: FIPA ACL Code from mams.MAMSAgent class

The snippet of code in Listing 3 relates to the support for FIPA ACL based
communication. The module on line 2 includes support for for converting functional term into JSON and vice-versa. The +!transmit() rule on lines 12–17
implement support for sending messages. This is matched by the rule on lines
4–7 which intercepts the raw CArtAgO signal relating to an incoming message.
The rule invokes a chain of subgoals that results in the conversion of the raw content of the message back into a form that corresponds more closely to a normal
ASTRA message event. The !message(...) goal generated on line 10 should be
could by the implementing agent to handle receipt of specific FIPA messages.

6   Illustration

To demonstrate our approach, a version of the Vickrey Auction example presented in [34] has been built using the framework described in Sect. 5. The resul-
tant code base is quite different because the original approach mixed code for
handling HTTP requests and responses with code for implementing the auctions. In contrast, the code in our approach is more focused on implementing
the auctions.

The implemented system exposes a set of virtual resources that are linked to specific agents within the implementation. As shown in Fig. 7, the `Manager` agent is associated with the `/clients` and the `/items` resources and the `Bidder` agents, which are created by the `Manager`, are each responsible for their own `/wanted` resource.

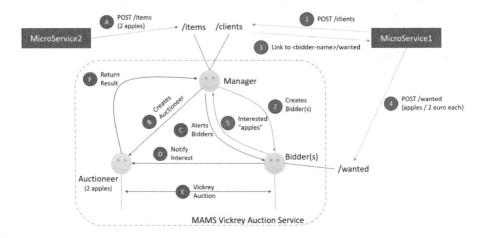

Fig. 7. Vickrey auction implementation (taken from [34])

```
1   agent PassiveMAMSAgent extends MAMSAgent {
2     rule +!listResource(string name, string cls)
3         : ~have(name) & artifact("base", string baseName, cartago.ArtifactId id2) {
4       string resName = baseName+"-"+name;
5       cartago.makeArtifact(resName, "mams.passive.PassiveListArtifact",
6           cartago.params([name, cls]), cartago.ArtifactId id);
7       cartago.linkArtifacts(id, "out-1", id2);
8       cartago.focus(id);
9       cartago.operation(id, createRoute());
10      +artifact(name, resName, id);
11      +listResource(name, cls);
12    }
13  }
14  agent Manager extends PassiveMAMSAgent {
15    rule +!init() {
16      MAMSAgent::!init();!created("base");
17      !listResource("clients", "auction.Client");
18      ...
19    }
20    rule $cartago.signal(string A,listItemCreated(string N,string T))
21        : bidder_count(int cnt) {
22      -+bidder_count(cnt + 1);
23      !monitorPassiveItem(N, T, A+"-"+N);
24      string BN = "bidder_"+cnt+"_"+N;
25      system.createAgent(BN, "Bidder"); +for_client(BN, A+"-"+N);
26    }
27  }
```

Listing 4: Part of the mams.PassiveMAMSAgent program

The `mams.PassiveMAMSAgent` agent program provides plans to support the creation of passively-managed artifacts. Listing 4 shows a plan that can be used to create a `list` resource. Below this, a second piece of code from the `Manager` agent program illustrates how to use this to create a list of clients. It also demonstrates how CArtAgO signals are used to alert the agent to the creation of new items. A templating mechanism is provided that uses Java classes (here the `auction.Client` class) as a schema for items.

7 Discussion

One of the main benefits of the approach presented in this paper is that it standardises how to build MAMS-based applications. This has led to a number of improvements compared against the initial implementation of MAMS as described in [34]:

- *Explicit Modelling of Resources:* The original MAMS model maintained an implicit model of resources whose state was represented within the agents' beliefs. The approach advocated in this paper models resources explicitly. A key benefit of this has been the ability to define explicit resource types (see Table 1), with associated semantics for valid HTTP requests, that are encoded within the the resource model.
- *Support for Extensibility:* The implementation of resources is designed to be extensible and permit the addition of other resource types as is necessary. This is essential as it permits the development of bespoke resource models and types. We view the creation of such resources as essential to support the implementation of concepts such as decentralised trust management [2] and social reputation [13].
- *Use of a Linked Data Model:* Linking of resources provides a way for external systems to discover and navigate complex APIs. Support for this has been realised through the use of the Hypertext Application Language (HAL) and through the adoption of agreed standards for representing the specific types of resource supported in this paper.
- *A Cleaner Approach to Resource Management:* The original MAMS model supported only one form of resource management, which was intimately linked to the agent program. The developer of the program was responsible for handling all HTTP requests. The model presented in this paper offers a more refined approach, where valid HTTP requests (those that are permitted for the given resource type) are vetted by the associated agent (invalid requests are automatically rejected). In this paper, we term this agent-in-the-loop approach *active resource management* (see Sect. 4.3).
- *A Passive Resource Management Model:* In addition to the active model, this paper introduces a *passive resource management* model that separates agents from resource updates. Instead, agents are passive observers that monitor their associated resources for changes or who can modify the state of their resources directly (through internal operations that are equivalent to those supported by HTTP Requests).

- *Language Independence:* Finally, a last key advantage of the approach described in this paper is that it is agnostic to the agent programming language used. This has been achieve by focusing on an artifact-based model of virtual resources that is language independent.

For this project, we chose HAL as the hypermedia resource representation as it has many beneficial qualities that were suitable for a project such as ours which is working towards the idea of Hypermedia MAS [4]. HAL enables ease of navigation around a set of resources by maintaining a set of links that describe relationships between individual resources. This lends itself to the idea of an agent exploring, discovering and reasoning about a given set of resources. HAL provided us with a very simplistic way of displaying how an agent's 'body' is made up of the virtual resources that it manages. HAL was very useful in terms of allowing us to showcase our theoretical model in a very simple view, however, it is not without its limitations. HAL does not support resource metadata for describing the semantics of resources and can only specify the media type expected when de-referencing a linked resource. Additionally, HAL does not support hypermedia controls other than simple links and so cannot describe the service-specific semantics of operations on resources.

After reviewing hypermedia APIs, [20] provides a great breakdown of the state of the art in this field. It describes two main approaches to implementing hypermedia APIs: a bottom-up approach as well as a top-down approach. Bottom up approaches include HAL as well as the Constrained RESTful Application Language (CoRAL). As this paper is written from a Web of Things (WoT) perspective, both HAL and CoRAL are described as being able to represent both Things in a WoT context but also to represent complex web resources, which ties in with our research. Interestingly, CoRAL provides a solution to some of the shortcomings of HAL in that it supports the representation of simple resource metadata, as well as providing hypermedia controls by describing operations that can be performed on resources via forms.

The top-down approaches include the W3C Web of Things Specification that describes the Thing Description (TD) and a Web Thing Description provided by Mozilla. The top-down approaches are quite restrictive, insofar as that they have to represent a 'thing' as a cohesive unit of data and functionality. A key difference between these two approaches from the perspective of this research is that in the examples of the top-down approaches, any navigation away from that cohesive unit results in a JSON object that represents data, not another resource. Based on the working examples provided, there seemed to be no clear navigation from generated data back to a description of the resource. In contrast, when navigating the hyperlinks provided in both HAL and CoRAL, one is navigating between resources, and each resource has its own set of relevant hyperlinks. It is the expressiveness of the bottom-up approaches that is key to allowing services and agents to navigate a resource. The top-down approaches, however, support semantic descriptions of resources using JSON-LD, which provides a level of context. Additionally, based on the latest draft specification of CoRAL [14], it also allows for the expressions of simple RDF statements. However, it currently does not support more extensive representations such as JSON-LD. CoRAL is still a working draft but is a forerunner for a resource representation that can represent complex web resources related to this research, as it contains many key attributes.

There are several positive elements to each of these approaches to implementing hypermedia APIs. However, from the perspective of this research, it is our view that a combination of these positive elements would be best suited as a mechanism for representing resources. Another popular resource that we believe should be considered when discussing the correct path to choose with regard to resource representation is the likes of the OpenAPI[6] specification and RAML[7]. These tools are used to build a representation of an API that is both human and machine-readable, in both JSON and XML. These tools have been used in industrial contexts in order to provide in-depth descriptions of how to interact with services with minimal implementation on the consumer side. These services provide very clear and detailed information on how to interact with a given resource, including the correct HTTP verb to use. This is very useful from a RESTful perspective as it allows each resource to define all the HTTP verbs each resource supports. It is this level of detail that we see being included in hypermedia resource representation in order to promote autonomous interaction among services and agents. Understanding which approach is most suitable, or combination there of, is a key challenge to the evolution of MAMS.

Finally, [15] presents recent work on CArtAgO that exposes artifacts through a Web API. This contrasts with the work presented in this paper as it focuses first on simply exposing artifacts and secondly does so as a web API rather than as REST resources. As discussed in Sect. 4, the MAMS approach is quite different to the CArtAgO approach. As a result of using CArtAgO, steps such as the exposing of an agent's virtual resource became a much more complicated process. This is due to the fact that artifacts in the CArtAgO framework are inherently shared among all the entities in the environment, and in order to portray the fact that an artifact 'belonged' to a given agent, each artifact had to be linked to the base artifact of each agent. Although using CArtAgO was a limitation from this perspective, using CArtAgO as an environment framework allowed us to showcase that MAMS has cross-compatibility with other agent programming languages and is not tightly-coupled with any particular language.

8   Conclusions

This paper presents a novel approach to the implementation of Multi-Agent MicroServices (MAMS), a model that sits at the intersection between Multi-Agent Systems and Microservices. The model embraces current industry best practice and technology stacks and proposes introduces the idea of virtual resources as a mechanism for facilitating the seamless integration of agents into microservices-based architectures. Through this, we gain access to a wealth of

---

[6] https://swagger.io/specification/.
[7] https://raml.org/.

technologies and experience in how to deploy systems at scale while at the same time situating those agents in a larger web-enabled ecosystem.

Future work will seek to address a number of limitations of the model described here. This includes some improvements to the underlying architecture, but more significantly, the decoupling of resources and representations to allow multiple representations to be returned for a given resource. A main goal of this research in the near future is to work towards creating a hypermedia resource representation that can provide semantically enriched navigational cues that describe possible actions on given resources with enough detail in order to allow for interaction with minimal implementation on the side of the consumer, a combination of the solutions discussed in Sect. 7, from our perspective, associated with the current working standards. Ultimately, the aim is to support all the linked data formats described in [20] as well as any others that evolve over time.

A specific target is the implementation of support for JSON-LD [31] representations which we intend to use in CONSUS[8]: a research project that seeks, in part, to develop multi-agent decision-support tools for smart agriculture.

Acknowledgements. This research is funded under the SFI Strategic Partnerships Programme (16/ SPP/3296) and is co-funded by Origin Enterprises Plc.

References

1. Ancona, D., Drossopoulou, S., Mascardi, V.: Automatic generation of self-monitoring MASs from multiparty global session types in Jason. In: Baldoni, M., Dennis, L., Mascardi, V., Vasconcelos, W. (eds.) DALT 2012. LNCS (LNAI), vol. 7784, pp. 76–95. Springer, Heidelberg (2013). https://doi.org/10.1007/978-3-642-37890-4_5
2. Aref, A.M., Tran, T.T.: A decentralized trustworthiness estimation model for open, multiagent systems (DTMAS). J. Trust Manag. **2**(1), 3 (2015). https://doi.org/10.1186/s40493-015-0014-4
3. Balalaie, A., Heydarnoori, A., Jamshidi, P.: Microservices architecture enables devops: migration to a cloud-native architecture. IEEE Softw. **33**(3), 42–52 (2016)
4. El Fallah-Seghrouchni, A., Ricci, A., Son, T.C. (eds.): EMAS 2017. LNCS (LNAI), vol. 10738. Springer, Cham (2018). https://doi.org/10.1007/978-3-319-91899-0
5. Ciortea, A., Mayer, S., Gandon, F., Boissier, O., Ricci, A., Zimmermann, A.: A decade in hindsight: the missing bridge between multi-agent systems and the world wide web. In: Proceedings of the 18th International Conference on Autonomous Agents and MultiAgent Systems, pp. 1659–1663. International Foundation for Autonomous Agents and Multiagent Systems (2019)
6. Collier, R.W., Russell, S., Lillis, D.: Reflecting on agent programming with AgentSpeak(L). In: Chen, Q., Torroni, P., Villata, S., Hsu, J., Omicini, A. (eds.) PRIMA 2015. LNCS (LNAI), vol. 9387, pp. 351–366. Springer, Cham (2015). https://doi.org/10.1007/978-3-319-25524-8_22

---

[8] http://www.consus.ie.

7. Decker, S., Melnik, S., Van Harmelen, F., Fensel, D., Klein, M., Broekstra, J., Erdmann, M., Horrocks, I.: The semantic web: the roles of XML and RDF. IEEE Internet Comput. **4**(5), 63–73 (2000)
8. Dhaon, A., Collier, R.W.: Multiple inheritance in agent speak (l)-style programming languages. In: Proceedings of the 4th International Workshop on Programming based on Actors Agents and Decentralized Control, pp. 109–120 (2014)
9. Dragoni, N., Lanese, I., Larsen, S.T., Mazzara, M., Mustafin, R., Safina, L.: Microservices: how to make your application scale. In: Petrenko, A.K., Voronkov, A. (eds.) PSI 2017. LNCS, vol. 10742, pp. 95–104. Springer, Cham (2018). https://doi.org/10.1007/978-3-319-74313-4_8
10. Fielding, R.T.: REST: Architectural Styles and the Design of Network-based Software Architectures. Doctoral dissertation (2000). http://www.ics.uci.edu/~fielding/pubs/dissertation/top.htm
11. Framework, Z.: Hypertext application language website (2019). https://weierophinney.github.io/hal/hal/. Accessed 29 Oct 2019
12. Griffiths, N., Chao, K.-M. (eds.): Agent-Based Service-Oriented Computing. AIKP. Springer, London (2010). https://doi.org/10.1007/978-1-84996-041-0
13. Hahn, C., Fley, B., Florian, M., Spresny, D., Fischer, K.: Social reputation: A mechanism for flexible self-regulation of multiagent systems. J. Artif. Soc. Soc. Simul. **10**(1), 1–8 (2007)
14. Hartke, K.: The constrained restful application language (coral) (2020). https://datatracker.ietf.org/doc/draft-ietf-core-coral/. Accessed 08 Apr 2020
15. International Foundation for Autonomous Agents and Multiagent Systems: Engineering Scalable Distributed Environments and Organizations for MAS (2019)
16. Kelly, M.: Json hypertext applicaion language specification (2016). https://tools.ietf.org/html/draft-kelly-json-hal-08. Accessed 29 Oct 2019
17. Kravari, K., Bassiliades, N.: Storm: a social agent-based trust model for the internet of things adopting microservice architecture. Simul. Model. Pract. Theory **94**, 286–302 (2019)
18. Krivic, P., Skocir, P., Kusek, M., Jezic, G.: Microservices as agents in IoT systems. In: Jezic, G., Kusek, M., Chen-Burger, Y.-H.J., Howlett, R.J., Jain, L.C. (eds.) KES-AMSTA 2017. SIST, vol. 74, pp. 22–31. Springer, Cham (2018). https://doi.org/10.1007/978-3-319-59394-4_3
19. Lillis, D.: Internalising Interaction Protocols as First-Class Programming Elements in Multi Agent Systems. Ph.D. thesis, University College Dublin (2012)
20. Martins, J.A., Mazayev, A., Correia, N.: Hypermedia APIs for the web of things. IEEE Access **5**, 20058–20067 (2017)
21. Mascardi, V., Weyns, D.: Engineering multi-agent systems Anno 2025. In: Weyns, D., Mascardi, V., Ricci, A. (eds.) EMAS 2018. LNCS (LNAI), vol. 11375, pp. 3–16. Springer, Cham (2019). https://doi.org/10.1007/978-3-030-25693-7_1
22. O'Brien, P.D., Nicol, R.C.: FIPA-towards a standard for software agents. BT Technol. J. **16**(3), 51–59 (1998). https://doi.org/10.1023/A:1009621729979
23. O'Connor, R.V., Elger, P., Clarke, P.M.: Continuous software engineering-a microservices architecture perspective. J. Softw. Evol. Process **29**(11), e1866 (2017)
24. O'Neill, E., Lillis, D., O'Hare, G.M., Collier, R.W.: Explicit modelling of resources for multi-agent microservices using the cartago framework. In: 2020Proceedings of the 18th International Joint Conference on Autonomous Agents and Multi-Agent Systems, Auckland, NZ. International Foundation for Autonomous Agents and MultiAgent Systems (IFAAMAS) (2020)

25. De la Prieta, F., Rodríguez-González, S., Chamoso, P., Corchado, J.M., Bajo, J.: Survey of agent-based cloud computing applications. Future Gener. Comput. Syst. **100**, 223–236 (2019)
26. Rao, A.S.: AgentSpeak(L): BDI agents speak out in a logical computable language. In: Van de Velde, W., Perram, J.W. (eds.) MAAMAW 1996. LNCS, vol. 1038, pp. 42–55. Springer, Heidelberg (1996). https://doi.org/10.1007/BFb0031845
27. Ricci, A., Bordini, R.H., Hubner, J.F., Collier, R.: Agentspeak (er): An extension of agentspeak (l) improving encapsulation and reasoning about goals. In: The 17th International Conference on Autonomous Agents and Multiagent Systems (AAMAS 2018). International Foundation for Autonomous Agents and MultiAgent Systems (IFAAMAS) (2018)
28. Ricci, A., Viroli, M., Omicini, A.: CArtAgO: framework for prototyping artifact-based environments in MAS. In: Weyns, D., Parunak, H.V.D., Michel, F. (eds.) E4MAS 2006. LNCS (LNAI), vol. 4389, pp. 67–86. Springer, Heidelberg (2007). https://doi.org/10.1007/978-3-540-71103-2_4
29. Roy, C.: Restful API design: Microserices. https://medium.com/@cknextmove/restful-api-design-microservices-f983e3ea3563. Accessed 25 Oct 2019
30. Savaglio, C., Ganzha, M., Paprzycki, M., Bădică, C., Ivanović, M., Fortino, G.: Agent-based internet of things: State-of-the-art and research challenges. Future Gener. Comput. Syst **102**, 1038–1053 (2020)
31. Sporny, M., Longley, D., Kellogg, G., Lanthaler, M., Lindström, N.: Json-ld 1.0. W3C Recomm. **16**, 41 (2014)
32. Thönes, J.: Microservices. IEEE Softw. **32**(1), 116–116 (2015)
33. Villamizar, M., et al.: Evaluating the monolithic and the microservice architecture pattern to deploy web applications in the cloud. In: 2015 10th Computing Colombian Conference (10CCC), pp. 583–590. IEEE (2015)
34. Collier, R.W., O'Neill, E., Lillis, D., O'Hare, G.: Mams: Multi-agent microservices. In: Companion Proceedings of The 2019 World Wide Web Conference, pp. 655–662. ACM (2019)
35. Xu, C., Zhu, H., Bayley, I., Lightfoot, D., Green, M., Marshall, P.: Caople: a programming language for microservices SaaS. In: 2016 IEEE Symposium on Service-Oriented System Engineering (SOSE), pp. 34–43. IEEE (2016)

Aplib: Tactical Agents for Testing Computer Games

I. S. W. B. Prasetya[1]([✉]) [iD], Mehdi Dastani[1] [iD], Rui Prada[2] [iD], Tanja E. J. Vos[3,4] [iD], Frank Dignum[5] [iD], and Fitsum Kifetew[6] [iD]

[1] Utrecht University, Utrecht, The Netherlands
s.w.b.prasetya@uu.nl
[2] Inst. de Engenharia de Sistemas e Computadores - Investigação e Desenvolvimento, Lisbon, Portugal
[3] Universidad Politecnica de Valencia, Valencia, Spain
[4] Open University, Heerlen, The Netherlands
[5] Umeå University, Umeå, Sweden
[6] Fondazione Bruno Kessler, Trento, Italy

Abstract. Modern interactive software, such as computer games, employ complex user interfaces. Although these user interfaces make the games attractive and powerful, unfortunately they also make them extremely difficult to test. Not only do we have to deal with their functional complexity, but also the fine grained interactivity of their user interface blows up their interaction space, so that traditional automated testing techniques have trouble handling it. An agent-based testing approach offers an alternative solution: agents' goal driven planning, adaptivity, and reasoning ability can provide an extra edge towards effective navigation in complex interaction space. This paper presents aplib, a Java library for programming intelligent test agents, featuring novel tactical programming as an abstract way to exert control over agents' underlying reasoning-based behavior. This type of control is suitable for programming testing tasks. Aplib is implemented in such a way to provide the fluency of a Domain Specific Language (DSL). Its embedded DSL approach also means that aplib programmers will get al.l the advantages that Java programmers get: rich language features and a whole array of development tools.

Keywords: Automated game testing · AI for automated testing · Intelligent agents for testing · Agents tactical programming · Intelligent agent programming

1 Introduction

With the advances of technologies, computer games have become increasingly more interactive and complex. Modern computer games improve realism and user experience

This work is supported by European Union's Horizon 2020 research and innovation programme under grant agreement No 856716 Project iv4XR (Intelligent Verification/Validation for Extended Reality Based Systems).

© Springer Nature Switzerland AG 2020
C. Baroglio et al. (Eds.): EMAS 2020, LNAI 12589, pp. 21–41, 2020.
https://doi.org/10.1007/978-3-030-66534-0_2

Fig. 1. A 3D game called Lab Recruits where aplib were deployed aid testing.

by allowing users to have fine grained control/interactions. A downside of this development is that it becomes increasingly difficult to test computer games. For example, to test that a computer game would maintain the correctness invariant of a certain family of states, the tester will first need to operate the game to bring it to at least one of such states. This often requires a long series of fine grained interactions with the game. Only then the tester can check if the said invariant does hold in that state. Such a test is hard, error-prone, and fragile to automate. Consequently, many game developers still resort to expensive manual play testing. Considering that the game industry is worth over 100 billions USD, speeding up testing by effectively automating manual testing tasks is a need that cannot be ignored.

As indicated above, a common manual expensive test related task is to bring the game under test to a certain state of interest (goal state), either because we want to check if the state is correct, or because we need to do a specific action on this state that is required for the given test scenario. In principle this task is a search problem, for which solutions exist. However, in the context of computer games the problem is challenging. A game often employs randomness and it often consists of many entities that interact with each other and with the user. Some interactions might be cooperative while others can be adversarial. These and other factors lead to a vast and fine grained interaction space which is hard to deal with for the existing automated testing techniques such as search based [20,29], model based [15,43], or symbolic [4,42]. The key to handle such a space, we believe, is to have an approach that enables the programming of *domain reasoning* to express which parts of the interaction space of a particular game are relevant to consider, and likewise what kinds of plans (for reaching given goal states) are needed. This allows the underlying test engine to focus its search on the parts of the interaction and plan spaces that semantically matter. We propose to base such a solution on a *multi-agent approach* since autonomous distributed planning and reasoning based interactions with environments are already first class features.

Contribution. This paper presents aplib[1], a Java library for programming intelligent agents suitable for carrying out complex testing tasks. They can be used in conjunction

---

[1] "Agent Programming Library", https://iv4xr-project.github.io/aplib/.

with Java testing frameworks such as JUnit, e.g. to collect and manage test verdicts. Figure 1 shows a 3D game we use as a pilot where aplib was used to automate testing (we will also use it later as a running example). Aplib features BDI (Belief-Desire-Intention [23]) agents and adds a novel layer of *tactical programming* that provides an abstract way to exert control on agents behavior. Declarative reasoning rules express when actions are allowed to execute. Although in theory just using reasoning is enough to find a solution (a plan that would solve the given goal state) if given infinite time, such an approach is not likely to be performant enough. For testing, this matters as no developers would want to wait for hours for their test to complete. The tactical layer allows developers to program an imperative control structure over the underlying reasoning-based behavior, allowing them to have greater control over the search process. So-called *tactics* can be defined to enable agents to strategically choose and prioritize their short term actions and plans, whereas longer term strategies are expressed as so-called *goal structures*, specifying how a goal can be realized by chosing, prioritizing, sequencing, or repeating a set of subgoals.

While the concept of a hierarchical goal is not new, e.g. it can be solved by Hierarchical Task Networks (HTN) and Behavior Trees (BT), or can be encoded directly as BDI reasoning rules [9], aplib allows it to be expressed in terms of imperative programming idioms such as **SEQ** and **REPEAT**, which are more intuitive for programming control. The underlying reasoning based behavior remains declarative. Our tactical programming approach is more similar to tactical programming in interactive theorem proving, used by proof engineers to script proof search [12,22,40]. The use of this style in BDI agents and for solving testing problems is as far as we know new.

As opposed to dedicated agent programming languages [37,41] aplib offers a Domain Specific Language (DSL) *embedded* in Java. This means that aplib programmers will program in Java, but they will get a set of APIs that give the fluent appearance of a DSL. In principle, having a native programming language for writing tests is a huge benefit, but only if the language is rich enough and has enough tool and community support. Otherwise it is a risk that most companies will be unwilling to take. On the other hand, using an embedded DSL means that the programmers have direct access to all the benefit the host language, in this case Java: its expressiveness (OO, λ-expression etc.), static typing, rich libraries, and wealth of development tools.

Paper Structure. Section 2 first introduces the concept of testing tasks; these are the tasks that we want to automate. Section 3 explains the basic concepts of aplib agents and shows examples of how to create an agent with aplib and how to write some simple actions. Section 4 introduces the concept of goal structures, to express complex test scenarios, and our basic constructs for tactical programming. The section also explains aplib's 'deliberation cycle', which necessarily deviates from BDI's standard due to its tactical programming. Large scale case studies are still future work. However, Sect. 5 will briefly discuss our experience so far. Section 6 discusses related work, and finally Sect. 7 concludes and mentions some future work.

2   Testing Task

This section will introduce what we mean by a 'testing task', and what 'automating' it means. The typical testing task that we will consider has the form:

$$\underbrace{\phi}_{\text{situation}} \Rightarrow \underbrace{\psi}_{\text{invariant}} \tag{1}$$

where ϕ is a state predicate characterizing a situation and ψ is a state predicate that is expected to hold on all instances of the situation ϕ (that is, on all states satisfying ϕ). We call ψ an *invariant*, which is the term used by Ernst et al. [16] to refer to a predicate that is expected to hold at a certain control location in a program, e.g. when a program enters its loop, or when it exits; ϕ would then be a predicate that characterizes the control location of interest. This concept generalizes the well known pre- and post-conditions. E.g. if ϕ captures the exit of a method m, the invariant ψ then describes m's post-condition.

Since game testing typically has to be done in the so-called blackbox setup [3] where we abstract away from the source code (because it would otherwise be too complex), and hence also away from concepts such as programs' control location, we further generalize Ernst et al. by allowing ϕ to describe a family of game states that are semantically meaningful for human users; we call this a *situation*. For example ϕ could characterize the situation where a certain interactable game element, e.g. a switch, is visible, and ψ could then express the expectation that the switch should be in its 'off' state.

Since ϕ can potentially describe a very large, even infinite, set, the specification $\phi \Rightarrow \psi$ is tested by sampling a finite number of states, and then checking whether the invariant ψ holds in these states. Obviously such tests are only *relevant* when applied on sample states that satisfy the situation ϕ. Getting the game into a relevant state for testing $\phi \Rightarrow \psi$ is a non-trivial task for a computer. Since a game typically starts in specific initial states, it first *needs to be played* to move it to any specific other state. Consequently, when we want to automate the testing of $\phi \Rightarrow \psi$, the hard part is typically not in checking its invariant part, but in finding relevant states to test the implication.

Playing a game can be seen as the execution of a sequence of actions, e.g. moving up or down, interacting with some in-game entity, etc. The set of available actions might be different on different states. We will call a sequence of actions a *plan*. A *solution* is a plan that, when executed, would drive the game under test to a state relevant for $\phi \Rightarrow \psi$. In manual testing, a human is employed to search for such a solution. There are tools that can be used to record a script that can execute the plan and replay it whenever we need to re-test the corresponding situation. A major challenge, however, with script-based test automation is the manual effort required for maintaining the scripts when they break [2]. If the game designers introduce even a small change in a the game layout (e.g. an in-game door is moved to a different position), which happens very often during the development, a recorded script would typically break. Moreover, games are non-deterministic due to all sorts of random behavior (e.g. random moves by computer controlled enemies, or randomness due to timing effect). This makes such automation scripts for games even more fragile.

By 'automated testing' of $\phi \Rightarrow \psi$ we mean to replace the human effort by letting an *agent* search for solutions. This is a *search problem*: the space of possible plans is searched to find at least one that would solve ϕ. We can define the *robustness* of an automated test as how well it can cope with the non-determinism of the system under test. Since agents are typically reactive to the environment, agent-based test automation can thus be expected to be robust; this will be discussed later in Sect. 4.3.

Testing tasks can be generalized to test 'scenarios':

$$\underbrace{\phi_0 \; ; \; \dots \; ; \; \phi_{k-1}}_{\text{scenario}} \Rightarrow \underbrace{\psi}_{\text{invariant}} \tag{2}$$

Each ϕ_i is a state predicate describing a situation. The sequence $\phi_0; \dots ; \phi_{k-1}$ describes a scenario where executions of the game under test passes through the states satisfying each ϕ_i in the same chronological order as the sequence. In the state where ϕ_{k-1} is satisfied, the invariant ψ is expected to hold. For example, if developers employ UML Use Cases, these can be converted to the above form: each flow in a use case can be translated to a scenario, and its post condition to ψ. Testing a scenario is not fundamentally harder than testing a situation, since the next situation ϕ_{i+1} in the scenario defines the same kind of search problem as we had in situation testing where ϕ_i describes the starting states for the search.

3   Aplib **Agency**

This section will introduce our agent programming framework aplib and show how to use it to automate testing tasks.

Preliminary: Java functions. Since Java 8, functions can be conveniently formulated using so-called λ-expressions. E.g. the Java expression:

$$x \rightarrow x+1$$

constructs a nameless function that takes one parameter, x, and returns the value of $x+1$. Unlike in a pure functional language like Haskell, Java functions can be either *pure* (has no side effect) or impure/effectful. An *effectful* function of type $C{\rightarrow}D$ takes an object $u{:}C$ and returns some object $v{:}D$, and may also alter the state of u.

Importantly, a λ-expression can be passed as a parameter. Since as a function a λ-expression defines behavior, passing it as a parameter to a method or object essentially allows us to inject new behavior to the method/object. This allows us to extend the behavior of an agent without having to introduce a subclass. While the latter is the traditional OO way to extend behavior, it would clutter the code base if we plan to create e.g. many variations of the same agent. Our use of λ-expressions to inject behavior is essentially a generalization of the well-known Strategy Design Pattern [21].

3.1   Agent, Belief, and Goal

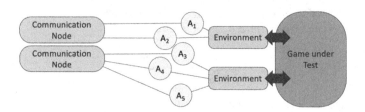

Fig. 2. Typical deployment of aplib agents. A_i are agents, controlling the game under test through an interface called *Environment*. A *communication node* allows connected agents to send messages to each other.

Figure 2 illustrates the typical way aplib agents are deployed. As common with software agents, aplib agents are intended to be used in conjunction with an external environment (in our case, this is the game under test) which is assumed to run independently. In aplib, the term 'Environment' refers, however, to a Java interface between the agents and the game. Aplib agents do *not* directly access nor control the game. Having the Environment in between keeps aplib neutral with respect to the technology used by the game under test. Developers do have to provide an implementation of this interface for each game what they want to test with aplib. This indeed requires effort, but it is a one-off investment, after which the developers would benefit from aplib's automation for the rest of the development process, as well as that of future versions of the game. The minimum functionality that an Environment should provide is a function to let an agent obtain relevant information about the current game state visible to it, and to send a command to some in-game entity that it is allowed to control.

Multiple agents can be deployed if the game is multi-player. In such a setup, agents may want to work together. A group of agents that wish to collaborate can register to a 'communication node' (see Fig. 2). This enables them to send messages to each other (singlecast, broadcast, or role-based multicast).

BDI with Goal Structure. As typical in BDI (Belief-Desire-Intent) agency, an aplib agent has a concept of belief, desire, and intent. An agent's state reflects its belief. It contains information on the current state of the game under test. Such information is a 'belief' because it may not be entirely factual. E.g. the game may only be willing to pass current information of in-game entities *in the close vicinity* of the agent. So, the agent's information on far away entities might over time become obsolete. The agent can be given a *goal structure*, defining its desire. Unlike flat goal-based structures used e.g. in 2APL [9] and GOAL [24], in this paper we employ a richly structured goal structure, with different nodes expressing different ways a goal could be achieved through its subgoals; more on this will be discussed Sect. 4. Abstractly, an aplib agent is a tuple:

$$A = (s, E, \Pi, \beta)$$

where s is an object representing A's state and E is its environment.

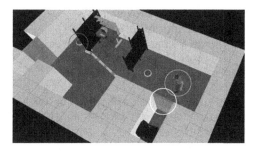

Fig. 3. A setup where we have to test that a closet door (circled white) can be opened.

Π is a goal structure, e.g. it can be a set of goals that have to be achieved sequentially. Each goal is a pair, let's denote it with $g \leftarrow\!- T^*$, where g is the goal itself and T is a 'tactic' intended to achieve g. In BDI terms, T reflects intention. When the agent decides to work on a goal $g \leftarrow\!- T^*$, it will commit to it: it will apply T *repeatedly* over multiple execution cycles until g is achieved, or the agent has used up its 'budget' for g.

The β in the tuple represents the agent's computing **budget**. Budget is used to control how long the agent should persist on pursuing its current goal. Executing a tactic consumes some budget. So, this is only possible if $\beta > 0$. Consequently, a goal will automatically fail when β reaches 0. Budget plays an important role when dealing with a goal structure with multiple goals as the agent will have to decide how to divide the budget over different goals. This will be discussed later in Sect. 4.

Example. Figure 3 shows a scene in a game called *Lab Recruits*[2]. Imagine that we want to test that the door (white circled) works (it can be opened). Two buttons (red circled) are present in the room. In a correct implementation, the door can be opened by activating the button closest to the door. A player (yellow circled) can activate a button by moving close to it and interacting with it. Suppose the door is identified by $door_1$ and its corresponding button $button_1$. The testing task above can be specified as follows:

$$\underbrace{button_1 \text{ is active}}_{\text{situation}} \Rightarrow \underbrace{door_1 \text{ is open}}_{\text{invariant}} \tag{3}$$

Figure 4 shows how we create a test agent named Smith to perform the aforementioned testing task. First, lines 1–3 show the relevant part of the environment the agent will use to interface with the Lab Recruits game; it shows the primitive commands available to the agent. The method interact(i, j) will cause an in-game character with id i (this would be the character controlled by the agent) to interact with another in-game entity with id j (e.g. a button). The method also returns a new'Observation', containing information on the new state of game-entities in the visible range of i. The method moveToward(i, p, q) will cause the character i to move *towards* a position q, given that p is i's current position. Simply teleporting to q is not allowed in most games. Instead, the method will only move i some small distance towards q (so, it may take multiple update cycles for a to actually reach q). The method also returns a new observation.

---

[2] https://github.com/iv4xr-project/labrecruits.

```
class LabRecruitsEnv extends Environment {                        1
    Observation interact(String id₁, String id₂) ...            2
    Observation moveToward(String id, Vec₃ p, Vec₃ q) ...       3
}                                                                4
var Smith = new TestAgent() ;                                    5
var Π = testgoal("g", Smith)                                      6
        . toSolve   (s → isActive(s.getEntity("button1")))       7
        . invariant(s → isOpen(s.getEntity("door1")))            8
        . tactic(activateButton₁Tac)                             9
        . lift() ;                                              10
Smith . withState(new AgentState())                             11
        . withEnvironment(labrecruitsEnv)                       12
        . setGoal(Π)                                            13
        . budget(200)                                           14
```

Fig. 4. Creating an agent named Smith to test the Lab Recruits game. The code is in Java, since Aplib is a DSL embedded in Java. The notation $x \rightarrow e$ in line 7 is Java lambda expression defining a function, in this case a predicate defining the goal.

Line 5 creates an empty agent. Lines 11–13 configure it: line 11 attaches a fresh state to the agent; then, assuming labrecruitsEnv is an instance of LabRecruitsEnv (defined in lines 1–3), line 12 hooks this environment to the agent. Line 13 assigns a goal named Π to the agent. The goal is defined in lines 6–10, stating that the desired situation the agent should establish is one where the in-game button$_1$ is active (line 7). Line 9 associates a tactic named activateButton$_1$Tac to this goal, which the agent will use to achieve the latter. Line 10 lifts the defined goal to become a goal structure. More precisely, line 6 creates a 'test-goal'. An ordinary goal, created using a constructor named **goal** rather than **testgoal**, simply formulates desired states to be in. A test-goal *additionally* specifies an invariant (line 8). It formulates a testing task as discussed in Sect. 2. E.g. lines 7 and 8 formulate the testing task in (3). When the goal part is achieved, the invariant will be tested on the current agent state. If this returns true, the test passes, otherwise it fails. Its automation is provided by the tactic activateButton$_1$Tac that should specify some strategy to go towards the button and activate it.

3.2 Action (Elementary Tactic)

A tactic is made of 'actions', composed hierarchically to define a goal-achieving strategy. Such composition will be discussed in Sect. 4.1. In the simple case though, a tactic is made of just a single action. An *action* is an effectful and guarded function over the agent's state. The example below shows the syntax for defining an action.

$$\text{var } \alpha = \textbf{action}("id") \cdot \underbrace{\textbf{do}_2(f)}_{\text{behavior}} \cdot \underbrace{\textbf{on}\_(q)}_{\text{guard}} \tag{4}$$

```
var approachButton₁ = action(" approachButton1 ").                              1
  . do₂((AgentState s) → (Entity button₁) → {                                   2
        var o = s.env.moveTowards(s.id ,s.position ,button₁.position) ;         3
        s.markObservation(o) ;                                                  4
        return s }                                                              5
    )                                                                           6
  . on_((AgentState s) → {                                                      7
        var e = s.getEntity ("button1") ;                                       8
        if (e==null) return null ;                                              9
        if (distance(s.position ,e.position) < 0.01) return null ;              10
        return e ;                                                              11
    ) ;                                                                         12
```

Fig. 5. An action that would move an agent closer to button$_1$. Notice that we again use λ-expressions (lines 3 and 7) to conveniently introduce functions without having to create a class.

This statement[3] defines an action with "id" as its id, and binds the action to the Java variable α. The f is a function defining the behavior that will be invoked when the action α is executed. This function is effectful and may change the agent state. The q, is a pure function, called the 'guard' of the action, specifying when the action is eligible for execution. Notice that the pair f, q can be seen as expressing a *reasoning rule* $q \to f$.

The guard q can be a predicate or a *query*. More precisely, let Σ be the type of the agent state and R the type of query results. We allow q to be a function of type $\Sigma \to R$. Whereas a predicate would inspect a state $s{:}\Sigma$ and simply return a true or a false, a query inspects s if it contains some object r satisfying a certain property. E.g. q might be checking if s contains a closed door. If such a door can be found, q returns it, else it returns **null**. This gives more information than just a simple true or false.

More precisely, the action α is executable on a state s if it is both control and guard-enabled on s. For now we can ignore control-enabledness. The action is *guard-enabled* on s when $q(s)$ returns some non-null r. The behavior function f has the type $\Sigma \to R \to V$ for some type V. When the action α is executed on s, it invokes $f(s)(r)$[4]. The result $v = f(s)(r)$, if it is not null, will then be checked if it achieves the agent's current goal.

For example, Fig. 5 shows an action that can help agent Smith from Fig. 4. In the game Lab Recruits, to interact with a button a player character needs to stand close to the button. Although in Fig. 3 the character seems to stand close to button$_1$, it is not close enough. The tactic in Fig. 5, when invoked, will move the character closer to the button (but will not interact with it, yet). It may take several invocations to move the

---

[3] Note that **action**, **do₂**, and **on_** are not Java keywords. They are just methods. However, they also implement the Fluent Interface design pattern [19] commonly used in embedded Domain Specific Languages (DSLs) to 'trick' the syntax restriction of the host language to allow methods to be called in a sequence as if they form a sentence to improve the DSL's fluency.

[4] This scheme of using r essentially simulates *unification* a la pgrules in 2APL. Unification plays an important role in 2APL. The action in (4) corresponds to pgrule $q(r)? \mid f(r)$ The parameter s (the agent's state/belief) is kept implicit in pgrules. In 2APL this action is executed through Prolog, where q is a Prolog query and r is obtained through unification with the fact base representing the agent's state.

```
class AgentState extends StateWithProlog {                              1
    ... addRules(                                                       2
        clause(openDoors("B","D1","D2"))                               3
        . IMPby(                                                        4
        or(and(close("D1"),connected("B","D1")),                       5
            and(open("D1")  ,unConnected("B","D1"),                    6
                close("D2"),connected("B","D2"))))                     7
}                                                                       8
action("open_doors_1and2")                                             9
  . do₂((AgentState s) →                                              10
        (Result r) → {                                                11
            var b = s.getEntity(stringval(r.get("B")))  ;             12
            if (distance(s.position,b.position) > 0.01)               13
                o = s.env.moveTowards(s.id,s.position,b.position)  ;  14
            else o = s.env.interact(s.id,b.id)  ;                     15
            s.markObservation(o)  ;                                   16
            return b })                                               17
  . on_((AgentState s) → s.query(openDoors("B",door₁,door₂)))        18
```

Fig. 6. An example action whose guard, line 18, is formulated declaratively in the Prolog style.

character close enough to the button. The action's guard specifies that the action is only enabled if button₁ exists (line 9) in the agent's belief. and furthermore its distance to the agent is ≥0.01 unit (line 3). The behavior part of the action, line 4, will then move the agent some small distance towards the button. Line 4 will incorporate the returned new observation (of the game state) into the agent's state.

Reasoning. Most of agent reasoning is carried out by actions' guards, since they are the ones that inspect the agent's state to decide which actions are executable. The reader may notice that the guard in the example in Fig. 5 is imperatively formulated, which is to be expected since aplib's host language, Java, is an imperative programming language. However, aplib also has a Prolog backend (using tuprolog [13]) to facilitate a declarative style of state query.

Figure 6 shows an example. To use Prolog-style queries, the agent's state needs to extend a class called StateWithProlog. It will then inherit an instance of a tuprolog engine to which we can add facts and inference rules, and then pose queries over these. Imagine a level in Lab Recruits where we have multiple doors and buttons. Some buttons may crank multiple doors when toggled. Suppose a test agent wants to get to a state where two doors, door₁ and door₂, are open. The example shows the definition of an action named "open_doors_1and2" that will do this. Note that after opening one of these doors, the agent should be careful when trying to open the second. It needs to find a button that indeed opens the second door, but without closing the first one again. The reasoning needed to handle this is formulated as a Prolog rule called openDoors defined in lines 3–7. With the help of this rule, the guard for the action "open_doors_1and2" can now be formulated as a Prolog query openDoors(B, door₁, door₂), which in aplib is expressed as in line 18. The predicate is true if door₁ is closed and B is a button connected to it (so, toggling the button would crank the door). Else, if door₁ is open,

B should be connected to door$_2$, but not to door$_1$ (so, toggling it will not close door$_1$ again). So, assuming a solution exists, invoking the action above multiple times will first open door$_1$, unless it is already open, and then door$_2$. Notice that the guard is *declarative*, as it only characterizes the properties that a right button should have; it does not spell out how we should iterate over all the buttons in the agent's belief to check it.

4   Structured Goals and Tactics

A goal can be very hard for an agent to achieve/solve directly. For example imagine a level in the game Lab Recruits, similar to Fig. 1, where we have to test some feature *F* located in some specific room. Let isInteracted$_F$ be the goal representing the agent is at *F* and manages to interact with it (and hence test it). To achieve this the agent will first need to reach the room where *F* is. To access this room a door D needs to be opened first. The door can be closed, in which case the agent first needs to find a specific button *B* that opens it. If the agent does not know all these steps, then directly solving isInteracted$_F$ will be very difficult.

We can help the agent by providing intermediate goals that it needs to solve first. We can formulate this as a 'goal structure' as the one below:

$$\textbf{SEQ}(\,\textbf{FIRSTof}(\,\text{isOpen}_D, \textbf{SEQ}(\text{isActivated}_B, \text{isOpen}_D)),$$
$$\text{isInteracted}_F)$$

where isOpen$_D$ and isActivated$_B$ are intermediate goals. **SEQ** and **FIRSTof** are examples of so-called goal combinators explained below.

In aplib a composite goal is called a *goal structure*. It is a tree with goals as the leaves, and goal-combinators as nodes. The goals at the leaves are ordinary goals or test-goals, and hence they all have tactics associated to each. The combinators do not have their own tactics. Instead, they are used to provide a high level control on the order or importance of the underlying goals. Available combinators are as follows; let *G* and $G_1, ..., G_n$ be goal structures:

- If $g \leftarrow\!-\!- T *$ is a goal with the tactic *T* associated to it, *g*.lift() turns it to a goal structure consisting of the goal as its only leaf. *T* is implicitly attached to this leaf.
- **SEQ**$(G_1, ..., G_n)$ is a goal structure that is achieved by achieving all the subgoals $G_1, ..., G_n$, and in that order. This is useful when G_n is hard to achieve; so $G_1, ..., G_{n-1}$ act as helpful intermediate goals to guide the agent. Goal structures of this form also naturally express test scenarios as in (2).
- $H = \textbf{FIRSTof}(G_1, ..., G_n)$ is a goal structure where, given *H* to achieve, the agent will first try to achieve G_1. If this fails, it tries G_2, and so on until there is one goal G_i that is achieved. If none is achieved, *H* is considered as failed.
- $H = \textbf{REPEAT}\ G$ is a goal structure where, given *H* to achieve, the agent will pursue *G*. If after sometime *G* fails, e.g. because it runs out of budget, it will be tried again. Fresh budget will be allocated for *G*, taken from what remains of the agent's total budget. This is iterated until *G* is achieved, or until *H*'s budget runs out.

Dynamic Subgoals. Rather than providing a whole goal structure to an agent, sometimes it might be better to let the agent dynamically introduce or cancel subgoals. For example imagine an agent A which initially is given a goal structure $\Pi =$ SEQ(isOpen$_D$, inRoom$_R$). As the agent works on the first subgoal, isOpen$_D$ imagine that it discovers that the door D is closed, and hence the subgoal cannot be reached before another subgoal is solved (i.e. activate the button that opens the door).

Rather than pre-programming how to handle this in Π we can let the tactic of isOpen$_D$ to make this decision instead. Since a tactic has access to the agent's state, it can inspect this state. Based on what it discovers it may then decide to insert a new subgoal, let's call it isActivated$_B$, that will cause the agent to first find the button B and activate it in order to open D. The agent can do this by invoking addBefore(isActivated$_B$), that will then change Π to:

$$\textbf{SEQ}(\textbf{REPEAT}(\textbf{SEQ}(\text{isActivated}_B, \text{isOpen}_D)), \text{inRoom}_R)$$

The **REPEAT** construct will cause the agent to move back to isActivated$_B$ upon failing isOpen$_D$. The sequence **SEQ**(isActivated$_B$, isOpen$_D$) will then be repeatedly attempted until it succeeds. The number of attempts can be controlled by assigning budget to the **REPEAT** construct (budgeting will be discussed below).

Budgeting. Since a goal structure can introduce multiple goals, they will be competing for the agent's attention. By default, aplib agents use the blind commitment policy [31] where an agent will commit to its current goal until it is achieved. However, it is possible to exert finer control on the agent's commitment through a simple but powerful budgeting mechanism.

When the agent was created, we can give it a starting computing budget β_0 (else it is assumed to be ∞). Let Π be the agent's root goal structure. For each sub-structure G in Π we can specify G.bmax: the *maximum* budget G will get. Else, the agent conservatively assumes G.bmax $= \infty$. By specifying bmax we control how much the agent should commit to a particular goal structure. This limit can be specified at the goal level (the leaves of Π), if the programmer wants to micro-manage the agent's commitment, or higher in the hierarchy of Π to strategically control it.

Once it runs, the agent will only work on a single goal at a time. The goal g it works on is called the *current goal*. Every ancestor of a current g is also current. For every goal structure G, let β_G denote the remaining budget for G. At the beginning, $\beta_\Pi = \beta_0$. When a goal or goal structure G in Π becomes current, budget is allocated to it as follows. When G becomes current, its parent either becomes current as well, or it is already current (e.g. the root Π is always current). Ancestors H that are already current keeps their β_H unchanged. Then, the budget for G is allocated by setting β_G to $\textbf{min}(G.\text{bmax}, \beta_{\text{parent}(G)})$, after we recursively determine $\beta_{\text{parent}(G)}$. This budgeting scheme is *safe*: the budget of a goal structure never exceeds that of its parent.

When working on a goal g, any work the agent does will consume some budget, say δ. This will be deducted from β_g and from the budget of its ancestors. If β_g becomes ≤ 0, the agent aborts g. It must then find another goal from Π.

```
1  var activateButton₁Tac = FIRSTof(
2      action("activateButton1").do₂(..).on_(..).lift()
3    . approachButton₁.lift()
4    . action("explore").do₂(..).lift()
5    )
```

Fig. 7. The tactic for agent Smith in Fig. 4, composed from three other tactics. The first (its full code is not shown) is an action to activate button₁ if it is close enough to the agent. Otherwise, the action *approachButton₁* (defined in Fig. 5) will move the agent towards the button, if it is visible to the agent (see the action's guard). Else, FIRSTof falls back to the last tactic that will explore the area around the agent to search the button. Note that without using a combinator like FIRSTof the control flow will have to be explicitly programmed into the actions' guards, resulting in a less abstract agent program, not to mention that the control flow would then be implicit, which makes the code harder to understand and more error prone.

4.1 Tactic

Rather than using a single action, Aplib provides a more powerful means to achieve a goal, namely tactic. A tactic is a hierarchical composition of actions. Methods used to compose them are also called *combinators*. Figure 7 shows an example of a tactic, composed with a combinator called FIRSTof. Structurally, a tactic is a tree with actions as leaves and tactic-combinators as nodes. The actions are the ones that do the actual work. Furthermore, recall that the actions also have their own guards, controlling their enabledness. The combinators are used to exert a higher level control over the actions, e.g. sequencing or choosing between them. This higher level control supersedes guard-level control[5]. The following tactic combinators[6] are provided; let $T_1, ..., T_n$ be tactics:

1. If α is an action, $T = \alpha.\textbf{lift}()$ is a tactic. Executing this tactic on an agent state s means executing α on s, which is only possible if α is enabled on s (if its guard results a non-null value when queried on s).
2. $T = \textbf{SEQ}(T_1, ..., T_n)$ is a tactic. When invoked, T will execute the whole sequence $T_1, ..., T_n$.
3. $T = \textbf{ANYof}(T_1, ..., T_n)$ is a tactic that randomly chooses one of enabled T_i's and executes it. A **SEQ** tactic is *enabled* if its first sub-tactic is enabled. For other combinators, it is enabled if one of its sub-tactic is enabled.
4. $T = \textbf{FIRSTof}(T_1, .., T_n)$ is a tactic. It is used to express priority over a set of tactics if more than one of them could be enabled. When invoked, T will invoke the first enabled T_i from the sequence $T_1, .., T_n$.

---

[5] While it is true that we can encode all control in action guards, this would not be an abstract way of programming tactical control and would ultimately result in error prone code.

[6] Earlier, in Sect. 1, we mentioned a relation with theorem provers. LCF-family theorem provers like HOL and Isabelle also have a concept of 'tactic', which basically is a function that constructs a proof of a given conjecture [12,22,40]. Since the solving proof is usually not known upfront, similar tactic combinators are used to control a search over the possible proof space. E.g. in HOL we have THEN, and ORLSE. These correspond to our SEQ and FIRSTof. HOL's REPEAT has no direct tactical counterpart in aplib, though aplib's deliberation cycles implicitly introduce a top-level repetition —this will be elaborated in Sect. 4.2.

4.2   Aplib Deliberation Cycle

Consider a goal $g \leftarrow -T^*$. When this goal becomes current, recall that the agent will then *repeatedly* execute T until g is achieved (or until its budget is exhausted). Aplib agents execute their tactics in cycles. In BDI agency these are called *deliberation cycles* [10,32,38]: in each cycle, an agent senses its environment, reasons which action to do, and then performs this action. To make itself responsive to changes in the environment, an agent only executes *one action per cycle*. So, if the environment's state changes at the next cycle, a different action can be chosen to respond to the change. However, if T contains a sub-tactic T' of the form $\textbf{SEQ}(T_1,..,T_n)$ things become more complicated. If T' is selected, the agent has to execute the whole sequence[7] which will take least n cycles, before it can repeat the whole T again. This makes the execution flow of a tactic non-trivial. We therefore have to deviate from the standard BDI deliberation [38].

Imagine an agent $A = (s, E, \Pi, \beta)$. At the start, A inspects its goal structure Π to determine which goal $g \leftarrow -T^*$ in Π it should pursue, and calculates how much of the budget β should be allocated for achieving g (β_g). A will then repeatedly apply T over multiple cycles until g is achieved, or β_g is exhausted. At every cycle, A does the following:

1. *Sensing.* The agent asks the Environment to provide a fresh state information.
2. *Reasoning.* The agent determines which actions α in T are executable on the current state s. This is the case if α is guard-enabled on s and furthermore also control-enabled. The definition of latter is somewhat complicated. Let us explain it with an example instead. Suppose $T = \textbf{ANYof}(\alpha_0, \textbf{SEQ}(\alpha_1, \alpha_2), \alpha_3)$. The first time T is considered for execution, α_0, α_1 and α_3 becomes control-enabled, but not α_2. If α_0 turns out to be *not* guard-enabled, and α_1, α_3 are, only the latter two are executable. Suppose α_1 is chosen for execution. At the next cycle only α_2 is control-enabled. If it is also guard-enabled it can be executed, else it remains control-enabled for the next cycle. After α_2 is executed, the execution of the whole T is completed, and it can be repeated again.

   If no action is executable, the agent will sleep until the next cycle. Note that since the game under test runs autonomously, it may in the mean time move to a new state, and hence in the next cycle some actions may become enabled.
3. *Execution and resolution.* Let α be the selected action. It is then executed. If its result v is non-null, it is considered as a candidate solution to be checked against the current goal g. If v achieves g (so, g is solved), the agent inspects the remaining goals in Π to decide the next one to handle. The whole cycle is repeated, but with the new goal. If there is no goal left, then the agent is done. If g is *not* achieved, it is maintained and the whole cycle is repeated.

4.3   Test Robustness

Let us now explain more concretely why aplib test automation is more robust. Recall the tactic activateButton$_{1Tac}$ (Fig. 7) to activate button$_1$. Notice that it uses the tactic

---

[7] Breaking off in the middle can be expressed using a combination of **FIRSTof** and **SEQ**.

approachButton$_1$.**lift**() (defined in Fig. 5) to approach the button first in case the agent is not standing next to it. Notice that the location is not hard-wired in this tactic, but instead queried from the button itself. Let us also replace the call to moveTowards in line 3 in Fig. 5 with navigateTo. This will cause the agent to use aplib's 3D-space path finding to guide itself towards the given location. If the game designer now moves the button elsewhere, e.g. to swap its position with the far button in Fig. 3, the tactic will still work, as long as there is a path that reaches the button. The tactic approachButton$_1$ requires however that the button is already in the agent's belief, which would not be the case if the developer moves it to a new position that is initially not visible to the agent. Fortunately the enclosing tactic activateButton$_{1Tac}$ can deal with that, by falling back to the 'explore' tactic to search the button first.

If the level contains some random fire hazard, we can replace approachButton$_1$ in activateButton$_{1Tac}$ with a more adaptive variant e.g.:

$$\textbf{FIRSTof}(\text{avoidHazardTac}, \text{approachButton}_1.\textbf{lift}())$$

If the agent now detects fire when it on its way to button$_1$, it will first try to evade the fire before resuming its navigation to button$_1$. Importantly, since the tactic executability is re-checked at every deliberation cycle, the agent will be able to timely invoke the above re-planning.

5 Proof of Concept

Lab Recruits	
C# scripts	64 files, 3524 sloc
animation control	12 files, 2763 lines
Implementation of Environment	
game-side	393 sloc C#
Java-side	1056 sloc Java
Support	
Domain specific tactics	505 sloc Java
General support (world representation, pathfinding)	1250 sloc Java
Utilities	240 sloc Java
Tests with aplib	
(game logic) button & door	74 sloc Java (28 sloc actual test-code)
(level test) state transitions (3)	117 sloc Java (61 sloc actual test-code)
(level test) simple reachability	69 sloc Java (19 sloc actual test-code)
(level test) complex reachability	98 sloc Java (46 sloc actual test-code)

Fig. 8. Some statistics of the experiment with the Lab Recruits game.

We conducted a pilot on the previously mentioned Lab Recruits game[8], as a proof of concept, and to get a preliminary idea on the effort to integrate aplib into the development cycle and to write tests. Lab Recruits is developed by a group of students using an established game development framework called Unity 3D. It consists of about 3500 lines of C# scripts. In Unity, not all dynamics are programmed in such scripts. E.g.

---

[8] https://github.com/iv4xr-project/labrecruits.

animation is designed with a separate tool, from which meta files ($\approx$ 2700 lines) are generated and compiled to behavior.

To extend their entertainment, most games are replayable on different instances of the playing world, so-called *levels*. Levels have unique layout, monsters and items drop, etc. The logic (game rules) is however the same over all levels. Levels are often meticulously hand crafted (it is an art that computers have not mastered yet), hence requiring significant human effort. A level in Lab Recruits represents a laboratory building, consisting of rooms, in one or multiple floors, populated by in-game objects, such as tables, and chairs. Some of them are interactable, such as buttons. Some of them represent hazard, such as, fire. In addition to testing the correctness of the general game logic, note that every newly crafted level also requires testing, e.g. to make sure that in-game entities which are necessary for completing the level are indeed reachable by the player.

Integration Effort. As remarked in Sect. 3.1 to use aplib the developers need to first provide an implementation of the interface Environment for their game. For Lab Recruits this amount to about 1400 lines of Java and C# —see Fig. 8. While this gives test agents basic control over the game, an important lesson we learned is that this is not enough. More abstract ways to control and navigate through the game are necessary. These are provided as a library of tactics ($\approx$ 500 lines) and support classes e.g. to do path-planning on a 3D surface ($\approx$ 1200 lines). Such tactics are quite game-specific, but much of the path-planning functionality is generic and will in the future be migrated to aplib's standard library.

While the amount of integration code is relatively substantial compared to the size of Lab Recruits itself, it does not mean that if we extend Lab Recruits with new game objects and new logic the integration code will grow as much. Moreover, the same integration can be used to test as many new levels as we have, no matter how large or complex they are.

Testing with aplib We used aplib agents to test Lab Recruits' general logic and a number of sample levels —an overview is given in Fig. 8. To test the general logic it is sufficient to make a minimalistic level exposing the aspects of the logic that we want to test. E.g. a button in Lab Recruits should open/close doors bound to it (and only those doors). This proves that if they are bound correctly, they will also interact correctly. This can be tested with a mini level with one button and several doors. The corresponding testing task takes 74 lines of code, though only a third of them describes the task itself.

A typical testing tasks when testing a level is to verify that every entity (or at least, the key entities) has the right behavior, e.g. that a button would open the right door (in other words, whether the level binds the correct doors to the button). In our experiment, testing three such buttons takes about 120 lines of code, but only about half of them actually describe the task.

Another typical testing task is to check if key entities in a level are actually reachable. In the simple case, an entity is reachable through an unobstructed path in the level. However, note that the entity might *not* be visible from the agent's initial position. So, solving such a task also involves searching the level. On the other hand, this contributes to the robustness of the test: if the developers change the level's layout or move the entity elsewhere, the test code will not break as long as the entity remains reachable. In our example, such a test takes about 70 lines. The code is reusable, irrespective the size and complexity of the level, as long as the target entity is reachable in the above sense.

In a more complex situation, reaching an entity requires opening a series of doors that block the path to it. To verify the entity's reachability, we simply translate the needed sequence of essential buttons (that should be toggled to open the guarding doors) into subgoals. For a setup that involves three buttons and three doors it takes about 100 lines of test code; only about half of them actually describe the task. The approach can be smarter (e.g. if we can eliminate the need to add subgoals), but this is not the goal of the current pilot, and left as future work.

6 Related Work

Software agents have been employed in various domains, e.g. computer games, health care, and control systems [26,27,30]. With aplib we have another usecase, namely automated testing. Using agents for software testing has actually been attempted before [5,33,35,36]. However, these works use agents to test services or web applications, which are software types that can already be handled by non-agent techniques such as model based [43] or search based [1,20] testing, whereas we argued that high interactivity of computer games poses a different level of challenge for automated testing.

To program agents, without having to do everything from scratch, we can either use an agent 'framework', which essentially provides a library, or we use a dedicated agent programming language. Examples of agent frameworks are JADE [6] and aplib for Java, HLogo [7] for Haskell, and PROFETA [18] for Python. Examples of dedicated agent languages are JASON [8], 2APL [9], GOAL [24], JADEL [25], and SARL [39]. HLogo is an agent framework that is specialized for developing an agent-based simulation. On the other hand, JADE and aplib are generic agent frameworks that can be connected to any environment. Aplib is light weight compared to JADE. E.g. the latter supports distributed agents and FIPA compliance which aplib does not have. JADE does not natively offers BDI agency, though BDI agency, e.g. as offered by JADEL, can be implemented on top of JADE. In contrast, aplib and PROFETA are natively BDI agent frameworks.

Among the dedicated agent programming languages, some are dedicated for programming BDI agents. The good thing is that they offer Prolog-style declarative programming. On the down side e.g. available data types are restricted (e.g. no support for collection and polymorphism), which is a serious hinderance if we are to use them for large projects. One with a very rich set of language features (collection, polymorphism, OO, lambda expression) is SARL, though it is non-BDI. PROFETA and aplib are somewhere in between. Both are BDI DSLs, but they are embedded DSLs rather than a native language as SARL. To improve its fluency as a DSL, aplib makes heavy use of design patterns such as Fluent Interface [19] and Strategy Pattern [21]. PROFETA and aplib's host languages are full of features (Python and Java, respectively), that would give the strength of SARL that agent languages like JASON and GOAL cannot offer.

Aplib's distinguishing feature compared to other implementations of BDI agency (e.g. JACK, JASON, 2APL, GOAL, JADEL, PROFETA) is its tactical programming of plans (through tactics) and goals (through goal structures). An agent is essentially set of actions. The BDI architecture does not traditionally impose a rigid control structure on these actions, hence allowing agents to react adaptively to changing environment. However, there are also goals that require certain actions to be carried out in a certain order over multiple deliberation cycles. Or, when given a hard goal to achieve, the agent might need to try different strategies, each would need to be given enough commitment by the agent, and conversely it should be possible to abort it so that another strategy can be tried. All these imply that tactics and strategies require some form of control structures, although not as rigid as in e.g. procedures. All the aforementioned BDI implementations do not provide control structures beyond intra-action control structures. This shortcoming was already observed by [17], stating domains like autonomous vehicles need agents with tactical ability. They went even further, stating that Agent Oriented Software Engineering (AOSE) methodologies in general do not provide a sufficiently rich representation of goal control structures. While inter-actions and inter-goals control structures can be encoded through pushing and popping of beliefs or goals into the agent's state, such an approach would clutter the programs and error prone. An existing solution for tactical programming for agents is to use the Tactics Development extension [17] of the Prometheus agent development methodology [34]. This extension allows tactics to be graphically modelled, and template implementations in JACK can be generated from the models. In contrast, Aplib provides the features directly at the programming level. It provides the additional control structures suitable for tactical programming over the usual rule-based style programming of BDI agents. When programming test agents, having an option to exert control helps the tester to narrow the agents' search space which may benefit their performance, which is important when we start to accumulate a large number of tests.

Let us also mention the agent language IndiGolog [11] from the Golog-family [28]. The original Golog [28] allows a model of an environment to be expressed in a mix of imperative statements and 'situation calculus' axioms (comparable to Hoare triples). A Golog agent solves goals *off-line*, using the model. The obtained plan (sequence of actions) are then executed on the environment. Such an approach is less suitable for testing a game due to the latter's non-determinism. In contrast, IndiGolog offers a mix of reactive programming and model-based off-line planning. If a test-goal can be broken into subgoals where some are robust against the game's non-determinism, off-line planning can be employed to handle the latter. Although testing is not a main use-case of IndiGolog nor Golog, their idea actually resembles a well known testing approach called Model Based Testing (MBT) [15] where Labelled Transition Systems (LTS) or Extended Finite State Machines (EFSMs) are often used as models. In MBT, a model also defines correctness (e.g. when the model specifies b to happen after a, the implementation is expected to behave in the same way), in addition to providing guidance on how to reach a given goal state as in Golog. Aplib currently has no MBT capability; this is future work. Extending aplib with MBT would benefit from aplib's tactical layer, which as pointed out in Sect. 4.3 improves agents' robustness against non-determinism, which in terms of MBT would allow more goals to be solved off line. Since requiring developers to provide detailed models is unlikely to scale up, future research should be focused on model learning [43], e.g. to learn the parts of the model that only serve to provide goal solving guidance, so that developers only need to focus on the parts that capture the game's correctness.

7 Conclusion and Future Work

We have presented aplib, a BDI agent programming framework featuring multi agency and novel tactical programming and strategic goal-level programming. We choose to offer aplib as a Domain Specific Language (DSL) embedded in Java, hence making the framework very expressive. Despite the decreased fluency, we believe this embedded DSL approach to be better suited for large scale programming of agents, while avoiding the high expense and long term risk of maintaining a dedicated agent programming language.

With the above features aplib would be a good choice to be used as a framework to program test agents for testing highly interactive software such as computer games. Our experience so far with the Lab Recruits case study (Fig. 1) shows that even a simple test agent that can navigate within a closed terrain already introduces automation that is previously not possible. Larger and more thorough case studies are still future work. We would also like to explore the use of emotion modelling framework such as FAtiMA [14] alongside aplib agents to allow us to test user experience (e.g. whether the game becomes too boring too quickly), which is an aspect of a great concern in the game industry.

While in many cases relying on reasoning-based intelligence is enough, there are also cases where this is not. Recently we have seen rapid advances in learning-based AI. As future work we seek to extend aplib to let programmers hook learning algorithms to their agents to teach the agents to make the right choices, at least in some situation, as an alternative when rule-based reasoning becomes too complicated (e.g. when it involves recognizing visual or audio patterns).

References

1. Alshahwan, N., Harman, M.: Automated web application testing using search based software engineering. In: 26th International Conference on Automated Software Engineering. IEEE (2011)
2. Alégroth, E., Feldt, R., Kolström, P.: Maintenance of automated test suites in industry: an empirical study on visual GUI testing. Inf. Softw. Technol. **73**, 66–80 (2016)
3. Ammann, P., Offutt, J.: Introduction to Software Testing. Cambridge University Press, New York (2016)
4. Anand, S., et al.: An orchestrated survey of methodologies for automated software test case generation. J. Syst. Softw. **86**(8), 1978–2001 (2013)
5. Bai, X., Chen, B., Ma, B., Gong, Y.: Design of intelligent agents for collaborative testing of service-based systems. In: 6th International Workshop on Automation of Software Test. ACM (2011)
6. Bellifemine, F., Poggi, A., Rimassa, G.: JADE-a FIPA-compliant agent framework. In: Proceedings of PAAM (1999)
7. Bezirgiannis, N., Prasetya, I., Sakellariou, I.: Hlogo: A parallel Haskell variant of NetLogo. In: 6th International Conference on Simulation and Modeling Methodologies, Technologies and Applications (SIMULTECH). IEEE (2016)

8. Bordini, R.H., Hübner, J.F., Wooldridge, M.: Programming Multi-agent Systems in AgentSpeak Using Jason, vol. 8. John Wiley & Sons, Hoboken (2007)
9. Dastani, M.: 2APL: a practical agent programming language. Auton. Agent Multi-Agent Syst. **16**(3), 214–248 (2008). https://doi.org/10.1007/s10458-008-9036-y
10. Dastani, M., Testerink, B.: Design patterns for multi-agent programming. Int. J. Agent-Oriented Softw. Eng. **5**(2/3), 167–202 (2016)
11. De Giacomo, G., Lespérance, Y., Levesque, H.J., Sardina, S.: IndiGolog: a high-level programming language for embedded reasoning agents. In: El Fallah Seghrouchni, A., Dix, J., Dastani, M., Bordini, R.H. (eds.) Multi-Agent Programming, pp. 31–72. Springer, Boston, MA (2009). https://doi.org/10.1007/978-0-387-89299-3_2
12. Delahaye, D.: A tactic language for the system coq. In: Parigot, M., Voronkov, A. (eds.) LPAR 2000. LNAI, vol. 1955, pp. 85–95. Springer, Heidelberg (2000). https://doi.org/10.1007/3-540-44404-1_7
13. Denti, E., Omicini, A., Calegari, R.: tuProlog: Making Prolog ubiquitous. ALP Newsletter, October 2013
14. Dias, J., Mascarenhas, S., Paiva, A.: FAtiMA modular: towards an agent architecture with a generic appraisal framework. In: Bosse, T., Broekens, J., Dias, J., van der Zwaan, J. (eds.) Emotion Modeling. LNCS (LNAI), vol. 8750, pp. 44–56. Springer, Cham (2014). https://doi.org/10.1007/978-3-319-12973-0_3
15. Dias Neto, A.C., Subramanyan, R., Vieira, M., Travassos, G.H.: A survey on model-based testing approaches: a systematic review. In: Proceedings of the 1st ACM International Workshop on Empirical Assessment of Software Engineering Languages and Technologies (2007)
16. Ernst, M.D., et al.: The daikon system for dynamic detection of likely invariants. Sci. Comput. Program. **69**(1–3), 35–45 (2007)
17. Evertsz, R., Thangarajah, J., Yadav, N., Ly, T.: A framework for modelling tactical decision-making in autonomous systems. J. Syst. Softw. **110**, 222–238 (2015)
18. Fichera, L., Messina, F., Pappalardo, G., Santoro, C.: A Python framework for programming autonomous robots using a declarative approach. Sci. Comput. Program. **139**, 36–55 (2017)
19. Fowler, M., Evans, E.: Fluent interface. martinfowler.com (2005). https://martinfowler.com/bliki/FluentInterface.html
20. Fraser, G., Arcuri, A.: EvoSuite: automatic test suite generation for object-oriented software. In: 19th ACM SIGSOFT Symposium and the 13th European Conference on Foundations of Software Engineering. ACM (2011)
21. Gamma, E., Helm, R., Johnson, R., Vlissides, J.: Design Patterns: Elements of Reusable Object-oriented Software. Addison-Wesley, Boston (1994)
22. Gordon, M.J., Melham, T.F.: Introduction to HOL A Theorem Proving Environment for Higher Order Logic. Cambridge University Press, New York (1993)
23. Herzig, A., Lorini, E., Perrussel, L., Xiao, Z.: BDI logics for BDI architectures: old problems, new perspectives. KI-Künstliche Intelligenz **31**(1), 73–83 (2017). https://doi.org/10.1007/s13218-016-0457-5
24. Hindriks, K.V.: Programming Cognitive Agents in GOAL (2018). https://goalapl.atlassian.net/wiki/spaces/GOAL/overview
25. Iotti, E.: An agent-oriented programming language for JADE multi-agent systems. Ph.D. thesis, Università di Parma. Dipartimento di Ingegneria e Architettura (2018)
26. Jennings, N., Jennings, N.R., Wooldridge, M.J.: Agent Technology: Foundations, Applications, and Markets. Springer Science & Business Media, Berlin (1998). https://doi.org/10.1007/978-3-662-03678-5
27. Leitão, P.: Agent-based distributed manufacturing control: a state-of-the-art survey. Eng. Appl. Artifi. Intell. **22**(7), 979–991 (2009)
28. Levesque, H.J., Reiter, R., Lespérance, Y., Lin, F., Scherl, R.B.: GOLOG: a logic programming language for dynamic domains. J. Log. Program. **31**(1–3), 59–83 (1997)

29. McMinn, P.: Search-based software test data generation: a survey. Softw. Test. Verif. Reliabi. **14**(2), 105–156 (2004)
30. Merabet, G.H., et al.: Applications of multi-agent systems in smart grids: a survey. In: International conference on multimedia computing and systems (ICMCS), pp. 1088–1094. IEEE (2014)
31. Meyer, J.J., Broersen, J., Herzig, A.: Handbook of Logics for Knowledge and Belief, chap. BDI Logics, pp. 453–498. College Publications (2015)
32. Meyer, J. J. C.: Agent technology. In: Wah, B.W. (ed.) Encyclopedia of Computer Science and Engineering. John Wiley & Sons (2008)
33. Miao, H., Chen, S., Qian, Z.: A formal open framework based on agent for testing web applications. In: International Conference on Computational Intelligence and Security (CIS). IEEE (2007)
34. Padgham, L., Winikoff, M.: Prometheus: a practical agent-oriented methodology. In: Agent-Oriented Methodologies. IGI Global (2005)
35. Paydar, S., Kahani, M.: An agent-based framework for automated testing of web-based systems. J. Softw. Eng. Appl. **4**(02), 86 (2011)
36. Qi, Y., Kung, D., Wong, E.: An agent-based testing approach for web applications. In: 29th International Computer Software and Applications Conference (COMPSAC), vol. 2. IEEE (2005)
37. Rafael, H., Mehdi, D., Jürgen, D., Amal, E.: Multi-Agent Programming-Languages. Platforms and Applications. Springer, Boston (2005). https://doi.org/10.1007/b137449
38. Rao, A.S., Georgeff, M.P.: An abstract architecture for rational agents. 3rd International Conference on Principles of Knowledge Representation and Reasoning (1992)
39. Rodriguez, S., Gaud, N., Galland, S.: SARL: a general-purpose agent-oriented Programming language. In: International Conference on Intelligent Agent Technology. IEEE (2014)
40. Schmidt, D.A.: A programming notation for tactical reasoning. In: Shostak, R.E. (ed.) CADE 1984. LNCS, vol. 170, pp. 445–459. Springer, New York (1984). https://doi.org/10.1007/978-0-387-34768-4_26
41. Seghrouchni, A.E.F., Dix, J., Dastani, M., Bordini, R.H.: Multi-Agent Programming: Languages Tools and Applications. Springer, Boston (2009). https://doi.org/10.1007/978-0-387-89299-3
42. Sen, K., Agha, G.: CUTE and jCUTE: concolic unit testing and explicit path model-checking tools. In: Ball, T., Jones, R.B. (eds.) CAV 2006. LNCS, vol. 4144, pp. 419–423. Springer, Heidelberg (2006). https://doi.org/10.1007/11817963_38
43. Vos, T., et al.: FITTEST: a new continuous and automated testing process for future internet applications. In: CSMR-WCRE. IEEE (2014)

Exploiting Simulation for MAS Development and Execution—The JaCaMo-Sim Approach

Alessandro Ricci[1(✉)], Angelo Croatti[1], Rafael H. Bordini[2], Jomi F. Hübner[3], and Olivier Boissier[4]

[1] DISI, University of Bologna, Cesena, FC, Italy
{a.ricci,a.croatti}@unibo.it
[2] POLI-PUCRS, Porto Alegre, Brazil
rafael.bordini@pucrs.br
[3] Federal University of Santa Catarina, Florianópolis, Brazil
jomi.hubner@ufsc.br
[4] Univ. Lyon, MINES Saint-Étienne, CNRS Lab., Saint-Étienne, France
olivier.boissier@emse.fr

Abstract. Simulation can be an important conceptual and practical tool to support the engineering of multi-agent systems (MAS), in different ways. In this paper we consider the case in which simulation is applied and exploited directly upon a MAS developed using an existing agent/MAS programming platform. That is: without requiring to model and simulate agents and their environment using a different platform, e.g. an agent-based simulation one. In particular, we describe the design of JaCaMo-sim, an extension of the JaCaMo platform that makes it possible to both run and simulate the execution of MAS programs based on BDI agents written in Jason, situated in artifact-based environments developed in CArtAgO. The tool can be useful for different aspects that concern MAS engineering, from MAS testing/debugging at development time to agent decision making support at runtime.

1 Introduction

As observed by Wooldridge and Jennings about two decades ago, "The development of any agent system - however trivial - is essentially a process of experimentation" [14]. Testing and simulation are two main classes of conceptual/practical tools developed through the years to support experimentation in engineering MAS. *Testing* accounts for running the system – or a part of it – either in real environments or test beds [11], so as to analyze its behaviour, evaluate its quality and improve it by identifying defects and problems [19]. Testing of agents and multi-agent systems is typically harder than conventional software systems, due to aspects such as autonomy, interaction, concurrency, distribution [18], and different kinds of testing levels and techniques have been developed in literature [19]. *Simulation* is – generally speaking – the process of designing a *model* of a real system and conducting experiments with this model for the purpose of either understanding the behaviour of the system or evaluating various strategies for the operation of the system [25,32]. It is pervasively applied in science and engineering, including software engineering [4] where it can be used for different purposes, e.g.

© Springer Nature Switzerland AG 2020
C. Baroglio et al. (Eds.): EMAS 2020, LNAI 12589, pp. 42–60, 2020.
https://doi.org/10.1007/978-3-030-66534-0_3

to improve system reliability, or to cut costs, providing insight into the design of processes, architecture, or product line before significant time and cost are invested. In the context of agents and MAS, the intersection between MAS and simulation has been widely explored in literature [29], both using MAS as a paradigm for modeling and simulating complex system, and using simulation as a tool for testing as well as for designing MAS. In particular, it is considered a more effective approach compared to classic testing when dealing with agent systems that display a situation-triggered or a time-triggered behaviour [23, 28, 30], making it possible to abstract from physical time and to create controlled experiments to analyse the behaviour of the system in scenarios that would be difficult (or expensive) to be reproduced in the real world.

Typically, compared to testing, simulation implies the extra burden of creating a model of the agent system/MAS, to be executed by corresponding simulators. In this paper we introduce and develop the idea of exploiting a simulation-based approach to support MAS development, without the need of creating a model of the system and using directly the agent/MAS program it self. This idea goes back to the *grand challenge* launched by Adelinde Uhrmacher in [30], where she pointed out that an important direction and challenge for simulation in AOSE is about having hybrid development/execution/simulation environments that would allow to execute agents *as they are*[1] and to switch arbitrarily between the execution in the real environment and test environment. This hybrid development/execution/simulation environments should allow agents to be an integral part of the experimental setting and as such perceivable and controllable. That is: having tools supporting a graceful transformation from *simulation* to *emulation* [30]. We argue that this challenge – even if suggested in literature almost two decades ago – is still an open issue, and more and more relevant, as soon as we consider the engineering of complex agent-based systems.

More in detail, in our research we aim at exploring and tacking this challenge in the context of agent-oriented programming and multi-agent oriented programming, in particular using the JaCaMo platform [3]. This platform allows for programming MAS integrating different and independent programming dimensions: agents are programmed using the Jason BDI agent programming language; the environment can be programmed using the CArtAgO framework, based on the A&A (agents and artifacts) conceptual model; and organisation can be specified and programmed using the Moise framework. In this paper we present and discuss the model, the design, and a first prototype of a platform that makes it possible to run a JaCaMo program both in real mode and simulation mode. When executing in simulation mode, the program is executed like a simulation by simulators, using a simulated time and environment. MAS execution in this case becomes a time-controlled simulation, based on the DES (Discrete Event Simulation) model [7]. Differently from existing simulation tools in MAS, in our case the *model* to be simulated is the MAS program itself.

We believe that the idea and the tool could be useful for three main aspects that concern MAS engineering. The first one already mentioned is *testing*. The tool would allow to test/observe a MAS behaviour in any conditions without being bound to the availability of specific execution/deployment environments. For instance, with this tool, a complex distributed MAS may be run in a simulated mode on a single computer,

---

[1] "As they are" here means, roughly speaking, considering their actual code and implementation.

where all aspects about user interaction, external environment, etc. are simulated. Like for every simulation/simulator, when running in simulated-time, the result of the simulation is independent from the computer or system used to run the simulation. Just, when using faster computers, the simulation is going to take less time. The second one – still related to the development time – is about supporting the development of specific application contexts where running agents in simulated environments is part of the design/engineering process. For instance, when agents need to be *trained* before being deployed, like in the case of reinforcement learning. The third case is about runtime, where the tool could be used by agents to help their decision making, in particular to predict the effect of their actions by running a simulation from the current state of the MAS.

The paper is organised as follows. After an account of related works (Sect. 2), we describe the idea behind the JaCaMo-sim platform, modeling MAS execution as a Discrete Event Simulation (Sect. 3), Then, we describe how the model has been implemented, i.e. the architecture of JaCaMo-sim platform (Sect. 4) and an example showing the tool at work (Sect. 5). We conclude the paper by sketching the road ahead that we see for this research line (Sect. 6).

2   Related Works

As remarked in the introduction, a main reference for our paper is the seminal work of Adelinde Uhrmacher and colleagues, in exploring the use of simulation for testing agents [23, 28, 30] and pointing out the grand challenge mentioned in the introduction. A main result of their research is the JAMES (JAva-based Multipurpose Environment for Simulation) platform, a Java framework for modeling and simulation [12]. This platform[2] is mostly used for agent-based and multi-agent based simulations; however, it has been applied also for testing agent systems, as in the case of the AUTOMINDER software [28]. As far as authors' knowledge, the platform does not provide specific features for integrating simulation and emulation of agents/MAS.

Besides JAMES, our work is related to existing approaches in the literature that explored the value and use of simulation for AOSE [29, 30]. These include proposals that use simulation to support the process of MAS development, such as PAS-SIM [5]; to support agent-based system development in general [24]; to define integrated approaches for the development and validation of MAS [8]; or, to engineer self-organising MAS [10]. Platforms such as Multi-Agent System Simulator (MASS) [31] and Sensible Agents [1] have been designed to investigate the performance of agents and multi-agent systems in complex environments.

Our contribution is especially related to those applying simulation to testing of agents and MAS – which is a main challenge in MAS engineering [18, 19] – and, in particular, with those that explore the integration of BDI agents and agent programming languages/purpose with simulation environments. In the literature, research works exploring such an integration have been proposed more in the context of agent-based simulation (ABS) and multi-agent based systems (MABS). A main example is [27], which

---

[2] At the time of writing, JAMES II is the reference version, available at http://jamesii.informatik. uni-rostock.de/jamesii.org/.

describes a three-tiered BDI-ABM architecture, to integrate existing simulation platforms (e.g., MATSim) and the BDI frameworks (e.g., JACK) as independent and uncoupled parts that interact by means of an action/perception interface, and using a time-step based approach to advance the execution. More recent examples include [6,16]. Our approach has a different scope, being not targeted to ABS/MABS but AOSE. In spite of the different perspective, from a technical point of view in our case a Discrete Event Simulation model is adopted and the BDI platform itself (JaCaMo in our case) is extended so as to support a simulation execution modality.

The specific DES-based approach used in JaCaMo-sim recalls the classic approach used in the context of PDES (Parallel Discrete Event Simulation) [9] and in distributed simulation of multi-agent systems [17]. In that context, JaCaMo-sim can be classified as a conservative approach, adopting agents, artifacts and workspaces as logical processes involved by a simulation, not sharing memory. Differently from PDES, in our case the objective is not to parallelise the simulation execution, by exploiting a network of processors, but to take into the account distribution at the model level, which – in our case – corresponds to the distributed MAS program itself.

Finally, a research work which is conceptually strongly related to our proposal is the Brahms framework [26]. Brahms has been primarily developed as modelling and simulation environment for work practices, but finally it has been used also as an agent-based platform to develop real systems. The same platform can be used for both simulating and running a MAS system. The path taken in our paper has been somewhat in the opposite direction: we started from a platform used for developing and running MAS and we extended it in order to support the simulation of the MAS – keeping the "agents as they are" [30], without the need of implementing the model using a different language.

3   The Approach

In this section we describe how the idea works at a model level, abstracting from implementation details. The idea is based on two main points. The first one is that, at the model level, the execution of a (JaCaMo) MAS, at the bottom level, is *event-driven*. The agent part (Jason) is based on a BDI reasoning cycle [20], which can be modelled as a well-defined sequence of events concerning the sense, deliberate and act stages. The communication part is managed by the Jason side – exploiting different ACL platforms, like Jade [2] – and can be modelled in terms of events as well. The environment part (CArtAgO) can be described too in terms of events [22], in which computations proceed as soon as a new operation is requested on artifacts (corresponding to action on the agent side). In order to have observable effects, the execution of operations updates artifact's observable state, generating events. The implementation of the organisation part (Moise) is based on agents and artifacts [13].

Being event-driven, it is straightforward to model the execution of a MAS program as a Discrete Event Simulation (DES) [7]. In particular, a MAS program execution can be modelled as a system in which state changes can be represented by a collection of discrete events, occurring at a certain time. In DES, a state change implies that an event occurs and the states of entities remain constant between events. In MAS program execution we can assume this, by choosing a proper level of abstraction about states and events, so as to abstract from changes that are not considered relevant. When executing a MAS program, events are scheduled and executed by the control flows used by the execution platform. On the agent side, there are control flows used to move on agents reasoning cycle, and, on environment side, there are control flows used to execute operations on artifacts. To execute a MAS in a *simulated mode*, event scheduling and execution are intercepted, so as to be governed by a DES-like simulation loop [7], deciding which events should be scheduled next, according to the time planned for them. A next-event approach for advancing time is used: after all state changes have been made at the time corresponding to a particular event, simulated time is advanced to the time of the next event and the event is executed. Differently from simple DES, in our case, being MAS generally a distributed system, we do not want to assume a single simulated timeline. Every agent, artifact and workspace have their own independent timeline.

The second main point on which the approach is based is about the *external* environment, how it is modelled and how the MAS interacts with it. In JaCaMo, any aspects that concern the external environment of a MAS are meant to be modelled/encapsulated into artifacts. These artifacts are also called *boundary artifacts*, since they are the boundary inside the MAS that enables/mediates the interaction with the external environment. Examples range from artifacts representing the GUI (enabling the interaction with human users) to external devices (e.g., a printer, a sensor) and services (e.g., Internet-based API for maps). In a simulated execution, boundary artifacts are replaced with a version that implements the simulated behaviour, however preserving the interface in terms of operations (actions) and observable state (percepts).

3.1 Execution Contexts, Events and Activities

In the following, we provide an overview of the set of main abstract concepts used to shape the idea, in spite of the specific agent platform/model adopted. We introduce the concept of execution context (EC) to model any locus of activity of the MAS, equipped with its own timeline. In our case, we have an EC for each agent, referred as agent EC, and for all basic abstractions of the MAS which have an independent existence and timeline with respect to agents. These elements include the environment and the communication medium used to enable agent communications. In the case of JaCaMo, the environment is modelled in terms of artifacts and workspaces, so an EC is introduced for each artifact (artifact EC) and workspace (workspace EC). An EC is introduced also for the communication medium (referred as comm EC), enabling speech-act based message passing among agents. Each EC is characterised by its own clock Ts to keep track of the (simulated) time.

The dynamics/behaviour of each EC is described in terms of events occurring there. Events have no duration, they occur in a precise time of the EC timeline. Each event is characterised by a timestamp ts, assigned using the clock Ts of the EC, representing when the event happened (or is scheduled to happen) inside the EC. It is worth remarking here the difference between event generation and even execution. Event generation concerns when the event is created and scheduled. Event execution concerns when the scheduled event actually happens, occurs. In normal MAS execution, event generation and execution almost coincide. When executing in simulated mode instead, events are scheduled to happen in the future, at a time which is defined by a *time assignment function*, used to shape the temporal evolution of the simulation.

Events occurring in the same EC are totally ordered. Instead, events of different EC can only be partially ordered, exploiting a *causal relationship* between them. For instance, the action request done by an agent – that appears in the agent EC – is the root of a chain of causally-related events, whose effect is the execution of the corresponding operation by the artifact – that appears in the artifact EC. The same holds for agent communication, involving the sending of a message and the receipt of the same message, two events that are part of the same causal chain across two different ECs. Events belonging to the same causal chain can be ordered by an happened-before relation [15].

The concept of *activity* is introduced to represent something relevant occurring between two causally-related events—that correspond to the beginning of the activity and the end of the activity. For instance: the beginning of a reasoning cycle and the end of the same reasoning cycle. For activities, a notion of *duration* can be defined, as the difference between the timestamps of the two events, being them part of the same EC. Activities can overlap or can be wrapped by other activities. For instance: a sense activity, marking the sense stage inside the reasoning cycle, is wrapped/included in the reasoning cycle activity.

Some activities may span over multiple ECs. A main example concerns agent communication, in which the beginning event is the *send* action executed in the act stage of the sender agent and the end event is the message receipt occurring in the sense stage by the receiver agent. Another main example concerns the execution of an external action, as an activity whose beginning event (the action request) and the end event (the perception about action completion or failure) occurs in the same EC (the agent EC), however involving a chain of events that occurs both in the EC of the artifact hosting the operation and the workspace hosting the artifact.

The duration of activities in these cases *cannot* be computed simply as the difference of the timestamps of the beginning and end events, because these two events or events in the causal chain belong to different ECs, possibly with independent clocks. To tackle this problem, we introduce a notion of *synchronisation events* that bind together two different ECs in chains of causally-related events. For instance, the event representing an action request on an agent EC and the notification of the same action to be dispatched on the workspace EC that hosts the artifact. In this case, the execution of the first event in one EC causes the synchronous execution of the second event in the other EC, where the concrete semantics of *synchronous* is defined by the model of time defined for specific simulation by the developer/modeller.

A Core Set of Events and Activities. We identified a first core set of events modelling the event-driven execution of a MAS program. These events can be split in three main categories:

- events concerning agent reasoning cycle execution, involving only the EC of a single agent;
- events concerning agent communication, involving the EC of two agents and of the communication medium; and

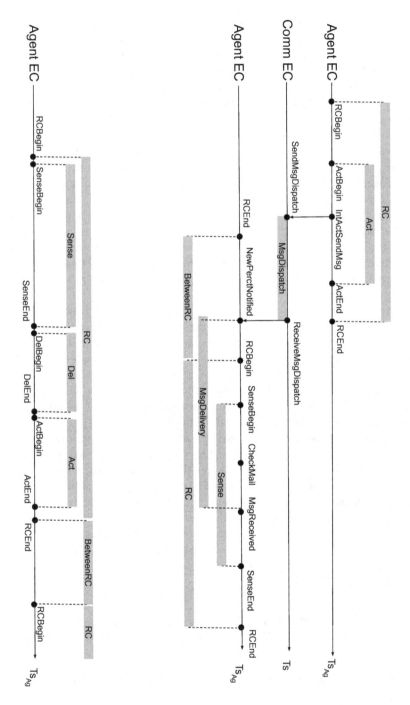

Fig. 1. Diagrams representing events and activities related to communication between agents, involving also the communication media EC. The name of events and activities have been shortened compared to the ones reported in Table 1.

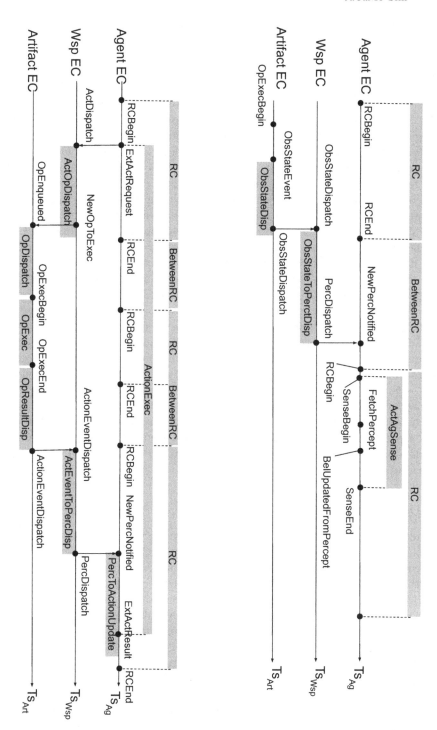

Fig. 2. Diagrams representing events and activities related to agent EC and artifact EC. The name of events and activities have been shortened compared to the ones reported in Table 3 and in Table 4.

– events concerning agent environment interaction, involving the EC of an agent, an artifact and the workspace hosting the artifact.

Table 1 (reported in the appendix) shows a partial list of events concerning the agent EC related to the agent reasoning cycle, including relevant activities connecting the events.

Figure 1 (on the left) shows events and activities on a timeline, including only main events concerning the beginning and end of the reasoning cycle and events marking the beginning and end of every stage. Events and activities related to agent communication are listed in Table 2 (in appendix) and shown on a time line in Fig. 1 (on the right). Agent communication involves three different ECs: the EC of the sender agent, of the receiver agent and of the communication medium exploited to deliver the message. Finally, the list of events and activities concerning agent-environment interaction is reported in Table 3 (events) and Table 4 (activities)—both in the appendix. The timeline is shown in Fig. 2. Agent-environment interaction involves three different ECs as well: the EC of the agent executing an external action or observing some artifact; the EC of the artifact providing the operation to be executed or the observable state to be observed; and the EC of the workspace hosting the artifact and joined by the agent, functioning as a glue. The agent-environment interaction concerns two scenarios, shown in Fig. 2. The first (on the left) concerns an agent requesting an action, which triggers the execution of an operation hosted by an artifact. When (if) the operation execution completes (or fails), an action event is generated and notified on the agent side. The second concerns the generation of an observable event on the environment side – that could concern either the update of observable properties of an artifact, or the generation of a signal – notified as a percept on the agent side. It is worth remarking that in CArtAgO, on which JaCaMo is based, even predefined actions (e.g., to create an artifact, to lookup artifact, and so forth) are modelled as actions provided by some existing artifact [21]. In this paper we do not consider events and activities that concern interaction between artifacts—that is, artifact executing operation over another artifact (called linked operation in CArtAgO).

3.2   The Simulation Loop

The execution of the simulation follows a classic event-scheduling approach as found in DES, adapted so that the MAS execution platform (JaCaMo in our case) is used to run the model (the MAS program). Each EC has its own *FES* (future event set), which represents the set of events that have been scheduled to be executed (i.e. to occur) in the future [7]. Given the event-driven behaviour, the dynamics/execution of each EC can be modelled/tracked as a state that atomically evolves given the execution (occurrence) of events. The execution of an event causes the generation of events that are scheduled in the FES of the EC of the event and possibly in other ECs. Each event is decorated with its timestamp ts computed by the time assignment function establishing when the event is going to happen in the future.

Like in the DES case, the simulator behaviour is given by a *loop*, run by its own control flow (depicted in Fig. 3). Differently from the DES case, the execution of events is carried by the JaCaMo platform (concurrently), by means of the EC control flows (that are part of the Jason and CArtAgO scheduler systems). This is more similar to

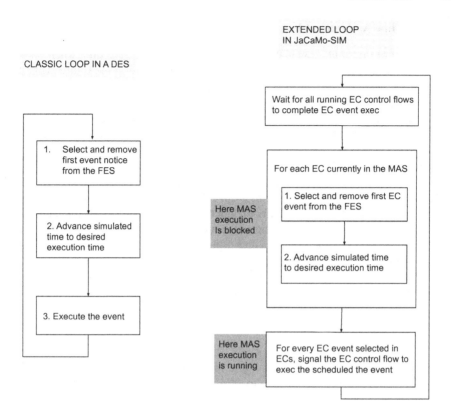

Fig. 3. The simulation loop – on the left: the classic DES version; on the right: the one adopted in JaCaMo-sim

what happens in PDES [9], where the simulation accounts for multiple logical processes which are executed in parallel on different processors. In JaCaMo, basically there are two kinds of EC control flows: the ones running the agent reasoning cycles and the ones running operation executions on artifacts in workspaces. In executing events, EC control flows may schedule EC events in different ECs. At each iteration, the simulator loop considers the (dynamic) set of all ECs currently in execution and, before choosing next event to be scheduled, the loop must be sure that all running control flows completed current event execution. This is a synchronisation point between the MAS execution platform and the simulation loop. This is what makes sure that there are not causality errors.

So at each iteration the simulation loop: *(1)* waits all control flows to be blocked (sync point); *(2)* selects the next event to be scheduled for every EC; and *(3)* unblocks the corresponding control flows on the platform side which is waiting to execute the event.

3.3   The Time Assignment Function

A key aspect of the simulation is the assignment of the (simulated) time when scheduling a new event, that is: specifying when it is going to happen in the future. This time could be any value greater or equal than the current time of the EC where the event occurs. If the event represents the end of some activity, then the event time is equal to the current time of the EC plus the duration that the activity is supposed to have. This time could be either random or not, could either depend on the specific state of the EC or not.

Actually, the specific strategy adopted to assign a time to events is application specific. Therefore, the simulator is meant to provide maximum flexibility to developers/-modellers for defining that function, to allow for recreating the specific situation to be tested/experimented. Such a flexibility includes also the possibility to implement different time/distribution models in defining the strategy—from a centralized case, where all agents and the environment are supposed to run in the same node, sharing a common clock, to fully decentralized and distributed cases, where agents and artifacts are running on different nodes, and the e.g. Internet is used as underlying network for enabling both agent communication and agent-environment interaction.

4   First Implementation

The JaCaMo-sim platform[3] provides a first implementation of the approach described before. The platform is a lightweight extension of the basic JaCaMo platform. A new component called JCM Execution Controller is added. This component is called by the main platform each time a new event – which is relevant, given the model discussed before – is going to be scheduled or executed. The calls are performed by the control flows that are used inside the JaCaMo platform (Jason side, CArtAgO side) to execute agents and artifacts.

The Execution Controller component could be configured to work in different modalities: (1) *normal mode*; (2) *tracking mode*; (3) *simulation mode* (see Fig. 4). In normal mode, the Execution Controller is almost an empty component, not creating any overhead over MAS execution. In *tracking mode*, the Execution Controller is a lightweight layer just tracking time of events in ECs. Some components (Viewer, Logger) are used to visualize/log tracked data. The clock of the ECs in this case is directly the clock of the machine(s) running the EC, so events are decorated with timestamps that are directly the wall time. This modality is useful for profiling purposes, in particular to check the duration of activities.

In *simulation mode* the Execution Controller contains the simulator loop described in previous section, controlling event scheduling and execution. In current API (available in Java), a `Simulation` class is provided to configure the parameters and temporal behaviour of the simulation. This base class is meant to be extended to define details of specific simulations. The interface of the `Simulation` class includes a method to be overridden (called `assignTime`) implementing the time assignment function described in previous section. The method is called each time an event is scheduled, so as to

---

[3] Available here: https://github.com/jacamo-lang/jacamo-sim.

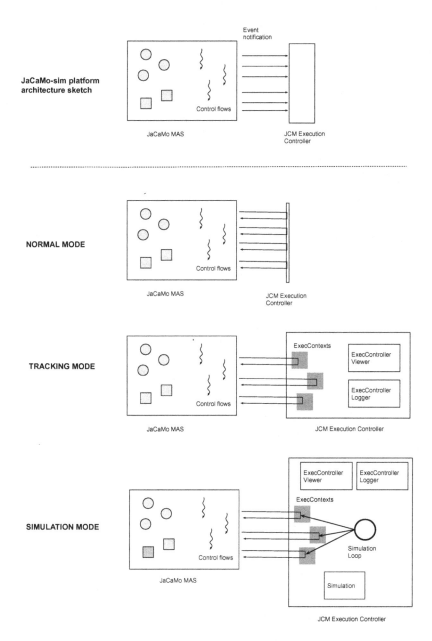

Fig. 4. A representation of the JaCaMo-sim Platform, with in evidence the JCM Execution Controller component. In normal mode this component does not perform any function. In tracking mode, it logs the timing of events. In simulation mode, it executes the extended simulation loop described in Sect. 3.

```
!main_test.

+!main_test
 <- println("start");
    makeArtifact("counter", "ex1.Counter", [], Id);
    focus(Id);
    inc.

+count(V) <- println("count value: ",V).
```

Fig. 5. Source code of the `tester_agent`, in example 1 (available in the repository).

```
class CentralizedSimulation extends Simulation {
  private Random gen;
  private long time;

  public CentralizedSimulation() {
    gen = new Random(1);
    time = 0;

    setActivityDuration("ActAgRC", (ECActivity act, ExecContext ctx) -> {
      return 1000 + gen.nextInt(1000); });

    setActivityDuration("ActArtOpExec", (ECActivity act, ExecContext ctx) -> {
      if (ctx.getId().equals("counter")) {
        return 5000 + gen.nextInt(1000);
      } else return 0;
    });}

  public void assignTime(ECEvent ev, ExecContext ctx) {
    long time = ctx.getCurrentTimeInMicroSec();
    if (ev.getName().equals("EvAgExtActResult")) {

      ECEvent evActReq = ev.getEventInTheCausalChain("EvAgExtActRequest");
      ECActivity act = ev.getActivityInTheCausalChain("ActArtOpExec");

      if (evActReq != null && act != null) {
        long dur = act.getDurationInMicroSec();
        long startedTime = evActReq.getTimeInMicroSec();
        long evt = startedTime + dur;
        ev.setTime(evt/1000, evt);
      }}
    ...}
  ...}

/* main spawning the simulation */

public class RunTest {
  public static void main(String args[]) throws Exception {
    ExecutionController contr = ExecutionController.getExecController();
    Simulation sim = new CentralizedSimulation();
    contr.initSimulationMode(sim);  /* initialize the execution in simulation mode */
    // contr.initTrackingMode();

    /* spawn the MAS */
    jason.infra.centralised.RunCentralisedMAS.main(
      new String[] { "src/test/jcmsim/example-1/main.mas2j" });
  }
}
```

Fig. 6. Source code of the main, configuring and launching the simulation.

decorate it with a specific time. Besides this method, the Simulation API includes also methods to directly specify the duration of activities, if available. Some concrete examples are shown in next section.

5 The Tool at Work

The JaCaMo-sim distribution includes some simple examples that can be used to play with the tool, involving agent-environment interaction and agent communication. Example 1 is a very simple case about agent-environment interaction, involving a tester_agent and a Counter artifact. The artifact provides an inc operation and a value observable property, which is update each time the operation is executed. The agent simply creates an instance of the artifact, called counter, start observing it and executes an inc action. When the agent perceives a change on the count observable property, it prints a current value on the console. Figure 5 shows the source code of the Jason agent and Fig. 6 a snippet of the Java application, configuring and launching the example. The simulation is configured so that: the duration of the ActAgRC activity (representing the reasoning cycle activity) is a random value between 1 and 2 ms; the duration of the inc operation execution is a random value between 5 and 6 ms; all the other activities (not specified) are meant to have a zero duration. A centralised model of time is adopted (this depends on the implementation of the assignTime method overridden from the Simulation class).

Figure 7 instead shows an excerpt of the output produced launching the example 1, in tracking mode (on left) and in simulation mode (on the right). It shows a portion of the events and activities concerning the tester_agent and the counter artifact, with in evidence the timings (in microseconds) related to events and activities concerning the reasoning cycle, the execution of actions and operations, the events related to the count observable property changes and corresponding percepts. The timings in the simulated mode, in particular the duration of reasoning cycles and of operation execution, correspond to the time assignment function configured in the simulation objects.

The other examples available in the distribution make it possible to test the tool in the case of agent communication (example 2) and agent-environment with boundary artifacts (example 3)—in particular a GUI artifact, enabling the interaction with human user.

6 The Road Ahead

We consider this paper just a first step of a broad research direction that aims at exploring the use of simulation for agent/MAS programming and execution. On the one hand, the idea presented in this paper should be general enough to be applied to any agent/-MAS programming platform, besides JaCaMo, for exploring any interesting scenarios related to that integration. On the other hand, current tool – which is based the specific JaCaMo platform – provides a very basic support to that purpose, suffering of limitations that will be tackled in future work.

The main directions that we see for the road ahead for this research line include, first of all, a deeper analysis and understanding of the specific use of simulation for MAS

```
AGENT: tester_agent - start time: 1582896117914        AGENT: tester_agent - start time: 0

Events:                                                Events:
[0] [event: reasoning cycle begin | num-cycle: 1 ]     [0] [event: reasoning cycle begin | num-cycle: 1 ]
[1] [event: fetch percept | num-cycle: 1 ]             [0] [event: fetch percept | num-cycle: 1 ]
[6] [event: check mail | num-cycle: 1 ]                [0] [event: check mail | num-cycle: 1 ]
[8] [event: ext action req                             [0] [event: ext action req
    | makeArtifact("counter","ex1.Counter",[],Id)]         | makeArtifact("counter","ex1.Counter",[],Id)]
[11] [event: reasoning cycle end | num-cycle: 1 ]      [1] [event: reasoning cycle end | num-cycle: 1 ]
[13] [event: new action event notified                 [1] [event: reasoning cycle begin | num-cycle: 2 ]
    | action id: 1 | makeArtifact succeeded ]          ...
[14] [event: reasoning cycle begin | num-cycle: 2 ]    [7] [event: ext action req | inc]
...                                                    [9] [event: reasoning cycle end | num-cycle: 6 ]
[20] [event: ext action req | inc]                     ...
[20] [event: reasoning cycle end | num-cycle: 4 ]      [11] [event: reasoning cycle begin | num-cycle: 8 ]
[20] [event: new obs state notified                    [11] [event: fetch percept | num-cycle: 8 ]
    | percept id: 10 | counter ]                       [11] [event: new obs state notified
[20] [event: reasoning cycle begin | num-cycle: 5 ]        | percept id: 10 | counter ]
[20] [event: fetch percept | num-cycle: 5 ]            [13] [event: reasoning cycle end | num-cycle: 8 ]
[21] [event: new action event notified                 [13] [event: reasoning cycle begin | num-cycle: 9 ]
    | action id: 3 | inc succeeded ]                   [13] [event: fetch percept | num-cycle: 9 ]
[21] [event: BB updated with obs state event           [13] [event: BB updated with obs state event
    | percept 10 from counter]                             | percept 10 from counter]
                                                       ...
...                                                    [13] [event: new action event notified
                                                           | action id: 3 | inc succeeded ]
Activities:                                            ...
[0] [activity: reasoning cycle | num-cycle: 1 ]        [15] [event: fetch percept | num-cycle: 10 ]
    duration: 11 ms ( 10713 us )                       [15] [event: ext action result | act-id: 3 | success ]
[8] [activity: action exec | act-id: 1
    | makeArtifact | succeeded ]                       Activities:
    duration: 6 ms ( 6209 us )                         [0] [activity: reasoning cycle | num-cycle: 1 ]
[11] [activity: between reasoning cycles                   duration: 1 ms ( 1985 us )
    | num-cycles: 1 - 2 ]  duration: 3 ms ( 3117 us )  [0] [activity: action exec | act-id: 1
...                                                        | makeArtifact | succeeded ]
[20] [activity: action exec | act-id: 3                    duration: 3 ms ( 3573 us )
    | inc | succeeded ]  duration: 1 ms ( 1783 us )    [1] [activity: between reasoning cycles
...                                                        | num-cycles: 1 - 2 ]  duration: 0 ms ( 0 us )
                                                       ...
                                                       [7] [activity: action exec | act-id: 3
                                                           | inc | succeeded ]  duration: 8 ms ( 7064 us )
                                                       ...
```

```
-----------------------------------                    -----------------------------------
ARTIFACT: counter - start time: 1582896117934          ARTIFACT: counter - start time: 7

Events:                                                Events:
[0] [event: art new op to dispatch | act-id: 3         [0] [event: art new op to dispatch | act-id: 3
    | inc on counter by tester_agent]                      | inc on counter by tester_agent]
[0] [event: op exec begin | act-id: 3                  [0] [event: op exec begin | act-id: 3
    | inc on counter by tester_agent]                      | inc on counter by tester_agent ]
[0] [event: art new obs state event | counter]         [0] [event: art new obs state event | counter]
[1] [event: op exec end | act-id: 3                    [6] [event: op exec end | act-id: 3
    | inc on counter ]                                     | inc on counter ]
[1] [event: action event dispatch | act-id: 3 | inc ]  [6] [event: action event dispatch | act-id: 3 | inc ]
...                                                    ...
Activities:                                            Activities:
[0] [activity: op dispatched | act-id: 3               [0] [activity: op dispatched | act-id: 3
    | inc on counter by tester_agent]                      | inc on counter by tester_agent]
    duration: 0 ms ( 62 us )                               duration: 0 ms ( 0 us )
[0] [activity: op execution | act-id: 3                [0] [activity: op execution | act-id: 3
    | inc on counter by tester_agent]                      | inc on counter by tester_agent]
    duration: 1 ms ( 931 us )                              duration: 6 ms ( 5606 us )
[1] [activity: op result dispatch                      [6] [activity: op result dispatch | act-id: 3
    | act-id: 3 | inc]  duration: 0 ms ( 17 us )           | inc]  duration: 0 ms ( 0 us )
...                                                    ...
```

Fig. 7. Output logged by the tool running the MAS of example 1 both in tracking mode (on the left) and in simulation mode (on the right).

programming, eventually using some reference case studies to give more concreteness to the exploration. This includes testing and validation, but also *debugging*. Besides, we aim at exploring the use of simulation at runtime, to support agent decision making, to reason about the effect of actions. Another main direction is about defining a formalisation of the tool, capturing main concepts beyond the specific platform used, eventually exploring the use of existing formal frameworks such as DEVS [32], and related tools. A further interesting direction concerns the organization dimension, which has not been considered in this paper, that is: introducing a set of events and activities that concern the organisation level and exploiting simulations to analyse the behaviour of the system at that level of abstraction. A generalisation of this point is about making the tool extensible enough so that it would allow to define new custom layers of events and activities – on top of the core set one – corresponding to higher levels of abstraction, closer to the domain level.

A   Events and Activities

Table 1. Agent EC events and activities concerning the reasoning cycle, and the sense stage in particular (excluding those involving agent communication and agent-environment interaction). The same names are used in the current JaCaMo-sim implementation (in particular, for each event a Java class with the same name is defined).

EvAgRCBegin/EvAgRCEnd	Reasoning cycle begin and end
EvAgSenseBegin/EvAgSenseEnd	Sense stage begin and end
EvAgDelBegin/EvAgDelEnd	Deliberate stage begin and end
EvAgActBegin/EvAgActEnd	Act stage begin and end
EvAgFetchPercept	Agent checking for percepts in the sense stage
EvAgCheckMail	Agent checking for mails in the sense stage
ActAgRC	reasoning cycle activity
ActAgBetweenRC	activity between two subsequent reasoning cycles
ActAgSense	Sense stage activity
ActAgDel	Deliberate stage activity
ActAgAct	Act stage activity

Table 2. Events and activities involved in agent communication.

EvAgIntActMsgSend	A new send action has been performed (act stage)
EvCommSendMsgDispatch	The dispatch of new message has been requested to the Comm medium by a sender agent. This is the synchronous event (as defined in Sect. 3) created in the Communication EC corresponding to EvAgIntActMsgSend event occurring in the agent EC
EvCommReceiveMsgDispatch	A message is ready to be delivered to some target agent. This event is caused by the EvCommSendMsgDispatch event
EvAgNewMsgNotifier	A new message is asynchronously notified to an agent. This is the synchronous event on the agent side of the EvCommSendMsgDispatch event
EvAgNewMsgReceived	The agent has received the message in the sense stage. This event is caused by the EvAgCheckMail event
ActCommMsgDispatch	Activity devoted to deliver the message by the Communication medium

Table 3. Events involved in agent-environment interaction.

EvAgExtActRequest	An external action request, to execute an operation on some artifact
EvWspActDispatch	A new request of action be dispatched by the workspace to the target artiact. This is the synchronous event created in the workspace EC corresponding to EvAgExtActRequest event occurring in the agent EC
EvWspNewOpToExec	Event representing a new op execution to be served inside the workspace. This event is caused by the EvWspActDispatch event
EvArtOpEnqueued	Event generated when the operation request has been enqueued in the artifact. This is the synchronous event on the artifact side of the EvWspNewOpToExec event on the workspace side
EvArtOpExecBegin	Event representing the beginning of operation execution on the artifact side. This event is caused by the EvArtOpEnqueued event
EvArtObsStateEvent	Event representing a change to the observable state of the artifact (including the generation of a signal)
EvWspObsStateDispatch	Event representing a obs state event to be dispatched from an artifact. This is the synchronous event on the workspace side of the EvArtObsStateEvent event on the artifact side
EvArtOpExecEnd	Event representing the end of operation execution on the artifact side
EvWspActionEventDispatch	Event representing an action event to be dispatched from an artifact, representing action/operation success or failure. This is the synchronous event on the workspace side of the EvArtOpExecEnd event on the artifact side
EvWspPerceptDispatch	Event representing a new percept ready to be dispatched to an agent, either representing a new observable event or an action event. This event is caused either by the EvWspActionEventDispatch event or the EvWspObsStateDispatch event
EvAgNewPerceptNotified	A new percept notified to the agent percept queue. This is the synchronous event of with EvWspPerceptDispatch on the workspace side
EvAgBelUpdatedFromPercept	Agent updating a belief from a percept (sense stage). This event is caused by the EvAgNewPerceptNotified event (about a new observable state event)
EvAgExtActResult	Agent perceiving the success or failure of an action previously requested (sense stage). This event is caused by the EvAgNewPerceptNotified event (about a new action event)

Table 4. Activities involved in agent-environment interaction.

ActWspOpDispatch	Activity on the workspace side to deliver a new operation to be executed on an artifact
ActArtOpDispatch	Activity to deliver an enqueued operation to an artifact to be executed
ActArtOpExec	Activity concerning the execution of an operation
ActArtObsStateDispatch	Activity to dispatch of a new observable event to the worskpace
ActArtActionEventDispatch	Activity to dispatch an operation/action result to the workspace
ActWspActEventToPerceptDispatch	Activity on the workspace side to deliver an operation/action result as a percept to the agent that executed the action
ActWspObsStateToPerceptDispatch	Activity on the workspace side to deliver an new observable event as a percept to an agent observing the artifact

References

1. Barber, K.S., et al.: Sensible agents: an implemented multi-agent system and testbed. In: Proceedings of the Fifth International Conference on Autonomous Agents, pp. 92–99. ACM, New York (2001)

2. Bellifemine, F.L., Caire, G., Greenwood, D.: Developing Multi-Agent Systems with JADE. Wiley Series in Agent Technology. Wiley, Hoboken (2007)

3. Boissier, O., Bordini, R., Hübner, J.F., Ricci, A., Santi, A.: Multi-agent oriented programming with JaCaMo. Sci. Comput. Program. **78**(6), 747–761 (2013)

4. Christie, A.: Simulation: an enabling technology in software engineering. CrossTalk J. Def. Softw. Eng. (1999)

5. Cossentino, M., Fortino, G., Garro, A., Mascillaro, S., Russo, W.: PASSIM: a simulation-based process for the development of multi-agent systems. Int. J. Agent-Oriented Soft. Eng. **2**(2), 132–170 (2008)

6. Davoust, A., et al.: An architecture for integrating BDI agents with a simulation environment. In: EMAS 2019 (2019)

7. Fishman, G.: Discrete-Event Simulation: Modeling, Programming, and Analysis. Springer, New York (2001). https://doi.org/10.1007/978-1-4757-3552-9

8. Fortino, G., Garro, A., Russo, W.: An integrated approach for the development and validation of multi-agent systems. Comput. Syst. Sci. Eng. **20** (2005)

9. Fujimoto, R.M.: Parallel discrete event simulation. Commun. ACM **33**(10), 30–53 (1990)

10. Gardelli, L., Viroli, M., Omicini, A.: On the role of simulations in engineering self-organising MAS: the case of an intrusion detection system in TuCSoN. In: Brueckner, S.A., Di Marzo Serugendo, G., Hales, D., Zambonelli, F. (eds.) ESOA 2005. LNCS (LNAI), vol. 3910, pp. 153–166. Springer, Heidelberg (2006). https://doi.org/10.1007/11734697_12

11. Hanks, S., Pollack, M.E., Cohen, P.R.: Benchmarks, test beds, controlled experimentation, and the design of agent architectures. AI Mag. **14**(4), 17–42 (1993)

12. Himmelspach, J., Uhrmacher, A.M.: Plug'n simulate. In: 40th Annual Simulation Symposium (ANSS 2007), pp. 137–143 (2007)

13. Hübner, J.F., Boissier, O., Kitio, R., Ricci, A.: Instrumenting multi-agent organisations with organisational artifacts and agents: "giving the organisational power back to the agents". J. Auton. Agents Multi-Agent Syst. **20**(3), 369–400 (2010)

14. Jennings, N.R., Wooldridge, M.: Applications of intelligent agents. In: Jennings, N.R., Wooldridge, M.J. (eds.) Agent Technology: Foundations, Applications, and Markets, pp. 3–28. Springer, Berlin Heidelberg, Berlin, Heidelberg (1998)

15. Lamport, L.: Time, clocks, and the ordering of events in a distributed system. Commun. ACM **21**(7), 558–565 (1978)

16. Larsen, J.B.: Going beyond BDI for agent-based simulation. J. Inf. Telecommun. **3**(4), 446–464 (2019). https://doi.org/10.1080/24751839.2019.1620024

17. Logan, B., Theodoropoulos, G.: The distributed simulation of multiagent systems. Proc. IEEE **89**(2), 174–185 (2001)

18. Miles, S., et al.: Why testing autonomous agents is hard and what can be done about it, January 2010. http://www.pa.icar.cnr.it/cossentino/AOSETF10/docs/miles.pdf. AOSE Technical Forum

19. Nguyen, C.D., Perini, A., Bernon, C., Pavón, J., Thangarajah, J.: Testing in multi-agent systems. In: Gleizes, M.-P., Gomez-Sanz, J.J. (eds.) AOSE 2009. LNCS, vol. 6038, pp. 180–190. Springer, Heidelberg (2011). https://doi.org/10.1007/978-3-642-19208-1_13

20. Rao, A.S.: AgentSpeak(L): BDI agents speak out in a logical computable language. In: Van de Velde, W., Perram, J.W. (eds.) MAAMAW 1996. LNCS, vol. 1038, pp. 42–55. Springer, Heidelberg (1996). https://doi.org/10.1007/BFb0031845

21. Ricci, A., Piunti, M., Viroli, M.: Environment programming in multi-agent systems: an artifact-based perspective. Auton. Agents Multi Agent Syst. **23**(2), 158–192 (2011)
22. Ricci, A., Viroli, M., Piunti, M.: Formalising the environment in MAS programming: a formal model for artifact-based environments. In: Braubach, L., Briot, J.-P., Thangarajah, J. (eds.) ProMAS 2009. LNCS (LNAI), vol. 5919, pp. 133–150. Springer, Heidelberg (2010). https://doi.org/10.1007/978-3-642-14843-9_9
23. Röhl, M., Uhrmacher, A.M.: Controlled experimentation with agents — models and implementations. In: Gleizes, M.-P., Omicini, A., Zambonelli, F. (eds.) ESAW 2004. LNCS (LNAI), vol. 3451, pp. 292–304. Springer, Heidelberg (2005). https://doi.org/10.1007/11423355_21
24. Sarjoughian, H., Zeigler, B., Hall, S.: A layered modeling and simulation architecture for agent-based system development. Proc. IEEE **89**, 201–213 (2001)
25. Shannon, R., Johannes, J.D.: Systems simulation: the art and science. IEEE Trans. Syst. Man Cybern. **SMC-6**(10), 723–724 (1976)
26. Sierhuis, M., Hoof, R.: Brahms: a multi-agent modelling environment for simulating work processes and practices. Int. J. Simul. Process. Model. **3** (2007)
27. Singh, D., Padgham, L., Logan, B.: Integrating BDI agents with agent-based simulation platforms. Auton. Agents Multi-Agent Syst. **30**(6), 1050–1071 (2016)
28. Uhrmacher, A., Röhl, M., Himmelspach, J.: Unpaced and paced simulation for testing agents. In: Simulation in Industry, 15th European Simulation Symposium, January 2003
29. Uhrmacher, A.M., Weyns, D.: Multi-Agent Systems: Simulation and Applications, 1st edn. CRC Press, Inc., Boca Raton (2009)
30. Uhrmacher, A.: Simulation for agent-oriented software engineering. In: Proceedings of the 1st International Conference on Grand Challenges for Modeling and Simulation, San Antonio, Texas, USA, 27–31 January (2002)
31. Vincent, R., Horling, B., Lesser, V.: An agent infrastructure to build and evaluate multi-agent systems: the Java agent framework and multi-agent system simulator. In: Wagner, T., Rana, O.F. (eds.) AGENTS 2000. LNCS (LNAI), vol. 1887, pp. 102–127. Springer, Heidelberg (2001). https://doi.org/10.1007/3-540-47772-1_11
32. Zeigler, B.P., Kim, T.G., Praehofer, H.: Theory of Modeling and Simulation, 2nd edn. Academic Press, Inc., Cambridge (2000)

Fragility and Robustness in Multiagent Systems

Matteo Baldoni⬥, Cristina Baroglio^(✉)⬥, and Roberto Micalizio⬥

Dipartimento di Informatica, Università degli Studi di Torino, Turin, Italy
{matteo.baldoni,cristina.baroglio,roberto.micalizio}@unito.it

Abstract. Robustness is an important property of software systems, and the availability of proper feedback is seen as crucial to obtain it, especially in the case of systems of distributed and interconnected components. Multiagent Systems (MAS) are valuable for conceptualizing and implementing distributed systems, but the current design methodologies for MAS fall short in addressing robustness in a systematic way at design time. In this paper we outline our vision of how robustness in MAS can be granted as a design property. To this end, we exploit the notion of accountability as a mechanism to build reporting frameworks and, then, we describe how robustness is gained. We exemplify our vision on the JaCaMo agent platform.

Keywords: Robustness · MAS engineering · Accountability · JaCaMo

1 Introduction

Robustness is an important property of software systems. The Systems and Software Engineering Vocabulary ISO/IEC/IEEE 24765 international standard defines it as the degree to which a system or component can function correctly in the presence of invalid inputs or stressful environmental conditions [1]. In many cases, robustness refers to a system property rather than to the system as a whole: a property of a system is robust if it is invariant with respect to a set of perturbations [2]. This makes it possible to interpret many system properties as types of robustness: reliability as robustness to component failures; efficiency as robustness to lack of resources; scalability as robustness to changes to the size and complexity of the system as a whole; modularity as robustness to structured component rearrangements; evolvability as robustness of lineages to changes on long time scales.

The availability of feedback is seen as crucial in gaining robustness [2], yet not easy to obtain as is the case of multi-scale systems or of distributed systems of interconnected components. We see feedback as a piece of information, broadly speaking some facts that are obtained retroactively, that objectively concern an execution of interest, and that are passed from one component to another. The significance and the quality of feedback are crucial, as well, in making a system robust: one would not want any kind of information to be returned but only

C. Baroglio et al. (Eds.): EMAS 2020, LNAI 12589, pp. 61–77, 2020.
https://doi.org/10.1007/978-3-030-66534-0_4

information that is functional to the desired kind of robustness, and that comes from a reliable source.

Coming to Multiagent Systems (MAS), the current architectures and methodologies for their design and development (see e.g., [3,44,47]) fall short in addressing robustness in a systematic way at design time. For instance, they do not foresee mechanisms for exception handling, as instead is done for programming languages like Java, or in the actor model (e.g., see [30]). This happens because traditional approaches to exception handling do not accommodate some important features of MAS, like openness, heterogeneity, agent encapsulation, and distribution [37]. The common assumption is that software components are "collaborative", and that the code will be available for inspection. But introspection is often impossible when dealing with agents, and collaboration cannot be given for granted. As maintained in [37], in the case of MAS this sort of mechanisms should leverage on the proactivity of the agents.

Nevertheless, it is already possible to see in action elements that support the systematic introduction of robustness. For instance, agents often rely on reputation and trust to estimate how reliable another agent is before using (in their deliberative cycle) a piece of information that was produced by that agent [33]. When the MAS is enriched with an organizational infrastructure, that same infrastructure can be exploited to state the authority of the agents on given scopes. However, in order to support robustness something more is still needed. Alderson and Doyle [2] suggest that a possible strategy to achieve robustness in complex systems consists in "using feedback interconnection of sensors and actuators". That is, by exploiting the feedback coming from a (network of) system sensor(s), a component (in our case, an agent) can properly activate its actuators to complete its task. In this paper we aim at mapping this vision in the context of Multiagent Organizations (MAO). In MAO, is our opinion, feedback and feedback networks must be encompassed at the institutional level, through mechanisms that, on the one hand, are seamlessly integrated in the organizational ones (basically, the use of norms to regulate the functioning of the organization) and, on the other hand, capture the interconnectedness of feedback production and its propagation.

In the next section we explain the difficulties of gaining robustness in MAS. In Sect. 3 we introduce accountability and lay the basics for building reporting frameworks through it; in Sect. 3.1 we introduce a possible architecture, extending that of JaCaMo [13], for robust MAO.

2   Fragility in Distributed Systems and MAS

Many systems "are complex networks of multiple algorithms, control loops, sensors, and human roles that interact over different time scales and changing conditions" [43]. In sociology, such a complex network becomes a set of constraints that make a system, which comprises many parts, to act as a whole [24]. The combination of individuals and relationships produces emergent powers that enable the organization to achieve goals that otherwise would not be achievable (or not as easily). And the same holds for MAO.

However, the greater complexity introduces also new fragilities, that need to be coped with. More generally, "... this complexity itself can be a source of new fragility, leading to 'robust yet fragile' tradeoffs in system design" [2]. For example, consider the autonomous vehicle described in [43]. It is equipped with eighteen sensor packages, basic sensor processing/actuator controls, software or reasoning on temporal logic, sensor fusion, multiple path, traffic, and mission planners, conflict management, health monitoring, fault management, optimization, classifiers, models of the environment (maps), obstacle detection, road finding, vehicle finding, and sensor validation checks. Here, the use of protocols, of layering, and of feedback creates a complex, multi-scale modularity that *per se* is exposed to many risks of failure in presence of abnormal conditions. How to gain robustness?

It is possible to resort to MAS abstractions and methodologies to tackle the realization of robust complex systems of the described kind. These methodologies typically assume that agents coalesce in *organizations* to coordinate their interactions and tasks: system-level goals can be accomplished by taking advantage of the contribution of each agent [41]. An organization, thus, encompasses a functional decomposition of a global goal into subgoals. Subgoals are, then, assigned to agents by means of *norms*, that orchestrate the execution of the functional decomposition: as soon as a specific organizational goal is needed, the normative system generates an *obligation* toward some agent to achieve that goal. Agents' acceptance of the organizational constraints enables them to act in a shared environment, and achieve results unachievable if they acted in isolation. The agents' autonomy is an enabler of the system adaptability, which, in turn, is crucial to achieve robustness: a robust system is one that adapts to stressful environmental conditions, and components can adapt to changing contextual conditions and perturbations only if they are autonomous in their decision process. Adaptability, however, requires the system to be equipped with the ability to produce proper feedback, propagate it, and process it, so as to enable the selection and enactment of behavior that is appropriate to cope with the situation. The lack of such mechanisms makes the system fragile.

A functional decomposition describes what is expected of the agents for achieving a global goal, based on their supposed capabilities, but agents may fail the expectations. When this happens, a normative system would typically take the involved agents as *violators of some obligation*, and react to the violation by issuing sanctions toward the misbehaving agent. Consequently, on one hand, we can see the normative system as a means that enables the orchestration of the activities of a group of autonomous agents, while on the other hand, in some sense we can see it also as a means that tries to produce robustness. This because the agents are pushed to do *what is expected of them*, and thus to tackle the situations the system is facing. The rationale is to guide the agents toward the interest of the organization. The problem is that sanctions are not generally accompanied by feedback and feedback handling mechanisms, and thus they do not provide a means that supports robustness. Indeed, to be effective, sanctions must at least (1) be sufficiently "strong" to contrast the agents' self-interest in pursuing different goals of their own, and (2) target agents that actually have the resources and capabilities needed to face the situation of interest. In both cases robustness would be gained only by propagating through the system information about the *reasons* that caused the violation, and by revising the norms accordingly. Otherwise, for what concerns the first condition, how to identify a right trade-off that works for any agent without making assumptions of the agents' internals? For what concerns the second condition, how to propagate the reasons that cause the failure of some agent? Suppose, for instance, the agent is requested to deliver a parcel but the address is wrong. The parcel will not be delivered, but it is not the agent's fault. In such a case, sanction would be pointless because it would not help to achieve the result, and the organization would have no information of the reasons of the failure.

The problem is always the same: *the lack of, broadly speaking, a feedback framework*. Such a lack, for instance, makes it impossible to acquire information about possible conflicts (that remain internal to the agents), and hinders the identification of other agents to which reassign the goal because they have the skills that are needed to cope with a perturbation. As a consequence, the organization will generally be unable of selecting alternative strategies for pursuing its goals in presence of unfavorable conditions. To tackle these conditions effectively as a consequence of a good design, we need new conceptual tools. Inspired by what is often done in human organizations [25,40,46], we claim that *accountability* [10,12,22,27,28] provides such a new tool. As we will discuss in detail in the next section, accountability allows a designer to specify how feedback, that is collected by an agent, is passed to another agent, who is in position to react to the perturbation. Thanks to the former agent's accountability, the other agent, who would not otherwise know of the situation, becomes aware of the perturbation, and triggers its internal deliberative process for deciding how to tackle it (with a straightforward benefit to the whole organization). In our view, accountability is the key to design and develop robust MAS and organizations; we justify this claim in the following section.

3   Robustness Through Accountability

The term accountability has its roots in Latin, where it is related to the verb *computare*, to compute or calculate. Roughly speaking, an accountable person has the capability to provide an account about a condition of interest [21], that is, a person can be accountable for a condition, only if she has some competence, or knowledge, about the very same condition. Accountability "emerges as a primary characteristic of governance where there is a sense of agreement and certainty about the legitimacy of expectations between the community members." [22]. Accountability is, therefore, a mechanism and instrument of administrative and political power. It can be the means through which organizations can ensure the compliance of their processes to predefined standards as well as the force that enables changes aimed at improving the organization [14,25].

In many cultures, accountability is associated with blame [20], either *post factum* (who is to blame for an act or an error that has occurred), or *pre factum* (who is blameworthy for errors not yet occurred), but this is a very partial view that disregards the potential involved in relationships concerning the ability and the designation to provide response about something to someone who is legitimated to ask. In sociology, and in ethnomethodology in particular, it is seen as a basic mechanism that allows individuals to constitute societies [27,38]. Basically, it supports sense-making and coordination in a group of interacting parties, all of whom share an agreement on how things should be done [27], and can be reduced to two key features that connect two parties: one of the parties (the "account taker" or *a-taker*) can legitimately ask, under some agreed conditions, to the other party an account about a process of interest; the other party (the "account giver" or *a-giver*) is legitimately required to provide the account to the a-taker [5,6,19]. We can also say that the relationship between a-giver and a-taker is a relationship between a power-wielder and those holding them accountable, that expresses a general recognition of the *legitimacy of the authority of the parties* that are involved: one to exercise particular powers and the other to hold them to provide an account [28]. Consequently, we see accountability as having two main dimensions:

1. *normative dimension* (expectation), capturing the legitimacy of asking and the availability to provide accounts, yielding expectations on the agents' behavior;
2. *structural dimension* (control), capturing that, for being accountable about a process, an agent must have control over that process and have awareness of the situation it will account for.

Control often is interpreted as the ability to bring about events, possibly through other agents (see e.g., [36,45]), that is, to have power over a situation of interest. In the case of accountability, this means that agents can build the account themselves, either because they were directly involved in the attempt of bringing about some event, or because they can get the information that is necessary to build an account through other agents (see also [12]).

We denote accountability as $\mathbb{A}(x, y, r, u)$, where x is the a-giver, y is the a-taker. When condition r holds, y has the claim-right to ask x for an account about u, and x is in position to provide substantive and authoritative accounts about u. Condition r is not related to the state of u, but rather it represents the circumstance in which the a-giver is held to account (see [12]). When such a condition is not met, the a-giver is not obliged to produce the account. For instance, a buyer may hold a seller to account for some goods, but the seller will have to provide a feedback only if the purchase actually occurred, that is, only if the payment took place. Here, payment is the contextual condition that gives the buyer the right to have the account.

Notably, $\mathbb{A}(x, y, r, u)$ does not imply that x is the agent that brings about u; rather, x must report about the state of u when r holds and a request from y is received. Thus, $\mathbb{A}(x, y, r, u)$ entails an agreement between x and y: x accepts the legitimacy of y to ask about u, as well as, y recognizes the power of x to account about u (normative dimension). Such an account can be produced either because x was involved in first person in the attempt of bringing about u, or because it can reach the information that is necessary to build the account because it plays the role of a-taker in some accountability relationships that concern the parts of u (structural dimension).

3.1   Exemplification in JaCaMo

To accommodate the two dimensions of accountability within a MAO, to the aim of increasing robustness, one needs to operate at different levels of the organization model. First, at the conceptual level, the organization model has to be extended to encompass concepts related to the reporting of facts, and to their treatment. Second, at the normative level, we need to introduce the norms that regulate these new concepts. In particular, robustness relies on delivering feedback about perturbations to agents in charge of handling such perturbations so as to maintain invariant a system property [2]. In the rest of this section, we exemplify a possible realization in the well-known JaCaMo platform [13].

An Organizational Conceptual Model. We exemplify how the accountability dimension can be taken into account within a MAO model by exploiting the conceptual model of JaCaMo [13]. It is worth noting that our approach is not strictly dependent on JaCaMo, but it is applicable in any organizational model where a *Business Task* is structured in terms of organizational goals, or tasks, and where there is an explicit representation of the responsibilities taken up by the agents. To this aim, the conceptual model in Fig. 1 generalizes JaCaMo's concepts Scheme, Mission, and Goal respectively into Business Task, Responsibility, and Task (terms inspired by [26]). The mapping between Responsibility and Mission deserves some argumentation. In a JaCaMo organization goals are grouped in missions, which are then subject to norms. Specifically, the organization will issue obligations to achieve a mission goal to the agents. The organization can exert such a power on the agents because they are asked to *commit* to a mission at the beginning the execution. That is, if an agent does not fulfill an obligation, the organization is legitimated to sanction the agent by virtue of its commitment to the mission. The rationale is that, since it is not possible, in general, to inspect agents, it is also impossible to know whether the agent possesses the right capabilities to play a role, not even whether the agent will be compliant to the norms. To fill this knowledge gap, agents in JaCaMo are asked to commit to a mission as an implicit declaration that they possess the right behaviors for enacting the mission role, and that they will be receptive to the obligations the organization will issue about the goals in that mission. We interpret such a commitment as a declaration of *responsibility* assumption.

Note that in JaCaMo, an agent fulfills an obligation from the organization by mapping it into an internal goal: the satisfaction of such an internal goal will amount to an achievement of a mission goal, and hence will gain an institutional value. This approach guarantees a strong decoupling between the agents and the organization, allowing the agents to autonomously determine how they accomplish the organizational goals.

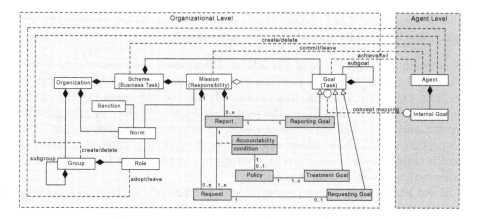

Fig. 1. The enhanced conceptual model. (Color figure online)

Finally, to the sake of generality, in Fig. 1 we also highlight `Sanction` as related to `Norm`, even though in JaCaMo this concept is just implicitly modeled.

Extending the Organization Conceptual Model. The green boxes in Fig. 1 highlights the concepts we add for modeling accountability. We capture the a-giver's side of accountability by means of `Report` as a component of `Mission`. The intuition is that an a-giver provides a report (i.e., an account) which is always contextualized by a mission: a report cannot exist on its own, but it refers to a specific mission to which the a-giver is committed. The association between `Report` and `Reporting Goal` makes it clear that a report is produced by some internal agent goal, mapping the `Reporting Goal`. The result of such an internal goal is a set of facts that gain an institutional meaning as a `Report`.

The a-taker's side of accountability is captured via `Request`, a component of `Mission`. An agent is legitimated to ask for a report only when the mission it is committed to includes at least one `Request`. The right of asking for a report can become an obligation when `Request` is associated with `Requesting Goal`. The organization can, in fact, issue obligations to achieve these goals pushing the agent to act as a-taker.

The relationships between `Report` and `Request` is captured as an association class `Accountability`, whose field `condition` represents the contextual condition that must be satisfied for granting the right of asking a report. It is important to underline that such an association class is usually defined between `Report` and `Request` instances that belong to different missions, and hence are under the responsibility of different agents. In this way, the association models the channel through which a report flows from the a-giver (who produces it) to the a-taker (who uses it). `Accountability` may be related to one (or more) `Policy`, that abstracts a strategy the organization has for copying with a specific report. `Policy`, in turn, is associated with one or more `Treatment Goals` that realize it. These further goals, when defined, are related to the mission of the agent behaving as a-taker: indeed, they capture how the report, provided by the a-giver, is addressed by the a-taker that asked for it.

Accountability Normative and Structural Dimensions. Accountability comes actually into play when the new concepts introduced above are regulated by specific norms. In particular, these norms should not only map the normative dimension of accountability (i.e., the legitimacy –*a-taker*'s side– of asking for an account, and the obligation –*a-giver*'s side– of producing such an account), but also capture its structural dimension. That is, it must be granted that when an agent is obliged to produce a report, that agent has the means for producing an authoritative report, i.e., an *account*.

In JaCaMo, norms are represented and interpreted by the Moise layer by using the Normative Programming Language (NPL) [32]. A norm in this language has the following syntax: **norm** $id : \varphi$ -> ψ, where id is an identifier of the norm, φ is the activation condition of the norm, and ψ is the consequence of the norm. A consequence can either be an obligation, or a failure. The former is used to raise obligations toward agents about goals to be achieved. The latter is used to model regimented norms; e.g., conditions that are prohibited. Intuitively, when ϕ is **fail**, any agent action that makes φ true will fail, too (and no change in the organization occurs).

We can reproduce the normative dimension of accountability by means of norms in NPL. For instance, the following norm template induces the accountability $\mathbb{A}(x, y, r, u)$.

```
1 norm reportProduction:
2    accountability(Request_u, Report_u, R) &
3    reportRequest(Y, Request_u) & R &
4    mission(M1, Y) & request(M1, Request_u) &
5    report(M2, Report_u) & mission(M2, X)
6    ->
7    obligation(X, ReportProduction, reportingGoal(Report_u),
8          Deadline)
```

The rule specifies that, when there exists an accountability relating a report about u and a request for the very same report in the context r (line 2), and agent y asks for a report on u under condition r (line 3), and y is legitimated to ask such a report because the request is part of its mission (line 4), and x is competent for producing an authoritative report about u because this is part of its mission (line 5), then an obligation on x is issued about goal reportingGoal(Report_u), through which the agent will provide y with the requested report.

Another norm can be defined to grant y the permission to ask for a report only when the request is part of its mission, and condition r holds. Indeed, in NPL we have to express a norm for prohibiting y to ask for a report when the context does not hold or when it has not a request for that report in its mission.

```
1   norm requestNotAllowed:
2      accountability(Request_u, Report_u, R) &
3      reportRequest(Y, Request_u) & ( not R |
```

```
4         (not (mission(M1, Y) & request(M1, Request_u)))
5    ->
6    fail (notLegitimateRequest(Y, R, U) )
```

The argument of the `fail` operator, `notLegitimateRequest(Y, R, U)`, represents the reason for the failure.

Following [5], the structural dimension of accountability requires that for each accountability $\mathbb{A}(x, y, r, u)$ defined in the system, either x has control over u, and hence can generate an account by producing facts, or there exists another accountability of the form $\mathbb{A}(z, x, r, u)$ supporting x. In terms of norms, thus, the structural dimension is a property that can be verified by assessing whether for each obligation that agent x has about reporting on u, x has the means for generating a report either from direct control over u, or from a report that x is legitimated (by norms) to ask to another agent. When both the structural and normative dimensions of accountability hold, x is an accountable agent for condition u, that is, x has the power to produce an *account* about u (i.e., an authoritative and reliable collection of facts).

It is worth noting that, although accountability is conceptually a directed relationship between agents, it is realized by means of undirected obligations. This happens because in our discussion we talk about accountability within the context of an organization, and rely on the organization's normative system to realize accountability by way of concepts like obligations and goals. Other approaches, such as [11,18], do not take the organizational perspective, but allow agents to establish their accountability relationships by means of protocols. In these cases, the notion of accountability is usually realized by means of social commitments, that differently from obligations, are always directed from a debtor agent towards a creditor agent.

Adding Robustness Through Accountability. The structural dimension of an accountability $\mathbb{A}(x, y, r, u)$ implies that accountability be grounded on control requirements. However, since it is not generally possible to assume that agents can be inspected, it is also generally impossible to know whether an agent has control over a specific condition when it enacts a role. To fill this knowledge gap, we assume that agents joins an organization only if they take on, explicitly, the *responsibility* of some of the organizational goals. As explained, responsibility is not directly represented in JaCaMo, but we can see the commitment to a mission as a declaration of responsibility assumption. Accountability and responsibility support robustness when the account about a perturbation is reported to the agent who is responsible for treating that perturbation. This is, in fact, a possible mapping of "the feedback interconnection of sensors and actuators" [2] into the organizational setting: the account of a perturbation (feedback) is the response that an a-giver produces as a consequence of a failure of a goal g (perturbation), that is of "interest" to an a-taker. The "interest" stems by the fact that the a-taker is responsible for an organizational goal, G, which cannot be accomplished due to the failure of g. By virtue of its responsibility on G, the a-taker is also responsible for treating any perturbation affecting G. Generally speaking, treating a perturbation means restoring a normal execution flow disrupted by that perturbation, but favorable opportunities could be handled, as well. TreatmentGoal abstracts such a task of treating perturbations by means of the mapping with the internal goals of a responsible agent.

4   Related Works

In this paper, we argued that accountability is instrumental for the realization of distributed systems that show some robustness property by design. Other works in literature have advocated the importance of accountability in the design of complex systems. The proposal in [15, 16] takes into account Sociotechnical Systems (STS), where multiple, autonomous principals interact with each other. They show how accountability plays a fundamental role in balancing the principals' autonomy. Their point is that accountability does not limit autonomy, since a principal can decide to violate any expectation for which it is accountable. However, by way of accountability, the principal would be held to account about that violation. Accountability relationships have, in fact, a normative stance, and hence they can be used to model the requirements of any STS. Accountability requirements serve as high-level representation of protocols, favoring the modularity of an STS development: a principal just needs to know its accountability requirements, and then can implement its software independently from others.

The work in [17] considers the ethical dimension in the design of STS. The authors argue that social norms provide a standard for correct behavior. Ethics is, in fact, a system-level concern; the point is that whether an agent's actions are ethical depends upon whether the system as a whole is ethical. An ethical system is capable of assessing the violation of an norm, and see it as an opportunity for innovation. An important aspect raised by the authors is that autonomy is not only a matter of intelligence and capabilities, but also involves the ability to violate norms. The rationale is that innovation presupposes the deviation from norms, that is to say, violating norms is not always bad, but sometimes it can lead to improving the whole system. In order to do this, it is necessary to align norms and agents, by relying on explanations that violators are expected to give. So, if the explanation hints a lack in the normative system, the violator is not sanctioned but rather the norms are updated. This approach is pretty different than ours. First of all, there is no explicit distinction between responsibility and accountability. The two concepts are merged within a single notion somehow aligned with liability. In [17], in fact, the normative dimension associated with accountability refers to the expectation that an a-taker has on what the a-giver will do (i.e., be ethical by adhering to norms). When the a-giver does not comply with the expectations, it is implicitly considered responsible for the violation, and hence held to explain the reasons for its behavior.

In our approach, the notion of accountability is not tied to liability, but has a wider understanding, since an accountable agent is not necessarily one to be blamed. To achieve this result we separate the responsibility of action from the accountability about situations [26]. The responsibility to act inside an organization is captured by the commitment to a mission: an agent accepts all the obligations that may be subsequently issued by the normative system of the organization. On the other hand, accountability is characterized by two dimensions: normative and structural. In our case, the normative dimension refers to the expectation an a-taker has on what accounts (i.e., reports) the a-giver is capable to provide. Such a dimension, however, must be supported by the structural dimension, that assures an a-giver has the proper means for producing the accounts it is expected to. Grounding the structural dimension on the assumption of responsibility allows agents to report legitimately about outcomes brought about by other agents [12]. This is essential when, in a distributed system, the perturbation detected by an agent may have to traverse many agents before reaching the one capable of handling it.

Moreover, explanations are not reports: an explanation in [17] is a justification of the agent's norm-violating behavior, while a report, in our understanding, does not have this specific interpretation. Then, a-givers in our approach are not seen as rule-violators: they are agents that meet perturbations and provide information about the encountered situation. The a-takers, on their hand, will interpret the received reports at the callee's level, possibly combining them with further information not available to the agents which met the perturbations. The adaptation process in [17] can, however, be seen as a type of robustness, and hence it bears similarities with the approach presented in the paper. Our objective, however, is not to change the norms, but to support the achievement of the organizational goal despite the occurrence of anticipated perturbations. In [17], instead, accountability enables the process of norms adaptation by feeding outcomes back into the design-phase. The two approaches are not in contrast, rather, they complement each other. They are both exemplifications of the perspective put forward in [2], for which a property of a system is robust if it is invariant with respect to a set of perturbations. The difference lies in the type of perturbations the two approaches aim at.

On the conceptual modeling side, ReMMo (Responsibility MetaModel) by Feltus [26] is one of the few attempts, to the best of our knowledge, of conceptualizing how responsibility can be structured in the frame of an enterprise architecture. There are some interesting similarities, but also substantial differences between ReMMo and the conceptual model we propose. Both in ReMMo and in our proposal, responsibilities originate from (professional) norms agents are held to respect. The two approaches agree that accountability refers to the obligation to report the achievement, maintenance, or avoidance of some given state to an authority [39]. ReMMo relates a responsibility to an aggregate of accountabilities. The rationale is that a responsibility is composed of duties, and an agent assigned to that responsibility is answerable, via accountabilities, for these duties. The same relationship emerges, indirectly, also in our conceptual model. In fact, a `Mission` can be composed by several `Report` and `Request`, and `Accountability` is an association class between them.

There are, however, some important differences. First of all, in ReMMo every responsibility is always associated with one or more accountabilities. We instead allow missions (sources of responsibility) that are not related with reports, and hence with accountabilities. This discrepancy stems from the different aims and scopes of the two models. ReMMo captures the complexity of a human organization, and aims at tracing who is responsible for some task and hence is held to account for what she does (or does not) concerning that task. The goal, thus, is to single out the person(s) who should provide an account for a specific business task performed within the enterprise. In our case, instead, we aim at achieving robustness by way of accountability as a mechanism for modeling feedback flows. But not for every mission feedback may be required, or can possibly be specified, and hence the model lets the definition of missions that are not in relation with reports. In addition, in our model `Report`, `Request`, and `Policy` are explicitly represented not only to specify who has to provide an account to whom, but also how such an account should be used by the a-taker for the robustness purpose. All these concepts are missing in ReMMo, where accountability is substantially overlapped with liability, and hence associated with a sanction. In our view, it is restrictive to see accountability just as a way to find a culprit to be sanctioned; rather, it is an important tool to get a better understanding of what is going on in the system, and possibly take proper action. Sanctions, if necessary, follow from normative decisions, and hence they are associated with the `Norm` concept. This is also the position put forward in [17], where it is observed how sanctions, although may serve as deterrent, remove accountability: by paying its sanction, an agent needs no longer to provide an account about its violation. This of course prevents one to know the causes of the violation, and hence blocks the adaptation process at the basis of robustness.

MOCA [12] is another attempt to model accountability from a computational point of view which deserves some discussion. MOCA is an information model that captures what kind of data (facts) must be available to develop systems that, in any situation of interest arising in a group of interacting agents, permit the identification of account-givers. The model is given in Object-Role Modeling (ORM) [31] due to the relational nature of the represented concepts, and enables automatic verification of consistency of a specific domain description. This allows a designer to establish whether all the relevant pieces of information for supporting accountability have been considered. MOCA builds the information model for accountability around two basic concepts: *just expectation* and *control*. For just expectation it is intended a mutual awareness and acceptance of an accountability relationships between the involved a-giver and a-taker agents. For control, instead, it is intended the power, possibly exerted indirectly by means of other agents, of achieving a condition of interest. These two features are properly captured in our proposal by, respectively, the normative and structural dimensions of accountability. Through the normative dimension, in fact, agents are aware of what obligations they may be subjected as a-giver, and what permissions they have as a-taker. The structural dimension, instead, grounds accountability relationships over an explicit assumption of responsibility from the agents via the commitment to missions. We consider such a commitment as a declaration of direct control (i.e., expressed in MOCA as the relation *can realize*).

Accountability is sometimes put in relation with other properties a system can exhibit, such as transparency, explainability and trust. In particular, the theme of trustful AI is rapidly gaining attention in the last few years. Although some authors consider accountability as opposite to trust [29], others posit that accountability may improve trust when interactions are structured around a clear set of standards [23]. In this paper, we have not focused on this topic, and leave the study of how trust may come into play in our accountability conceptual model to future research. It is worth noting, however, that the two notions are quite different. As we have discussed, accountability is a social relationships between two agents that requires mutual acceptance of rights and duties. Trust, instead, is not necessarily a social relationship: an agent trusts others on the basis of its internal decisions (that usually depend on what others did in the past). For instance, some works propose a strategy for computing trust by assessing how frequently an agent satisfies its commitments [35]. In doing this, however, trust emerges as a local perspective of a single agent, rather than a social relationship.

We conclude this section with a remark about robustness via reactive behaviors. In this paper we have shown how accountability plays a fundamental role in the case of agents because of their autonomy. Autonomy here means that agents are opaque: their beliefs cannot be inspected and their deliberative cycle cannot be known. As pointed out in [17], accountability helps because it defines public relationships that exist outside the agents, regardless of what agents may believe or intend. Of course, there are other settings where robustness can be gained via a purely reactive behavior and where neither accountability nor autonomy come into play. This is, for instance, the case of robustness via control engineering (see e.g., [34]), where a system is modeled as a set of mathematical equations that approximate the system expected outputs for any given inputs. Robustness is gained by means of a controller that, receiving constant feedback of the system outputs, automatically update some system parameters so as to meet its expected performance requirements. This approach is only possible, however, when we are able to design a model of the whole system knowing the (possible approximated) behavior of each of its components. This is not the case in software engineering, however.

5   Conclusions

In this paper, we have posited that an explicit representation of accountability relationships and responsibility declarations form a solid ground upon which a property of robustness can be achieved by design. We have taken into account agent organizations as background of our discussion, and hence we presented an organizational conceptual model apt to capture accountability and responsibility notions. The JaCaMo conceptual model served as a starting point for our extension, but our contribution is not strictly dependent on the JaCaMo model. An important result of this work is a normative characterization for capturing accountability relationships: accountability is, in fact, inherently a normative relationship [17]. We have identified two dimensions featuring accountability:

normative and structural. With the normative dimension we model the relationships between a-takers and a-givers, thus capturing the legitimacy of the former to ask for an account, and the obligation of the latter to provide the account. The structural dimension is instead related to the control, or competence, of a-givers. The structural dimension assures that an agent who is a-giver has the proper means for producing an authoritative account of the situation of interest. Only when such a condition holds, the account represents a meaningful piece of information. We are implementing the approach outlined in the paper by extending the JaCaMo platform, and a first release is on the way.

A key point raised in the paper is that accountability has a positive impact on the agents' autonomy and, due to this, on their adaptability, consequently opening the way to making an organization more robust. On the one side, accountability improves the awareness of the a-taker about what is happening in the system, allowing it to deliberate its (counter)actions accordingly. On the other side, the a-giver's reputation is not automatically reduced when failures occur, because the reports will highlight possible perturbations, supporting the functioning of the organization. Actually, this increases both trust and autonomy [4,42].

This work sets the ground for several future directions. First of all, it represents a general schema that can be tailored to capture specific applications. For instance, it is possible to realize an exception handling mechanism in agent organizations, by constraining the way in which agents produce and consume reports. Specifically, an exception is a situation of interest whose occurrence is related to errors, and which should be urgently reported to the agent in charge of handling these errors. Such "urgency" implies that whenever an agent detects an error it is obliged to report it, even without an explicit request. On the other side, the agent receiving a report will be in charge (i.e., obliged) of tackling the report, that is, handling the exception. These behaviors can be obtained by acting at the normative level of the organization by generating automatically obligations on report and treatment goals. We are currently developing a system, inspired by JaCaMo+ [8] and of [7,9].

In conclusion, we think that the presented framework can be the base for capturing a wide range of non-functional requirements, besides robustness, such as adaptability, fault tolerance, reusability, and transparency. Our intuition is that these non-functional requirements are met in a distributed system when its components (agents in our perspective), can exchange information at a different level of that of the outcomes that are specified by functional requirements. As shown in the paper, accountability can be a valid conceptual tool for reaching this objective.

Acknowledgments. The authors would like to thank the anonymous reviewers for their feedback, that helped to improve the paper, and Olivier Boissier and Stefano Tedeschi for the helpful discussions and support.

References

1. ISO/IEC/IEEE International Standard - Systems and software engineering - Vocabulary. ISO/IEC/IEEE 24765:2010(E), pp. 1–418, December 2010. https://doi.org/10.1109/IEEESTD.2010.5733835
2. Alderson, D.L., Doyle, J.C.: Contrasting views of complexity and their implications for network-centric infrastructures. IEEE Trans. Syst. Man Cybern. Part A Syst. Hum. **40**(4), 839–852 (2010)
3. Aldewereld, H., Dignum, V., Vasconcelos, W.W.: Group norms for multi-agent organisations. ACM Trans. Auton. Adapt. Syst. **11**(2), 15:1–15:31 (2016)
4. Baarslag, T., Kaisers, M., Gerding, E.H., Jonker, C.M., Gratch, J.: When will negotiation agents be able to represent us? The challenges and opportunities for autonomous negotiators. In: Proceedings of the Twenty-Sixth International Joint Conference on Artificial Intelligence, IJCAI 2017, Melbourne, Australia, 19–25 August 2017, pp. 4684–4690 (2017)
5. Baldoni, M., Baroglio, C., Boissier, O., May, K.M., Micalizio, R., Tedeschi, S.: Accountability and responsibility in agent organizations. In: Miller, T., Oren, N., Sakurai, Y., Noda, I., Savarimuthu, B.T.R., Cao Son, T. (eds.) PRIMA 2018. LNCS (LNAI), vol. 11224, pp. 261–278. Springer, Cham (2018). https://doi.org/10.1007/978-3-030-03098-8_16
6. Baldoni, M., Baroglio, C., Boissier, O., Micalizio, R., Tedeschi, S.: Accountability and responsibility in multiagent organizations for engineering business processes. In: Dennis, L.A., Bordini, R.H., Lespérance, Y. (eds.) EMAS 2019. LNCS (LNAI), vol. 12058, pp. 3–24. Springer, Cham (2020). https://doi.org/10.1007/978-3-030-51417-4_1
7. Baldoni, M., Baroglio, C., Capuzzimati, F.: A commitment-based infrastructure for programming socio-technical systems. ACM Trans. Internet Technol. **14**(4), 23:1–23:23 (2014). https://doi.org/10.1145/2677206. http://doi.acm.org/10.1145/2677206
8. Baldoni, M., Baroglio, C., Capuzzimati, F., Micalizio, R.: Commitment-based agent interaction in JaCaMo+. Fundamenta Informaticae **159**(1–2), 1–33 (2018)
9. Baldoni, M., Baroglio, C., Capuzzimati, F., Micalizio, R.: Type checking for protocol role enactments via commitments. Auton. Agent. Multi-Agent Syst. **32**(3), 349–386 (2018). https://doi.org/10.1007/s10458-018-9382-3
10. Baldoni, M., Baroglio, C., May, K.M., Micalizio, R., Tedeschi, S.: Computational accountability. In: Chesani, F., Mello, P., Milano, M. (eds.) Deep Understanding and Reasoning: A Challenge for Next-Generation Intelligent Agents, URANIA 2016, Genoa, Italy, vol. 1802, pp. 56–62. CEUR, Workshop Proceedings, December 2016. http://ceur-ws.org/Vol-1802/
11. Baldoni, M., Baroglio, C., May, K.M., Micalizio, R., Tedeschi, S.: Computational accountability in MAS organizations with ADOPT. Appl. Sci. **8**(4), 489 (2018)
12. Baldoni, M., Baroglio, C., May, K.M., Micalizio, R., Tedeschi, S.: MOCA: an ORM model for computational accountability. J. Intell. Artif. **13**(1), 5–20 (2019). https://doi.org/10.3233/IA-180014
13. Boissier, O., Bordini, R.H., Hübner, J.F., Ricci, A., Santi, A.: Multi-agent oriented programming with JaCaMo. Sci. Comput. Program. **78**(6), 747–761 (2013). http://www.sciencedirect.com/science/article/pii/S016764231100181X
14. Bovens, M.: Two concepts of accountability: accountability as a virtue and as a mechanism. West Eur. Polit. **33**(5), 946–967 (2010)

15. Chopra, A.K., Singh, M.P.: The thing itself speaks: accountability as a foundation for requirements in sociotechnical systems. In: IEEE 7th International Workshop RELAW. IEEE Computer Society (2014). https://doi.org/10.1109/RELAW.2014.6893477

16. Chopra, A.K., Singh, M.P.: From social machines to social protocols: software engineering foundations for sociotechnical systems. In: Proceedings of the 25th International Conference on WWW (2016)

17. Chopra, A.K., Singh, M.P.: Sociotechnical systems and ethics in the large. In: Furman, J., Marchant, G.E., Price, H., Rossi, F. (eds.) Proceedings of the 2018 AAAI/ACM Conference on AI, Ethics, and Society, AIES 2018, New Orleans, LA, USA, 02–03 February 2018, pp. 48–53. ACM (2018)

18. Chopra, A.K., Singh, M.P.: Clouseau: generating communication protocols from commitments. In: Proceedings of the Thirty-Fourth AAAI Conference on Artificial Intelligence (AAAI 2020), pp. 7244–7252. AAAI Press (2020)

19. Cranefield, S., Oren, N., Vasconcelos, W.W.: Accountability for practical reasoning agents. In: Lujak, M. (ed.) AT 2018. LNCS (LNAI), vol. 11327, pp. 33–48. Springer, Cham (2019). https://doi.org/10.1007/978-3-030-17294-7_3

20. Dubnick, M.J.: Blameworthiness, trustworthiness, and the second-personal standpoint: foundations for an ethical theory of accountability. Presented at EGPA Annual Conference, Group VII: Quality and Integrity of Governance, Edinburgh, Scotland, 11–13 September 2013

21. Dubnick, M.J.: Accountability as a Cultural Keyword, pp. 23–38. Oxford University Press, Oxford (2014)

22. Dubnick, M.J., Justice, J.B.: Accounting for accountability, September 2004. https://pdfs.semanticscholar.org/b204/36ed2c186568612f99cb8383711c554e7c70.pdf. Annual Meeting of the American Political Science Association

23. Ehren, M., Paterson, A., Baxter, J.: Accountability and trust: two sides of the same coin? J. Educ. Change **21**(1), 183–213 (2019). https://doi.org/10.1007/s10833-019-09352-4

24. Elder-Vass, D.: The Causal Power of Social Structures: Emergence, Structure and Agency. Cambridge University Press, Cambridge (2011)

25. Executive Board of the United Nations Development Programme and of the United Nations Population Fund: The UNDP accountability system, accountability framework and oversight policy. Technical report DP/2008/16/Rev.1, United Nations (2008)

26. Feltus, C.: Aligning access rights to governance needs with the responsibility metamodel (ReMMo) in the frame of enterprise architecture. Ph.D. thesis, University of Namur, Belgium (2014)

27. Garfinkel, H.: Studies in Ethnomethodology. Prentice-Hall Inc., Englewood Cliffs (1967)

28. Grant, R.W., Keohane, R.O.: Accountability and abuses of power in world politics. Am. Polit. Sci. Rev. **99**(1), 29–43 (2005)

29. Gundlach, G.T., Cannon, J.P.: "Trust but verify"? The performance implications of verification strategies in trusting relationships. J. Acad. Mark. Sci. **38**(4), 399–417 (2010). https://doi.org/10.1007/s11747-009-0180-y

30. Haller, P., Sommers, F.: Actors in Scala - Concurrent Programming for the Multicore Era. Artima, Walnut Creek (2011)

31. Halpin, T., Morgan, T.: Information Modeling and Relational Databases. Morgan Kaufmann Publishers, Burlington (2008)

32. Hübner, J.F., Boissier, O., Bordini, R.H.: A normative programming language for multi-agent organisations. Ann. Math. Artif. Intell. **62**(1), 27–53 (2011). https://doi.org/10.1007/s10472-011-9251-0

33. Huynh, T.D., Jennings, N.R., Shadbolt, N.R.: An integrated trust and reputation model for open multi-agent systems. Auton. Agent. Multi-Agent Syst. **13**(2), 119–154 (2006)

34. Ioannou, P.A., Sun, J.: Robust Adaptive Control. Courier Corporation, North Chelmsford (2012)

35. Kalia, A.K., Zhang, Z., Singh, M.P.: Estimating trust from agents' interactions via commitments. In: Schaub, T., Friedrich, G., O'Sullivan, B. (eds.) ECAI 2014 - 21st European Conference on Artificial Intelligence, 18–22 August 2014, Prague, Czech Republic - Including Prestigious Applications of Intelligent Systems (PAIS 2014). Frontiers in Artificial Intelligence and Applications, vol. 263, pp. 1043–1044. IOS Press (2014). https://doi.org/10.3233/978-1-61499-419-0-1043

36. Marengo, E., Baldoni, M., Baroglio, C., Chopra, A., Patti, V., Singh, M.: Commitments with regulations: reasoning about safety and control in REGULA. In: Proceedings of the 10th International Conference on Autonomous Agents and Multiagent Systems (AAMAS), vol. 2, pp. 467–474 (2011)

37. Platon, E., Sabouret, N., Honiden, S.: Challenges for exception handling in multi-agent systems. In: Choren, R., Garcia, A., Giese, H., Leung, H., Lucena, C., Romanovsky, A. (eds.) SELMAS 2006. LNCS, vol. 4408, pp. 41–56. Springer, Heidelberg (2007). https://doi.org/10.1007/978-3-540-73131-3_3

38. Rawls, A.W.: Harold Garfinkel, ethnomethodology and workplace studies. Organ. Stud. **29**(5), 701–732 (2008)

39. Sommerville, I., Lock, R., Storer, T., Dobson, J.: Deriving information requirements from responsibility models. In: van Eck, P., Gordijn, J., Wieringa, R. (eds.) CAiSE 2009. LNCS, vol. 5565, pp. 515–529. Springer, Heidelberg (2009). https://doi.org/10.1007/978-3-642-02144-2_40

40. Sustainable Energy for All Initiative: Accountability framework. https://sustainabledevelopment.un.org/content/documents/1644se4all.pdf

41. Timm, I.J., Scholz, T., Herzog, O., Krempels, K.H., Spaniol, O.: From agents to multiagent systems. In: Kirn, S., Herzog, O., Lockemann, P., Spaniol, O. (eds.) Multiagent Engineering. INFOSYS, pp. 35–51. Springer, Heidelberg (2006). https://doi.org/10.1007/3-540-32062-8_3

42. Winikoff, M.: Towards trusting autonomous systems. In: El Fallah-Seghrouchni, A., Ricci, A., Son, T.C. (eds.) EMAS 2017. LNCS (LNAI), vol. 10738, pp. 3–20. Springer, Cham (2018). https://doi.org/10.1007/978-3-319-91899-0_1

43. Woods, D.D.: The risks of autonomy: Doyle's catch. J. Cogn. Eng. Decis. Mak. **10**(2), 131–133 (2016)

44. Wooldridge, M., Jennings, N.R., Kinny, D.: The GAIA methodology for agent-oriented analysis and design. Auton. Agent. Multi-Agent Syst. **3**(3), 285–312 (2000). https://doi.org/10.1023/A:101007191086910.1023/A:1010071910869

45. Yazdanpanah, V., Dastani, M.: Distant group responsibility in multi-agent systems. In: Baldoni, M., Chopra, A.K., Son, T.C., Hirayama, K., Torroni, P. (eds.) PRIMA 2016. LNCS (LNAI), vol. 9862, pp. 261–278. Springer, Cham (2016). https://doi.org/10.1007/978-3-319-44832-9_16

46. Zahran, M.: Accountability Frameworks in the United Nations System (2011). https://www.unjiu.org/sites/www.unjiu.org/files/jiu_document_files/products/en/reports-notes/JIU%20Products/JIU_REP_2011_5_English.pdf. UN Report

47. Zambonelli, F., Jennings, N.R., Wooldridge, M.: Developing multiagent systems: the Gaia methodology. ACM Trans. Softw. Eng. Methodol. **12**(3), 317–370 (2003)

Fault Tolerance in Multiagent Systems

Samuel H. Christie V$^{(\boxtimes)}$ⓘ and Amit K. Chopraⓘ

Lancaster University, Bailrigg, Lancaster LA1 4YW, UK
{samuel.christie,amit.chopra}@lancaster.ac.uk

Abstract. A decentralized multiagent systems (MAS) is comprised of autonomous agents who interact with each other via asynchronous messaging. A protocol specifies a MAS by specifying the constraints on messaging between agents. Agents enact protocols by applying their own internal decision making.

Various kinds of faults may occur when enacting a protocol. For example, messages may be lost, duplicates may be delivered, and agents may crash during the processing of a message. Our contribution in this paper is demonstrating how information protocols support rich fault tolerance mechanisms, and in a manner that is unanticipated by alternative approaches for engineering decentralized MAS.

1 Introduction

Like any software system, a multiagent system is vulnerable to a variety of faults resulting from any number of root causes: bugs, hardware failure, environmental conditions, etc. If handled poorly or not at all, such faults could propagate through the system and ultimately cause an *error*, or deviation from the specified behavior of the system.

This paper is concerned with decentralized multiagent systems (MAS) in which autonomous agents communicate via asynchronous messaging and coordinate their computations by following an interaction protocol. The decision making of agents being private, the protocol is in fact the fundamental operational specification of a MAS. Indeed, it is meaningless to talk about the computations of a MAS except in terms of messages sent and received by its agents.

Agents enact a protocol by plugging in their private decision making, as encoded in their policies. Although there has been significant work on protocol specification [3,10] and engineering protocol-conformant agents [1], there is little work that addresses protocol enactment under various kinds of faults. The faults may correspond to communication infrastructure failures, e.g.., message loss, corruption, duplication, and so on, or to agent failures, e.g.., crashes.

We would expect that a fault-tolerant MAS has the following two properties. One, no fault causes an agent to send a message that would be noncompliant with the protocol. We refer to this property as *compliant-despite-faults*. Two, agents, if they choose to, can recover from faults by sending additional messages. We refer to this property as *progress-despite-faults*. Naturally, any additional message must be protocol-compliant.

© Springer Nature Switzerland AG 2020
C. Baroglio et al. (Eds.): EMAS 2020, LNAI 12589, pp. 78–86, 2020.
https://doi.org/10.1007/978-3-030-66534-0_5

Listing 1. The Ridesharing *RFQ* Protocol

```
RFQ {
  role Rider, Service
  parameter out ID key, out location, out destination, out price

  Rider -> Service: Request[out ID key, out location, out destination]
  Service -> Rider: Offer[in ID key, in location, in destination, out price]
}
```

Our contribution in this paper is illustrating how fault-tolerant MAS with the above properties can be constructed. We illustrate our ideas in the framework of information protocols [9]. In fact, we show that whereas information protocols are naturally compatible with fault-tolerance mechanisms, alternative approaches are not. In particular, although alternatives can ensure compliance, progress despite faults would be challenging.

2   Basic Fault Handling with Information Protocols

Throughout this paper, we will be developing examples based on a hypothetical ridesharing service.

Listing 1 gives the BSPL specification for a simple RFQ interaction, in which a rider shares their location and desired destination, which the service can use to estimate the cost of a journey.

In the *RFQ* protocol in Listing 1, there are two roles an agent may play: RIDER and SERVICE. The RIDER can send *Request*, which has a payload of three parameters: ID, location, and destination. These parameters are adorned ⌜out⌝, which means that RIDER produces new bindings for them upon sending *Request*. SERVICE can also send one message, *Offer*, with a payload of four parameters: ID, location, destination, and price. The first three parameters are adorned ⌜in⌝, which means SERVICE must observe a binding for them before sending *Offer*. In *RFQ*, all of the messages have ID as the only key, which uniquely identifies the enactments of *RFQ*. Each parameter may only have one binding for a given value of ID.

2.1   Message Reordering

Message reordering is a fault in several protocol specification languages, because they depend on ordering guaranties from the communication infrastructure [2].

For example, the *RFQ* protocol specified as a trace expression [3] is given as the following:

$$\text{RIDER} \xrightarrow{\textit{Request}} \text{SERVICE} \cdot \text{SERVICE} \xrightarrow{\textit{Offer}} \text{RIDER}$$

This specifies the simple requirement that a trace (log of messages) of the system match the concatenation of the traces of a single *Request* concatenated with the trace of a single *Offer*.

Although this matches exactly a single enactment of *RFQ*, since SERVICE cannot send *Offer* until it has received *Request*, there is minimal support for repeated enactments and no support for message reordering. Under Ferrando et al.'s [3] assumption of FIFO channels, if RIDER sends multiple *Requests*, it can expect to receive several *Offer* messages in the same order; multiple enactments are indistinguishable from isolated enactments. However, if something breaks and the messages are delivered out of order, RIDER would erroneously correlate the wrong *Offer* with its *Request*. Although message IDs could be automatically added by the infrastructure to help correlate requests with responses, such automatic IDs are only effective for two-party cases. A more detailed discussion of the limitations of such correlation IDs and FIFO queues is available at [2].

In contrast, systems specified by information protocols correctly associate messages with enactments without constraining the ordering, because the messages contain explicit keys that ensure correct correlation. Alternatively, information protocols are concerned with the cumulative information observed, and all information is explicitly communicated, so messages contain the same information regardless of the order they are received.

2.2 Message Duplication

Another common fault in communications is message duplication, in which a message is received multiple times, though it was sent only once.

In Sect. 2.1, the Trace specification of the *RFQ* protocol specifies exactly one transmission of *Request*, followed by exactly one transmission of *Offer*. If multiple *Request* are received, SERVICE will interpret them as multiple isolated enactments of *RFQ*, and presumably respond to each. Conversely, if multiple *Offer* messages are received, RIDER will incorrectly correlate them to its subsequent REQUEST messages.

In this case, the automatic addition of message IDs can identify and eliminate duplicate messages. However, relying on automatic correlation IDs imposes constraints on the infrastructure, and implicitly couples the agents to it.

Because all information in a message is explicit, information protocols are not affected by duplicate messages; they contain no new information regarding the enactment, and so do not affect the state of the agent. However, duplicate messages do potentially communicate implicit information about the environment; that something is wrong which would cause duplicates to occur. Thus, handling duplicate messages in the agent's policy instead of the infrastructure enables additional fault tolerance strategies and is important for ensuring progress despite faults, as we discuss further in Sect. 4.

2.3 Message Corruption

Message corruption damages the information content of a message, so information protocols alone do not provide a solution.

However, environmental message corruption can be easily detected and avoided using content-level techniques such as signatures and checksums. An unrecoverably corrupted message can be discarded and considered equivalent to message loss. As such, we do not consider accidental message corruption in detail.

2.4   Message Loss

A lost message contains no information, and is furthermore indistinguishable from delay or an agent's autonomous decision to not send the message. Therefore, an information protocol specification alone—or any protocol specification, for that matter—cannot correct message loss.

However, information protocols do enable the use of various strategies at the agent policy level for detecting and resolving message loss. The following sections discuss several causes for message loss, and strategies that can be taken to address them.

3   Internal Faults

In this section, we address faults that directly affect an agent itself, such as a bug in the agent's software implementation or a hardware failure. For simplicity, we consider that all of these faults can be abstracted to the worst case scenario of a *crash*, causing the agent to halt and cease further action. Strategies for handling lower-level faults and avoiding crashes are outside the scope of this discussion.

Figure 1 illustrates the architecture of a basic protocol-aware agent, to help identify the consequences of a crash at various points in its operation.

Fig. 1. An agent's internal architecture, showing how internal events and policy interact with the world through the protocol adapters.

Figure 1 shows the important components of a protocol-aware agent, and how it interacts with the world. Such an agent interacts with the world through its protocol adapters, which keep a history of all messages received and emitted, and check outgoing messages for consistency with that history. If a message is not consistent with the agent's history it will be dropped, ensuring compliance despite faults.

The agent's internal policy processes events and emits messages through the emission adapter. Events can be external, resulting from message receptions, or internal events such as sensory perception or timers.

The points at which a crash may occur include:

1. Before logging reception
2. After logging reception, before policy
3. During policy, before logging emission
4. After logging emission, before sending

Case 1 is indistinguishable from a network connection failure. Strategies for dealing with environmental network loss are discussed in Section 4.

Cases 2 and 3 are only distinguishable if the agent is stateful; that is, if processing the message produces side effects other than message emissions. As such, we instead discuss strategies for handling crashes during policy in stateless versus stateful agent implementations.

3.1   Crash During Stateless Policy

If the agent crashes after logging the reception but before policy, a new instance can be started using the logged history information. Because the history contains all messages that the agent has received or sent, it contains all of the information necessary for a new agent to resume where it left off.

There are several ways the restarted agent can resume computation. First, the agent could simply reprocess all of the messages in its history. This approach is inefficient, but very simple. Because the agent is stateless it will produce the same output for all of its inputs. As discussed in Sect. 2.2, information protocols can handle duplicate messages, though they could be checked against the history to avoid sending duplicates if desired.

Another option is querying the history for enabled messages. For example, consider the SERVICE role of the *RFQ* protocol in Listing 1. As SERVICE is stateless, it can compute a price using only the location and destination provided by RIDER. To identify prices that it needs to compute, it can search its database using the equivalent of the following SQL statement:

```
SELECT * FROM history WHERE
    location IS NOT NULL
    AND destination IS NOT NULL
    AND price IS NULL;
```

This query finds all enactments where a location and destination have been observed, but the price has not yet been computed. SERVICE can then compute and send these missing prices.

3.2   Crash During Stateful Policy

Consider the following rideshare protocol in Listing 2, in which RIDER hires the offered ride, and SERVICE replies with a description of the dispatched vehicle.

Listing 2. The *Hire* Protocol

```
Hire {
    role Rider, Service
    parameter in ID key, in price, out payment,

    Rider -> Service: Hire[in ID key, in price, out payment]
    Service -> Rider: Ride[in ID key, in payment, out rideID key, out
        description]
}
```

In Listing 2, SERVICE dispatches a vehicle and then announces the rideID and description to RIDER. If the crash happens after dispatching the vehicle but before the ride notification, SERVICE would not be able to remember that it had dispatched the ride from its message history alone. During restart, it may dispatch a second vehicle, wasting the first driver.

In general, and especially in cases involving side effects in the real world, there will be crashes that are unrecoverable. The only solutions are low-level atomic transactions, or detailed closed-loop sensor feedback to check the state of the system before proceeding.

For situations that are recoverable in software, we propose the following normalization of the agent architecture:

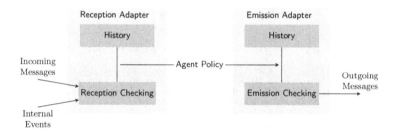

Fig. 2. Normalized agent architecture, with formerly internal events being handled as messages.

In Figure 2, the previously internal events are now treated like incoming messages, and handled by the agent's protocol adapter.

Normalizing an agent so that all of its events are handled as messages encourages proper protocol design. For example, SERVICE should be interacting with drivers via protocols. If so, those messages would be in the agent's history, and properly handled during restart.

4   External Faults

External faults are those due to environmental conditions, and therefore not the responsibility of any single agent.

Although the environment can cause any kind of error, information protocols are robust against reordering and duplication as we discussed in sections 2.1

and 2.2. Furthermore, messages corrupted by the environment are easily detected through the use of checksums and discarded, and so reduce to message loss. As such, we consider only strategies for handling message loss.

4.1 Retry Policies

If *Request* is lost during *RFQ*, it is as if the protocol had never begun—SERVICE is not aware of the request, and so is unable to respond. However, since an enactment is identified by unique key parameters (in this case the ID field), RIDER can resend the message until it gets through without confusing SERVICE.

Conversely, if *Offer* is lost, RIDER has no way to tell that SERVICE has received its message, and so this case is indistinguishable from the first. Thus SERVICE can expect to receive another copy of *Request* if the message was not received, and simply resend it.

This approach—the retry policy—is the basic pattern for handling message loss in information protocols, since agents may resend information without constraint. It is up to the agent's decision making when to resend a message.

This approach can also scale to larger protocols. Consider the three-party interaction in Listing 3.

Listing 3. The *Rideshare* Protocol

```
Rideshare {
  roles Rider, Service, Driver
  parameter out ID key, out loc, out dest, out payment, out rideID key, out
    description

  Rider -> Service: Hire [out ID key, out loc, out dest, out payment]
  Service -> Driver: Dispatch [in ID key, in loc, in dest, out rideID key]
  Driver -> Rider: Arrival [in ID key, in rideID key, out description]
}
```

In this simple protocol, RIDER hires a ride from location to destination, SERVICE dispatches DRIVER, who arrives to pick up the passenger. If all messages are transmitted successfully, no acknowledgements are required. However, even if some messages are lost, RIDER can resend its request until DRIVER arrives.

However, retry policies depend on the closed-loop nature of the protocol. If RIDER did not expect DRIVER to pick them up, and instead requested the ride on behalf of someone else, then they would have no way of detecting the fault and resending the message. If there is no way to detect a failure, there is no way to recover from it.

4.2 Role Replacement

An agent or connection (which are possibly indistinguishable to the other participants) may be permanently damaged, so that the only solution is to find a replacement.

At this point we discover the need for an extension to our protocol language: role adornments. Previously, roles were implicitly bound by the enactment of the protocol; perhaps all participants agreed before enacting it. However, now the selection and potential replacement of a role must be explicitly communicated within the protocol.

Listing 4. Multiple Dispatch Protocol

```
Multiple Dispatch {
  roles Rider, Service, Driver
  parameter out ID key, out loc, out dest, out payment, out rideID key, out
    description

  Rider -> out Service: Hire[out ID key, out loc, out dest, out payment]
  Service -> out Driver: Dispatch[in ID key, in Rider, out rideID key]
  Driver -> in Rider: Arrival[in ID key, in rideID key, out description]
}
```

In Listing 4, the roles are adorned ⌜in⌝ or ⌜out⌝ and may be included as parameters in a message. Specifically, RIDER selects SERVICE, who selects DRIVER, and DRIVER announces its arrival to the explicitly specified RIDER.

Treating the roles as parameters explicitly specifies which roles bind the other roles, giving SERVICE the opportunity to select a different shipper if the first proves unreliable.

5 Conclusion

In this paper, we have examined various kinds of faults that are relevant to MAS, and shown that depending on the fault information protocols either directly provide or enable strategies for both *compliance-despite-faults* and *progress-despite-faults*.

An in-depth classification of faults affecting multiagent systems has been done by Potiron et al. [7]. Our work focuses only on those faults relevant to a MAS specification, and suggests strategies for dealing with them using information protocols.

Limón et al. and Ricci et al. have discussed fault tolerance and JaCaMo [6, 8], but their suggestions have been limited to reconnecting nodes. Guessom et al. discuss fault tolerance for massive MAS [4], but focus on the architecture and replication of agents. Kumar et al. discuss fault tolerance for MAS [5], but focus on architectures for handling broker failures and recovery. None of these approaches involve specification of the MAS, let al.one protocol or information protocol based specifications.

For future work, we will consider cases where the roles act maliciously, either to defraud or attack the other participants in a protocol.

Acknowledgments. Thanks to the anonymous reviewers for helpful comments. Christie and Chopra were supported by EPSRC grant EP/N027965/1.

References

1. Baldoni, M., Baroglio, C., Martelli, A., Patti, V.: A priori conformance verification for guaranteeing interoperability in open environments. In: Proceedings of the 4th International Conference on Service-Oriented Computing, pp. 339–351, December 2006

2. Chopra, A.K., Christie V, S.H., Singh, M.P.: An evaluation of communication protocol languages for engineering multiagent systems. J. Artif. Intell. Res. (to appear)

3. Ferrando, A., Winikoff, M., Cranefield, S., Dignum, F., Mascardi, V.: On enactability of agent interaction protocols: towards a unified approach. In: Dennis, L.A., Bordini, R.H., Lespérance, Y. (eds.) EMAS 2019. LNCS (LNAI), vol. 12058, pp. 43–64. Springer, Cham (2020). https://doi.org/10.1007/978-3-030-51417-4_3

4. Guessoum, Z., Briot, J.-P., Faci, N.: Towards fault-tolerant massively multiagent systems. In: Ishida, T., Gasser, L., Nakashima, H. (eds.) MMAS 2004. LNCS (LNAI), vol. 3446, pp. 55–69. Springer, Heidelberg (2005). https://doi.org/10.1007/11512073_5

5. Kumar, S., Cohen, P.R.: Towards a fault-tolerant multi-agent system architecture. In: Sierra, C., Gini, M.L., Rosenschein, J.S. (eds.) Proceedings of the Fourth International Conference on Autonomous Agents, AGENTS 2000, Barcelona, Catalonia, Spain, June 3–7, 2000, pp. 459–466. ACM (2000). https://doi.org/10.1145/336595.337570

6. Limón, X., Guerra-Hernández, A., Ricci, A.: Distributed transparency in endogenous environments: the JaCaMo case. In: El Fallah-Seghrouchni, A., Ricci, A., Son, T.C. (eds.) EMAS 2017. LNCS (LNAI), vol. 10738, pp. 109–124. Springer, Cham (2018). https://doi.org/10.1007/978-3-319-91899-0_7

7. Potiron, K., Taillibert, P., El Fallah Seghrouchni, A.: A step towards fault tolerance for multi-agent systems. In: Dastani, M., El Fallah Seghrouchni, A., Leite, J., Torroni, P. (eds.) LADS 2007. LNCS (LNAI), vol. 5118, pp. 156–172. Springer, Heidelberg (2008). https://doi.org/10.1007/978-3-540-85058-8_10

8. Ricci, A., Ciortea, A., Mayer, S., Boissier, O., Bordini, R.H., Hübner, J.F.: Engineering scalable distributed environments and organizations for MAS. In: Elkind, E., Veloso, M., Agmon, N., Taylor, M.E. (eds.) Proceedings of the 18th International Conference on Autonomous Agents and MultiAgent Systems, AAMAS 2019, Montreal, QC, Canada, May 13–17, 2019, pp. 790–798. International Foundation for Autonomous Agents and Multiagent Systems (2019). http://dl.acm.org/citation.cfm?id=3331770

9. Singh, M.P.: Information-driven interaction-oriented programming: BSPL, the blindingly simple protocol language. In: Proceedings of the 10th International Conference on Autonomous Agents and MultiAgent Systems, pp. 491–498 (2011)

10. Winikoff, M., Yadav, N., Padgham, L.: A new hierarchical agent protocol notation. Auton. Agents Multi-Agent Syst. **32**(1), 59–133 (2017)

Multi-agent Control of Industrial Robot Vacuum Cleaners

Joe Collenette[1]($\boxtimes$) and Brian Logan[2]

[1] Department of Computer Science, University of Liverpool, Liverpool, UK
j.m.collenette@liverpool.ac.uk
[2] School of Computer Science, University of Nottingham, Nottingham, UK
brian.logan@nottingham.ac.uk

Abstract. In this paper, we describe a prototype multi-agent-based system for cleaning food production facilities developed as part of the Robo-Clean project. The prototype system is based on domestic robot vacuum cleaners equipped with infrared allergen sensors and Amazon echo dot speech interfaces. T.he robots are controlled by a multi-agent system implemented in Jason, which handles (ad hoc) task allocation and robot coordination. We briefly describe the architecture of the RoboClean system, how coordination is achieved using the contract net protocol, and the implementation of the current prototype.

1 Introduction

Hygiene and the avoidance of cross contamination, e.g., by allergens, is very important in food manufacturing. Production and/or specialist cleaning staff typically spend a significant amount of time cleaning food production facilities, following industry standards such as those specified by the British Retail Consortium [3]. This has a significant, and increasing impact on employee productivity and costs. The drive by manufacturers to provide more variety and alternative formulations (e.g., gluten free foods) increases the amount of time that must be spent cleaning, and the potential for accidents. For example, data from the UK Food Standards Agency shows that the number of food safety events relating to allergens approximately doubled between 2014/15 and 2017/18 [5].

One possible way of reducing the amount of time staff spend on cleaning is to use robots to automate part of the cleaning task. Cleaning robots, e.g., vacuum cleaners, are becoming increasingly common in domestic environments and are starting to appear in industrial settings. However, such robots are typically designed to operate in isolation rather than to assist human cleaners, and provide limited support for the integration of ad hoc cleaning tasks into a cleaning schedule. In addition, operation typically involves either physical contact with the robot (to push a button) or a touchscreen (e.g., app-based interfaces) which may be undesirable for reasons of hygiene. Finally, such systems are not designed for a food production environment, where the type of material being removed may be significant, e.g., an allergen.

In this demo paper, we describe a prototype multi-agent-based system for cleaning food production facilities developed as part of the RoboClean project.

© Springer Nature Switzerland AG 2020
C. Baroglio et al. (Eds.): EMAS 2020, LNAI 12589, pp. 87–99, 2020.
https://doi.org/10.1007/978-3-030-66534-0_6

The aim of the RoboClean project to investigate the potential of human-robot and multi-robot teams equipped with speech interfaces and allergen sensing capabilities for the cleaning of food production facilities. The RoboClean prototype system is based on domestic robot vacuum cleaners equipped with infrared (IR) allergen sensors and Amazon echo dot speech interfaces. The robots are controlled by a multi-agent system implemented in Jason [1], which handles (ad hoc) task allocation and robot coordination. We briefly describe the architecture of the RoboClean system, how coordination is achieved using the contract net protocol, and the implementation of the current prototype.

The remainder of the paper is organised as follows. In Sect. 2 we present the architecture of the RoboClean system. In Sect. 3 we briefly describe the implementation of current prototype and illustrate the operation of the task allocation system with an example. We conclude in Sect. 4 with some directions for future work.

2   The RoboClean Architecture

The focus of the RoboClean project is on human-robot interaction, flexible teamwork, and allergen monitoring rather than the practical issues related to cleaning in a food production facility, which may involve cleaning large amounts of semiliquid material. For simplicity, we assume the materials to be cleaned are dry powders, e.g., flours, spice blends, tea, coffee etc., possibly containing allergens, such as gluten or peanut flour, and the prototype system is based on domestic robot vacuum cleaners (Neato Botvac D7 Connected[1]) augmented with an near-infrared allergen sensor (NIRONE S2.0) and a basic speech interface (Amazon Echo Dot). Similarly, for ease of implementation, the agents run on a standard PC and communicate with the robots via an API, rather than on embedded processors on the robot vacuum cleaners. While simple and cheap, the use of off-the-shelf domestic vacuum cleaners introduces a number of challenges as detailed below. The RoboClean architecture is shown in Fig. 1.

2.1   Food Production Facility

A food production facility is assumed to have a variable number of cleaning robots, possibly of different types. Depending on the cleaning cycle and process, different types of robots may be used at different times (in the prototype system, all robots are of the same type, but the architecture does not rely on this), and robots may have to be taken out of service for maintenance, e.g., emptying the dust container. The production facility also defines a set of 'cleaning zones' specifying areas to be cleaned, for example, the area in front of a particular machine or alongside a production line. This zone information is used both by the speech interface to identify the location to be cleaned, e.g., "clean next to the

---

[1] https://www.neatorobotics.com/gb/robot-vacuum/botvac-connected-series/botvac-d7-connected/.

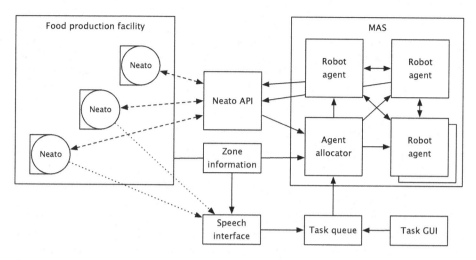

Fig. 1. The RoboClean architecture. The MAS communicates with Neato robots in the food production facility through the Neato API. Tasks are added to the Task queue via the Speech interface and the Task GUI. The Zone information represents the layout of Food production facility and is used by the Agent allocator and the Speech interface.

coffee roaster", and by the MAS during task allocation. A zone is a three-tuple and is defined as:

ID the identifier of the zone;
X, Y the coordinates of the top left hand corner of the zone; and
X1, Y1 the coordinates of the bottom right hand corner of the zone.

Zones can overlap and be nested one inside another. (The zone definition is based on that used by the Neato API.)

Regular cleaning of the facility is specified as a set of cleaning tasks.
A task is four-tuple defined as follows:

ID the identifier of the the task;
Zone the name of the zone to be cleaned;
Deadline the time by which the task should be completed; and
Priority the importance of the task is relative to other tasks (smaller numbers indicate a higher priority).

Tasks are specified using a simple GUI and added to a task queue.

The Neato Botvac D7 robots are internet connected robotic vacuum cleaners which can be controlled using mobile devices, e.g., smartphones, and other smart home devices such as Amazon Alexa and Google Home. The robots are battery powered, and recharge at a base station. Each robot is approximately 30 cm × 30 cm and weighs 3.5 kg. It has a front bumper that detects collisions and a top mounted laser used for both mapping and navigation. In the RoboClean system, each robot also has a speech interface which can be used to query and control the robot and the robot team, and an IR sensor. (In the interests of simplicity, the IR sensors are not shown; they are currently not integrated with the API and communicate indirectly with the MAS via a bluetooth connection.[2]) The speech interface can be used to give the robot (or a robot team) ad hoc cleaning tasks, which are added to the task queue.

2.2 Multi-agent System

The multi-agent system consists of an Agent allocator and a variable number of Robot agents. The *Agent allocator* has two main roles: it monitors the Neato API (described below) and, when a cleaning robot comes online, it allocates a robot agent to control the robot (creating the robot agent if necessary); it also monitors the task queue and dispatches new tasks to robot agents. Each *Robot agent* is responsible for monitoring and controlling a cleaning robot. The agent periodically polls its allocated cleaning robot to check its connection, battery and cleaning status, and issues commands as necessary to perform cleaning tasks allocated to it. Robot agents are also responsible for managing tasks dispatched to them by the agent allocator.

Robot agents allocate tasks they receive from the agent allocator using a version of the contract net protocol [9]. In the contract net protocol, each task has a manager who announces the task to other agents and requests bids, and then allocates an agent to perform the task. All agents able to perform the task (including the task manager itself) send a bid to the manager containing the agent's estimate of how long it would take it to perform the task, taking into account its current location relative to the task, charge level, dust container capacity and the tasks to which it is already committed. When all eligible agents have returned bids, the manager allocates the task to the agent that can perform the task in the least time. That agent then adds the task to its task list. The task will either be performed immediately (if the robot controlled by allocated agent is currently idle) or scheduled for future execution (e.g., after currently executing task(s) with earlier deadlines). When the task has been completed, the agent allocated the task notifies the task manager, which in turn notifies the agent allocator to update the interface. When a set of tasks is received, they are sorted so the highest priority are allocated first, then by the closest deadline, and finally by order received.

The *Task queue* is sorted first by the priority of the tasks, and secondly by their deadline. When a new task is generated, e.g., an ad hoc task requested by a member of the production staff via the Speech interface, it is added to the task queue in order. The agent allocator processes the task queue in order. For each task, it randomly selects a robot agent to act as task manager. The selected robot agent remains responsible for the task until the task is completed.

If the robot agent allocated the task is unable to complete it, e.g., because the cleaning robot it is controlling goes offline, it notifies the robot agents responsible for managing each of its allocated tasks so that the tasks can be re-advertised and

---

[2] For details of the sensor, see [8].

allocated to other robot agents. Once the task managers have been notified, the robot agent then notifies the agent alloctor that the robot that it is controlling is offline, and its status is changed to 'unallocated'.

2.3   Neato API

The Neato API forms the interface between the MAS and the cleaning robots. The Neato robots expose only a high-level webservice/IoT API, primarily intended for developing apps (e.g., for mobile devices). The API allows basic information about the robot to be queried, e.g., whether it is cleaning or charging at the base station, battery level etc., and provides some high-level commands, e.g., start/stop, clean zone X, etc. However, using the API, it is not possible to obtain sensor or position information from the robot, or execute low-level actions, e.g., moving to an arbitrary location. After cleaning a zone, the robot will return to the base station before starting to clean the next zone. These restrictions impact the coordination and control possible in the current prototype but not the overall architecture which is capable of finer coordination with more controllable robots. The architecture allows for other API's to be implemented with minimal changes.

3   RoboClean Prototype

To facilitate development and testing of the agent coordination, in the current prototype implementation of the RoboClean architecture, the Neato robots and Neato API are realised using a simulator. The simulator models the dynamics of the Neato robot vacuum cleaners, and provides the same query and control functionality as the Neato API. Similarly, the speech interface is modelled using a process that randomly generates ad hoc tasks which are added to the task queue. The architecture of the prototype is shown in Fig. 2, and each of the components is discussed in detail below.

3.1   Simulator

The environment is represented by a grid of cells, where each cell is 33 cm (i.e., the size of a robot). The layout of the environment and the number of robots to be simulated is specified in a text file. The first line of the file contains the key simulation parameters, and the remaining lines specify the contents of each cell. The simulation parameters are:

Dimensions the size of the environment in x and y (in cells);
Robot Count the number of robots; and
Simulation Speed the time between each simulation step in milliseconds.

The contents of each cell are specified using a simple textual encoding of size $x \times y$ where:

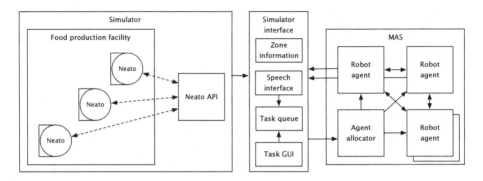

Fig. 2. The architecture of the RoboClean prototype. The Simulator simulates the food production facility and the Neato robots (including the Neato API), and communicates with MAS through the Simulator interface.

E represents an empty space;
O represents an obstacle (a space that a robot cannot occupy); and
B represents base station.

The number of base stations must be the same as the number of robots in the simulation and each robot is initially located at a base station to which it returns to recharge. In the simulator interface, robots are shown as blue circles, empty cells in light grey, obstacles in dark grey and base stations in yellow. During the simulation, the simulator randomly generates 'dirt' in empty cells, indicated by green cells. For example, the environment specified below is depicted in Fig. 3.

```
10 10 3 100
BEEEEEEEEB
EEOOEEEEEE
EOEEEEEEEE
EEEEEOEEEE
EEEEEEEEEE
EEEEEEEEEE
EEEEEEOEEE
EOEEEOEEEE
EOEEEEEEEE
EEEEEEEOEB
```

A more realistic environment, based on a food production facility is shown in Fig. 4: the dark grey curved lines represent the conveyor belts and processing stations where food is prepared.

As explained in Sect. 3.3 below, the task allocation algorithm assumes that the travel and cleaning times for a given zone are available. In the prototype, this information is computed by the simulator. When Neato robot receives a command from the Neato API to clean a zone, it uses its map of the environment to compute the shortest route to the top left corner of the zone. It then turns on

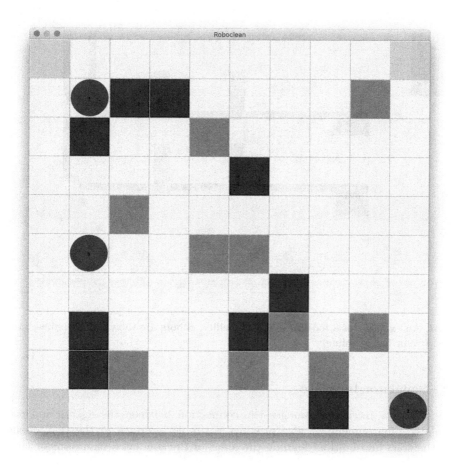

Fig. 3. An example of a simulation environment

the vacuum and begins cleaning the zone in a 'reverse S' pattern. That is, starting at the top left, it cleans the top row of cells left to right before moving down a row and cleaning the second row from the right to left and so on, continuing until the entire zone has been cleaned. The robots move more slowly when cleaning than when travelling between the base station and zone. The simulator mimics the behaviour of the physical robots, allowing relative travel and cleaning times to be calculated. The travel time is proportional to the minimum number of cells that must be traversed by the robot to reach its base station plus the number of cells from the base station to the first cell of the zone to be cleaned. The time required to clean a zone is assumed to be the size of zone times 10, as the Neato is approximately 10 times slower when the vacuum is engaged.

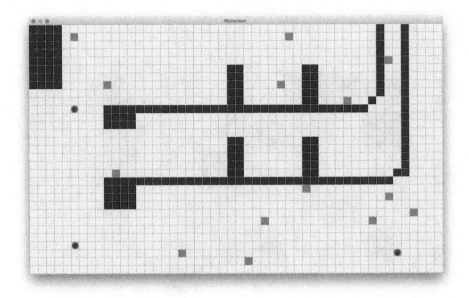

Fig. 4. An example of a food production facility; robots are shown at their base stations. (Color figure online)

3.2   Simulator Interface

The simulator interface manages the connection between the agents and the simulated environment. It also provides a simple interface to the task queue and the zone information defining the areas of the simulated environment that may be cleaned. The initial list of scheduled tasks can be updated at run time, simulating the effect of ad hoc tasks from the speech interface.

The simulator interface GUI is shown in Fig. 5. The panel on the left contains the zone definitions, and the panel on the right the current task queue. As explained above, each task is specified by a zone to be cleaned, a deadline and a priority.

3.3   Multi-agent System Implementation Prototype

The agent allocator and robot agents are implemented in Jason [1]. The contract net implementation makes use of the Jason contract net library. When an agent i receives an announcement of a task j, they compute a bid, i.e., the time it will take to complete the task, using a simple heuristic given by the the equation below:

$$Bid_i^j = \begin{cases} \infty & \text{if busy} \\ (MoveTime_i^j + CleanTime_i^j) * AllocatedTasks_i & \text{otherwise} \end{cases}$$

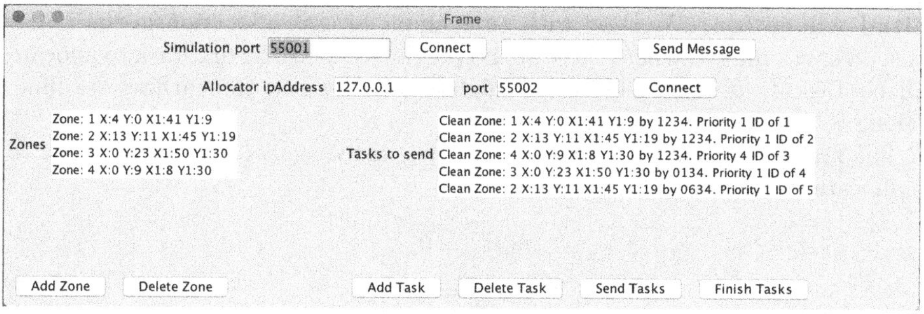

Fig. 5. The Task GUI of the Simulator interface showing the zones and tasks used in the examples.

where $MoveTime$ is the amount of time it would take to move to the zone to be cleaned and $CleanTime$ is the amount of time it would take to clean the zone. The total time required for zone j is weighted by the number of tasks already allocated to agent i; this approximates the time required to return to the base station after cleaning the zone, recharging time etc. While simplistic, this approach maximises the number of robots actively working on tasks (which users studies suggested was preferred by production staff, even if the resulting allocation is not optimal). To ensure that the agents are portable between different robots, environments, and tasks we assume that that times are available from the robot or the robot API (in the prototype, the simulator interface).

3.4   Example

As an example, we will show how the tasks are allocated when the task list is sent in two different scenarios. The first scenario is when the system is in the initial phase when no tasks have been allocated. The second scenario is when some, but not all, tasks that have been allocated have been completed. Before we can allocate the tasks we need to know what order they will be processed in. One possible ordering, where the first to be processed is at the top, is:

Task 4 Clean Zone 3, by 01:00 with a priority 1
Task 5 Clean Zone 2, by 06:00 with a priority 1
Task 1 Clean Zone 1, by 12:00 with a priority 1
Task 2 Clean Zone 2, by 12:00 with a priority 1
Task 3 Clean Zone 4, by 12:00 with a priority 4

The order in which tasks 1 and 2 are processed may be swapped, since they both have the same deadline and the same priority. The order in which they are processed depends on which task was received first by the agents. Below we assume that the tasks are received in the order given by the list.

Initial Allocation. We start with an example of task allocation in the initial start-up environment, where there are no previous tasks. The first task to allocate will be Task 4, as this task has the highest priority and the earliest deadline, making it the most important to allocate.

The first set of bids will come in from the three agents for the first task to be allocated (Task 4).

$$bid_{A1}^{T4} = 0,$$
$$bid_{A2}^{T4} = 0, \tag{1}$$
$$bid_{A3}^{T4} = 0,$$

All the bids are 0, as no task as been allocated to any of the agents. The bids being weighted against the number of previous tasks forces all the agents to place the best bid. The task can then be assigned to any of the agents, for our example we will assume that it has been assigned to Agent 1.

Task 5 is the next task to be allocated. Agent 1 will place a bid which is non zero, as this agent has been allocated a task. Agents 2 and 3 both place the best bids. For out example we will assume that Agent 2 has been allocated Task 5. Similarly for the next task, Task 1, Agent 3 will place the best bid, as this agent is the only one not allocated a task.

At this point the allocated tasks are:

Agent 1 Task 4
Agent 2 Task 5
Agent 3 Task 1

Task 2 is the next task to be allocated. The bids from the agents will now not be 0, as they all have at least one task allocated to them. For Task 2 the bids from the 3 agents will be shown in Eq. 2, which is Sect. 3.3 with variables solved for our example.

$$bid_{A1}^{T2} = (14 + 2560) * 1,$$
$$bid_{A2}^{T2} = (24 + 2560) * 1, \tag{2}$$
$$bid_{A3}^{T2} = (58 + 2560) * 1,$$

Agent 1 has produced the lowest bid as it is closest to the starting point of zone 2. Task 2 will be allocated to Agent 1. The final task to be allocated is Task 3. The bids for Task 3 will be:

$$bid_{A1}^{T3} = (7 + 2880) * 2,$$
$$bid_{A2}^{T3} = (24 + 2880) * 1, \tag{3}$$
$$bid_{A3}^{T3} = (63 + 2880) * 1,$$

While normally Agent 1 would be assigned Task 3, as it is the closest, the agent also has the most tasks allocated. The next closest is Agent 2, which has also put in the best bid for the task. The final allocation of tasks is therefore:

Agent 1 Task 4, Task 2
Agent 2 Task 5, Task 3
Agent 3 Task 1

Additional Task Allocation. The aim of the second example is to show how the agents and the contract net cope when presented with an additional list of cleaning tasks when they are currently working on a previously allocated set of tasks.

At this point in our example the agents will have sent their robot representative off to achieve one of the cleaning tasks that they have been allocated. The human operator in the food factory has noticed that there has been a spillage on the factory floor and have requested that another two tasks need to be allocated:

Task 1 Clean Zone 4, by 12:00 with a priority 1
Task 2 Clean Zone 3, by 12:00 with a priority 1

Both the tasks requested have the same deadline, they also have the same priority. Therefore the task that will be allocated first will the task that was received by the manager first. In this example we will assume that Task 1 is the task that will be allocated first.

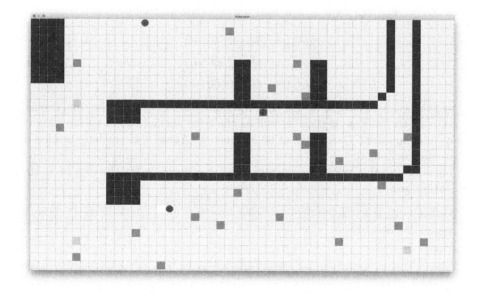

Fig. 6. The example food production facility showing the simulated agents moving around the environment working on cleaning tasks.

We will assume that the state of the environment is the same as presented in Fig. 6. The main feature to note is that no simulated robot is currently at the base station and all the agents are either working on one of their tasks or are moving back towards their base station. The agents are assumed to have the current tasks that still need to be completed:

Agent 1 Task 2
Agent 2 Task 3
Agent 3 All tasks completed

Each agent has completed a single task from the tasks that were allocated in the first example. Agents 1 and 2's robots are currently working on the next task, while Agent 3's robot heads back towards the base station.

The allocation for Task 1 is simple to calculate when the manager requests all the bids. Agent 3 will be the only agent to return the best bid of 0, since it is the only agent that has no tasks currently assigned to it. Task 1 will be assigned to Agent 3.

Agent 1 Task 2
Agent 2 Task 3
Agent 3 Task 1

Agent 3 now has a task to complete, but it is unable to send the robot to start the task until the robot has returned to the base station. The manager will move on to assigning Task 2. The bids for this task will be:

$$bid_{A1}^{T2} = (34 + 2560) * 1,$$
$$bid_{A2}^{T2} = (48 + 2560) * 1, \tag{4}$$
$$bid_{A3}^{T2} = (83 + 2560) * 1,$$

At this point it is worth noting that the simulation calculates the time needed to get back to the base station as well as the time needed to get to the zone to clean. In simulation, Task 2 would be assigned to Agent 2 as the base station is the closest to Zone 3.[3]

Therefore at this point the current tasks to complete for the agents in the simulation are:

Agent 1 Task 4, Task 2
Agent 2 Task 5
Agent 3 Task 1

All the tasks have been allocated. Given the speed at which the tasks can be allocated, we can assume that the state of the world has not changed between the start of allocation and the end of allocation. When the robot Agent 3 represents returns to the base station, the agent will be able to send the newly assigned task to its robot.

---

[3] When the prototype is implemented on real Neato robots, it will only be able calculate the move time based on the time it would take to move from the base station, as the Neato does not reveal its location through the API.

4   Discussion

We have presented a prototype allergen aware factory cleaning system, which is part of a larger RoboClean project that aims to facilitate effective and efficient cleaning through multi-agent and human-robot interactions. Our prototype system allows a queue of cleaning tasks to be distributed among a number of robots using the contract net protocol [9]. The contract net protocol was chosen due to its simplicity and the relatively small amount of information and communication required. There are a number of other task assignment protocols that extend contract nets, such as Alliance [7] and M+ [2], and scheduling approaches that focus on either minimising the number of late jobs [4] or taking, e.g., the battery life of the robot into consideration [6]. However, given the limited information available via the Neato API, we believe the contract net is a reasonable approach.

In future work, we plan to interface the MAS to the Neato API and hence to control the physical robots. This will provide a platform for user studies investigating human-robot interaction to be explored, e.g., in which situations does a human view themselves as interacting with a single robot and in which situations do they see themselves interacting with the team of robots through the robot being addressed. Another area of future work would be investigate alternative robot platforms which allow finer-grained control. This would allow a better allocation of tasks, e.g., in terms of minimising cleaning time, or ensure all tasks are completed before the deadline.

References

1. Bordini, R.H., Hübner, J.F., Wooldridge, M.: Programming Multi-agent Systems in AgentSpeak Using Jason, vol. 8. Wiley, New York (2007)
2. Botelho, S.C., Alami, R.: M+: a scheme for multi-robot cooperation through negotiated task allocation and achievement. In: Proceedings 1999 IEEE International Conference on Robotics and Automation (Cat. No. 99CH36288C), vol. 2, pp. 1234–1239. IEEE (1999)
3. British Research Consortium: Global standard food safety - issue 7 (2015)
4. Brucker, P.: Scheduling Algorithms. Springer, Heidelberg (2007). https://doi.org/10.1007/978-3-540-69516-5
5. Food Standards Agency: Annual report of food incidents 2016/17 (2018)
6. Luo, L., Chakraborty, N., Sycara, K.: Distributed algorithms for multirobot task assignment with task deadline constraints. IEEE Trans. Autom. Sci. Engi. 12(3), 876–888 (2015)
7. Parker, L.E.: Alliance: an architecture for fault tolerant multirobot cooperation. IEEE Trans. Robot. Autom. 14(2), 220–240 (1998)
8. Rady, A., Fischer, J., Reeves, S., Logan, B., Watson, N.J.: The effect of light intensity, sensor height, and spectral pre-processing methods when using NIR spectroscopy to identify different allergen-containing powdered foods. Sensors 20(1), 230 (2020)
9. Smith, R.G.: The contract net protocol: high-level communication and control in a distributed problem solver. IEEE Trans. Comput. 12, 1104–1113 (1980)

Orthos: A Trustworthy AI Framework for Data Acquisition

Moin Hussain Moti[1]([✉]) [iD], Dimitris Chatzopoulos[2] [iD], Pan Hui[2,3] [iD],
Boi Faltings[4] [iD], and Sujit Gujar[1] [iD]

[1] International Institute of Information Technology Hyderabad, Hyderabad, India
moin.moti@research.iiit.ac.in
[2] The Hong Kong University of Science and Technology, Hong Kong, China
[3] University of Helsinki, Helsinki, Finland
[4] Ecole Polytechnique Federale de Lausanne, 1015 Lausanne, Switzerland

Abstract. Information acquisition through crowdsensing with mobile agents is a popular way to collect data, especially in the context of smart cities where the deployment of dedicated data collectors is expensive and ineffective. It requires efficient information elicitation mechanisms to guarantee that the collected data are accurately acquired and reported. Such mechanisms can be implemented via smart contracts on blockchain to enable privacy and trust. In this work we develop *Orthos*, a *blockchain-based* trustworthy framework for spontaneous location-based crowdsensing queries without assuming any prior knowledge about them. We employ game-theoretic mechanisms to incentivize agents to report truthfully and ensure that the information is collected at the desired location while ensuring the privacy of the agents. We identify six necessary characteristics for information elicitation mechanisms to be applicable in spontaneous location-based settings and implement an existing state-of-the-art mechanism using *smart contracts*. Additionally, as location information is exogenous to these mechanisms, we design the *Proof-of-Location* protocol to ensure that agents gather the data at the desired locations. We examine the performance of *Orthos* on Rinkeby Ethereum testnet and conduct experiments with live audience.

Keywords: Trustworthy AI · Spatiotemporal data acquisition · Decentralised applications · Smart contracts

1 Introduction

Spatio-temporal data for modern applications and services can be acquired either by centralized entities (e.g., online reviews about a restaurant) or mobile agents (e.g., current queue length in a coffee shop). In the second case, information needs to be collected and reported in a trustworthy manner. The need for accurate location-based reports from mobile agents is, among others, highly motivated

---

In Greek, Orthos means correct and accurate.

© Springer Nature Switzerland AG 2020
C. Baroglio et al. (Eds.): EMAS 2020, LNAI 12589, pp. 100–118, 2020.
https://doi.org/10.1007/978-3-030-66534-0_7

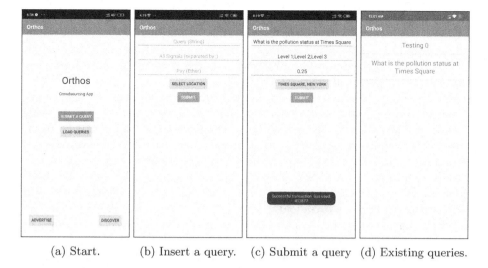

(a) Start.   (b) Insert a query.   (c) Submit a query   (d) Existing queries.

Fig. 1. Main activities of Orthos. The Orthos mobile application is connected to a set of Ethereum smart contracts.

by advances in smart cities, and more generally, smart infrastructure. Representative examples can be found on health monitoring systems (e.g., pollution levels in specific areas), smart farming, and others. For example, every year crop insurance firms receive numerous claims that need to be verified. The current solution is to send dedicated agents for on-field inspection. Trustworthy crowd-sensing frameworks can reduce the inspection cost by employing mobile agents in the vicinity of the crop plot to verify the claims.

Mobile agents have limited time to respond to queries in *spontaneous localized settings*/citefarm, therefore, it is probable for them to not have readily available prior knowledge. Also, depending on their location, agents may not be found in the vicinity. The potential unavailability of agents in locations of interest and the lack of prior knowledge motivates the need for trustworthy frameworks that can ensure the quality of the crowdsensed information. Mobile agents are expected to utilize their devices with multiple sensors to support services to *(i)* deploy resources, *(ii)* produce unbiased measurements, *(iii)* augment sparse data collected via static sensors, and *(iv)* supplement missing data caused by malfunctioning static sensors. There are three main challenges in acquiring information in spontaneous localized settings via mobile agents: *(i)* to ensure that they are truthful, *(ii)* to validate their presence in the examined settings, and *(iii)* to preserve their privacy while maintaining the transparency of the process.

To ensure agents' truthful participation, information elicitation mechanisms must guarantee non-negative utilities to agents and provide incentives to motivate them to submit accurate reports. Rational agents are expected to maximize their utility while not sacrificing a substantial amount of their resources. The existing literature consists of many mechanisms that induce agents to submit truthful reports [10,13,16,17,25–27]. We examine state-of-the-art information elicitation mechanisms and present the necessary conditions for them to be applicable in spontaneous localized settings. After comparing these mechanisms, we argue that the most applicable mechanism to the settings is the robust peer truth serum for crowdsourcing (RPTSC) [26].

Unfortunately, all these mechanisms take for granted that the agents are present at the requested area or assume that there exist parties (e.g., cellular network providers) that can assure the mechanism about the existence of an agent in the required location [7]. In the case where such location verification mechanisms does not exist, agents can abuse the system by faking their location. We design the *Proof-of-Location* (PoL) protocol, that does not require any fixed infrastructure to function, to force every mobile agent to provide a proof that their location is within a threshold.

Recent advances in blockchain-based architectures advance the design of decentralized incentive mechanisms. Such architectures are maintained by a network of peers, and motivate agents to participate in crowdsensing applications since their reports will not be controlled by centralized entities. Architectures like Ethereum, support the development of applications that are executed atop blockchain [5] based on *smart contracts*. We use Ethereum smart contracts to develop *Orthos*, a trustworthy framework for data acquisition in spontaneous localized settings. Orthos, via a set of smart contracts, *(i)* processes the submitted reports, *(ii)* estimates the ground truth using weighted averaging techniques and *(iii)* calculates the payments of the agents. Additionally, Orthos, via developed cryptographic techniques, hides agents' responses to guarantee that agents will not deviate from their honest behavior. Figure 1 depicts some activities of the implementation of Orthos on Android. Anyone can submit queries or load queries that request for spatio-temporal information at their location. Every query is defined by *(i)* a String (e.g., How is the availability in restaurant XYZ?), *(ii)* a set of possible answers, *(iii)* the GPS coordinates close to which the responded agents should be when answering the query, and *(iv)* the amount, in gas, the requester is willing to pay. The screenshots of the activities that allow agents to submit their answers to queries are presented after the description of Orthos in Sect. 5. The contributions of this work are multi-fold and are listed below:

1) We define six necessary characteristics required by any information elicitation mechanism to be used in spontaneous localized settings and investigate existing mechanisms regarding their applicability to these settings.
2) We develop *Orthos* for the development of incentive mechanisms for applications and services that elicit information. It acts as a wrapper for information elicitation mechanisms and facilitates the collection of agents' reports and the distribution of rewards in a decentralized and privacy-preserving fashion.
3) We design *Proof-of-Location (PoL)* protocol to detect and prevent malicious agents from faking their location. PoL is executed in the mobile devices of the agents to robustly verify that each interested agent can participate if she is located in the correct location.

4) We examine the applicability of Orthos by testing it with 27 participants.

In summary, Orthos works in the trinity of game theory for incentives, mobile computing for location validity, and blockchain technology.

2   Background

Orthos is a framework for information elicitation mechanisms that can be used efficiently in location-based applications and services such as mobile crowdsensing. Orthos leverages blockchain to provide transparency as well as privacy in a decentralized environment. In this section, we briefly explain what is mobile crowdsensing, blockchain and smart contract.

Mobile Crowdsensing. Mobile crowdsensing is a paradigm that utilizes the ubiquitousness of mobile users who are carrying smartphones and can collect and process data. Similar to Orthos, the authors of [22] develop Medusa, a framework to develop crowdsensing applications. However, the authors employ cloud resources instead of a blockchain and do not guarantee agents' privacy. The authors of [14], motivated by the fact that if the available mobile agents are fewer than the required ones, incentive mechanisms will lose efficacy, propose HySense. HySense combines mobile devices with static sensor nodes. Furthermore, the authors of [31] propose effSense, an energy-efficient and cost-effective framework to reduce the participation cost of mobile agents.

Blockchains. Blockchains is a distributed mechanism for storing data in the form of transactions. Bitcoin[1], Ethereum[2] and Ripple[3] are few notable public-distributed ledgers based on the blockchain architecture. These ledgers are maintained by their global peer-to-peer network of nodes. All transactions are stacked in a block and then the block is appended to the public-ledger. Each block contains a cryptographic hash of the previous block, a timestamp and transaction data. The data is hashed and encoded into a *Merkel Tree*. The cryptographic hash that forms the link to the previous block iteratively goes all the way back to the genesis block, this ensures the integrity of the whole blockchain. The data once recorded on a blockchain ledger is effectively immutable as any moderation would require alteration of all subsequent blocks which requires consensus of majority of the network nodes. Because of the decentralized nature of the blockchain, data is replicated across all nodes of the network. This protects the network from any threats to a particular node. However, publishing a block is a challenging process and requires a lot of resources, its termed as *mining* in blockchain nomenclature. A miner must validate all the transactions stacked in the block and solve a crytographic puzzle through bruteforce computations in

---

[1] https://bitcoin.org/.
[2] https://ethereum.org/.
[3] https://ripple.com.

order to mine a block, the solution obtained on solving the puzzle is termed as *proof-of-work*. The time taken to mine a block is variable and depends mainly on the difficulty level of the puzzle. The *block time* is the average time it takes for the network to generate one block in the blockchain. The block time for bitcoin is around 10 mins while the block time on Ethereum is around 15 seconds.

Smart Contracts. Nick Szabo [28] first coined the term and proposed the idea of a smart contract, "a set of promises, specified in digital form, including protocols within which the parties perform on the other promises". The idea was later adopted by blockchains to offer additional functionalities on the stored data. Each smart contract takes information as an input and processes that information using the set of rules defined in the contract. It can also trigger other smart contracts and access information stored on remote servers. Every smart contract is executed in a virtualized environment maintained by every peer in the blockchain. Whenever a smart contract is called, via a transaction, it is executed when the nodes that maintain the blockchain process the corresponding transaction. Every node has to execute the code of the contract and depending on its complexity and the capabilities of the peers, it may take a lot of time and resources. This contract execution paradigm motivates proposals for off-chain code execution. Blockchain-based mechanisms can execute parts of their modules on remote servers, also known as *oracles*, to improve their performance and increase the privacy of the agents [11]. Given that everything stored in the blockchain, including the code of smart contracts and the data stored on them, is visible to everyone, private information should be stored on oracles to motivate agents' participation. By building on top of a blockchain, smart contracts provide a trusted framework for many potential applications. For example, Bogner *et. al.* [3] present a decentralized application for sharing resources like Uber and Airbnb without the involvement of any trusted third party. Internet of Things (IoT) devices form a crucial part of any smart city project, however, privacy and security remain an issue. The authors of [36] and [38] propose smart contract based solutions for safe and secure access control of IoT devices. Unlike other online software applications, the code of a smart contract cannot be altered once deployed on the network. In [1], the authors have compared five different tools for detecting vulnerabilities in the smart contract, namely *Oyente* [19], *Securify* [30], *Remix* [12], *Smartcheck* [29] and *Mythril* [9], one can use these tools to safeguard the smart contracts against potential threats. Ethereum is one of the most popular smart contracts platform and Solidity[4] the most recommended language to develop smart contracts. Smart contracts are written in high-level-language code is then compiled to bytecodes. This bytecode is published to the Etheruem blockchain where it is executed on Ethereum Virtual Machine (EVM). The EVM consumes resources in the form of *gas* units to execute commands in the smart contract.

---

[4] https://docs.soliditylang.org/en/v0.7.5/.

3   Spontaneous Localized Settings

Considering an entity in question EiQ, a set of nearby mobile agents $\mathcal{U}$, and a budget B, we want to estimate a function f (e.g., EiQ can be the Eiffel Tower, f the current queue length in the tickets counter and B can be 1\$). $\mathcal{A}$ ($\mathcal{A} \subseteq \mathcal{U}$) agents choose to participate and assess EiQ. Every agent $i \in \mathcal{A}$ observes a signal $s_i \in S$ and reports a signal $r_i \in S$ which can be different from s_i. After submitting r_i, agent i collects a reward u_i ($\sum_{i \in \mathcal{A}} u_i \leq B$). If the equality holds and the budget is fully utilized, the mechanism is called *Strong Budget Balanced*. Orthos ensures this property while distributing rewards. The spontaneity of the requests and zero prior knowledge about the EiQ adds to the sophistication of the spontaneous localized settings. It, therefore, requires very specific mechanisms that can be used in such scenarios. Below, we list six essential characteristics a mechanism needs and discuss the applicability of seventeen mechanisms concerning these characteristics.

3.1   Essential Characteristics for Spontaneous Localized Settings

Before introducing existing information elicitation mechanisms and presenting Orthos' function in detail, we introduce the characteristics, these mechanisms should have to be applicable in spontaneous localized settings.

[C1] Bayesian Incentive Compatibility: A social choice function f : $\Theta_i \times ... \times \Theta_n \rightarrow X$ is said to be Bayesian incentive compatible (or truthfully implementable in Bayesian Nash equilibrium) if the direct revelation mechanism $\mathcal{D} = ((\Theta_i)_{i \in N}, f(.))$ has a *Bayesian Nash equilibrium* $s^*(.) = (s_i^*(), ..., s_n^*(.))$ in which $s_i^*(\theta_i) = \theta_i, \forall \theta_i \in \Theta_i, \forall i \in N$. As ground truth is not readily available in many scenarios, the verification of an agent's report depends on the reports of other agents. Therefore, the mechanism must induce *Bayesian Nash Equilibrium* where truthful reporting is the best response when agents are also truthful.

[C2] No Common Knowledge: Spontaneous localized settings refer to entities the information to which is difficult to access online. As a result, common knowledge parameters like *prior belief models* and *posterior expectations* used by most mechanisms are rendered futile for spontaneous localized settings.

[C3] Minimalistic Mechanism: A mechanism is *minimalistic* if the agents need to submit only the *information report* i.e. observed private signal for the EiQ. In addition to *information report*, many mechanisms require agents to submit a *prediction report*, that reflects the agents' belief about the distribution of information reports in the population. In the spontaneous localized settings, agents have limited time to respond to the request, therefore, we require a *minimalistic* mechanism where agents only have to submit the information report.

[C4] **Interim Individual Rationality (IIR):** Aggregated information from a few agents is less reliable and more prone to human error. Hence, to increase participation and guarantee information robustness, the mechanism must offer non-negative rewards to participating agents. If a mechanism ensures positive expected utility to the agents, it is said to satisfy IIR.

[C5] **Prevent Free-riders:** Free-riders can benefit from an IIR mechanism by submitting random responses and hence, the mechanism should not admit *uninformed equilibria* where free-riders benefit by abusing the mechanism.

[C6] **Collusion Resistant:** Agents must be located nearby the EiQ in spontaneous localized settings. Agents operating in close proximity expose the system to collusion. Therefore, the mechanism should be able to prevent such collusions.

Any mechanism that has the above set of attributes can be used in Orthos. We now investigate existing mechanisms in the literature to examine their applicability in spontaneous localized settings.

3.2   Information Elicitation Mechanisms

Many information elicitation mechanisms have been proposed but most of them are not applicable in spontaneous localized settings. Miller *et al.* [20], rely on the *common knowledge assumption* where every agent shares the same prior belief about an event, however, it is not possible to provide a prior belief model for all queries. Prelec *et al.* [21], on the other hand, proposes Bayesian Truth Serum (BTS), which does not require knowledge of any common prior information but is applicable only for a large number of agents. Since queries in spontaneous localized settings are strict location specific, not many agents are expected to participate all the time. Also, it suffers from free-riding and does not resist collusion. Witkowski *et al.* [34] propose Robust Bayesian Truth Serum (RBTS), which simplifies BTS but is only applicable for binary signals space and still suffers from free-riding and collusion. Radanovic *et al.* [23,24] improve RBTS by making it compatible with non-binary and continuous outcomes respectively but both of these mechanisms do not address free-riding and collusion. Similarly to BTS, Zhang *et al.* [37] and Lambert *et al.* [18] do not require common prior information but suffer from free-riding and collusion among agents. Furthermore, in the mechanism proposed in [18], the agents are indifferent between being honest and misreporting in the equilibrium.

Witkowski *et al.* [32,33] propose mechanisms that assume neither any common prior information nor a large number of agents and are robust to private beliefs of agents. However, they suffer from *temporal separation*. This requires the agent to submit one report before and one after executing the crowdsourced task. Temporal separation is not practical in many situations and slows down the crowdsensing process. Also, both the mechanisms lack provisions for resisting collusion among agents and free-riding. Riley *et al.* [27] propose a minimalistic mechanism under the assumption that all the agents with the same outcome have the same posterior expectations. Jurca *et al.* [16,17] propose mechanisms that are more suitable for interactive reputation markets where agents interact and rate each other. Both mechanisms are susceptible to collusion. Moreover, the former is not independent of agents' private beliefs and the latter assumes a prior belief distribution. Faltings *et al.* [13] introduce Peer Truth Serum (PTS), a minimalistic mechanism that assumes a prior belief model. The mechanism also admits uninformed equilibria where agents do not perform measurements. Such equilibria can result in free-riding agents that lower the quality of the collected information. Orthos requires a mechanism that does not depend on any of the aforementioned assumptions as the requests can arrive almost spontaneously and the mechanism must be robust to incorporate the report of as many nearby agents willing to participate as possible.

Considering the introduced essential characteristics we review four applicable mechanisms: **M1** by [10] is a strong incentive compatible mechanism that can only be applied to binary settings. It is worth mentioning however that binary outcomes limit the usability of Orthos in many scenarios and compromise with the quality of aggregated information.

	C1	C2	C3	C4	C5	C6
M1	✓	✓	–	✓	✓	–
M2 (LPTS)	✓	–	✓	✓	✓	✓
M3 (PTSC)	✓	✓	✓	✓	✓	✓
M4 (RPTSC)	✓	✓	✓	✓	✓	✓

Table 1. Comparison matrix of the examined mechanisms.

M2 by [25] improves PTS by introducing Logarithmic PTS and eliminating the dependency on a prior belief model. M2 produces worse payoff than truthful reporting for uninformed equilibria and against misbehaving agents acting on collusion strategies.

M3 & M4 by [26] are optimized versions of PTS. M3, Peer Truth Serum for Crowdsourcing (PTSC) is more robust than PTS in cases where the number of participating agents is small. M4, Robust PTSC (RPTSC) is a furthermore robust version of PTSC which excludes the possibilities of ill-defined results from PTSC. PTSC and RPTSC enable the agents to participate in multiple tasks, however, for our purpose, we will restrict to single tasks scenarios.

It is clear from the comparison matrix (Table 1) that M3 and M4 satisfy all the requirements for spontaneous localized settings, however, since M4 (i.e. RPTSC) is a more robust version of M3, we select it for our Orthos protocol.

3.3 Robust Peer Truth Serum for Crowdsourcing

Robust Peer Truth Serum for Crowdsourcing (RPTSC), proposed in [26] is a minimalistic payment mechanism that incentivizes the honest behavior of agents. It is a Bayesian incentive compatible mechanism and is independent of agents' private prior beliefs. Agents only announce their observation in their reports to participate in the process. For every report, RPTSC generates a non-negative score. Any uninformed equilibrium, where agents do not perform measurements, including random reporting or collusion on one value and collusion strategies that are based on agents' measurements, result in worse payoff than truthful reporting. Thus, agents are incentivized to submit honest reports. An agent i submits a report $r_i \in S$ to the system. Randomly select a peer agent p and let her report be r_p. RPTSC calculates the fractional frequency of agent i's report, R_i, as follows:

$$R_i(r_i, p) = \frac{num_{-i}(r_i)}{\sum_{s \in S} num_{-\{i,p\}}(s)} \tag{1}$$

where num is the function that counts occurrences of reported values among all the reports. The summation in the denominator reduces to total number of reports submitted. Given a constant $\alpha > 0$, the reward of agent i is

$$\tau(r_i, r_p) = \left(\frac{\alpha}{R_i(r_i, p)} \right) \text{ if } r_i = r_p \text{ and } R_i(r_i, p) \neq 0 \text{ and } 0 \text{ otherwise.} \tag{2}$$

4   Implementing Decentralized Data Acquisition Mechanisms

Information elicitation mechanisms can be integrated into decentralized applications (DApps) in the form of smart contracts. Ethereum smart contracts are compiled into bytecode and executed on EVM. For each computation, the EVM consumes some fuel, named *gas*. Gas is the unit of measurement for the resources consumed in Ethereum. The monetary expenditure depends on the consumed gas units and the gas price at that moment. The gas price is the valuation of gas units in terms of ether and it changes according to market dynamics.

Reading information from a contract is gas-free and nearly instant, however, writing into a smart contract requires gas proportional to the storage needs. Similarly, computations on a smart contract require gas proportional to the computational complexity. Transactions on Ethereum are executed in batches and stored in *blocks*. Each block has a *gas limit* that forces the sum of all the gas needs of the transactions stored on each block to not exceed this limit. Hence, it is not possible to accomplish complex tasks on smart contracts via a single transaction. Also, since storage on the blockchain is expensive, its impractical to maintain long logs of persistent data for a complex task to be carried out in disjoint transactions. It is also worth mentioning that Ethereum does not support floating-point numbers (i.e., all divisions are integer divisions) making computations that require floating-point numbers to be handled on a case by case basis that usually imposes additional computation overhead.

The two primary tasks of any data acquisition mechanism are collecting and storing reports from all agents and performing computations on those reports to determine rewards for the agents. Both of these tasks are anti-complimentary to the smart contract. In the previous sections, we discussed various information elicitation mechanisms and presented four that apply to spontaneous localized settings. However, among them, only M3 (PTSC) and M4 (RPTSC) are computationally feasible to implement on the smart contract. M1 is a very complex mechanism with dependency on multiple tasks while M2 uses a logarithm scoring rule which is difficult to implement on the smart contract because of no support for floating-point numbers. PTSC and RPTSC are very similar mechanisms but between them, RPTSC is a more robust mechanism as it excludes the possibility of ill-defined results from PTSC. Hence, we recommend using RPTSC for data acquisition on decentralized mechanisms. According to our measurements, the gas needs of RPTSC is 2495101, which corresponds to less than half USD.

5   Orthos

Orthos is a blockchain-based data acquisition mechanism applicable in spontaneous localized settings. RPTSC and any other mechanism that meets the essential criteria presented in Table 1 can be applied for crowdsensing in spontaneous localized settings securely and anonymously using Orthos. The architecture of Orthos is split into two parts: a mobile application and a DApp. We have designed a protocol, called *Orthos protocol*, to dictate the interaction between the two components during the data acquisition process. Figures 1 and 3 show a total of six screenshots of the developed mobile application that allows mobile agents to submit a query, load existing queries in their location and answer existing queries by submitting a report.

The Orthos protocol is composed of four phases: *commitment phase, reveal phase, scoring phase,* and *reward distribution phase.* In the commitment phase, each agent i assesses EiQ, observes signal s_i and commits to a report r_i. Figure 3a shows the screen of the mobile application after the submission of the commitment. No more agents are accepted once this phase ends. Only the final commitment of the agent is taken into consideration and is revealed in the reveal phase where the report is processed, as depicted in Fig. 3b. Participating mobile agents need to transact with the blockchain part of Orthos to submit their commitments and reveal their reports by calling the submit() and reveal() smart contract functions respectively.

In the scoring phase, each agent i is rewarded based on her report r_i and the payment mechanism. Information elicitation mechanisms for spatio-temporal queries are unable to detect if an agent commits a signal after assessing EiQ at the required location. Agents can attempt to manipulate their location by faking their GPS reading if it is beneficial. Orthos bypasses this limitation using *Proof-of-Location (PoL)*, a distributed protocol that is executed by the agents. PoLs have been used in the design of location-based cryptocurrencies, where agents are required to be either at a specific location to be rewarded [35] or the agents' interconnectivity affects their rewards [8].

5.1   Location Proofs in Spontaneous Localized Settings

Agents need to include a PoL whenever they submit an answer to a query for an EiQ. Using their mobile devices, an agent i that wants to produce a proof of her location broadcasts her *context* to all nearby mobile devices. Orthos is based on Google's Nearby Connections API to connect with mobile phones in

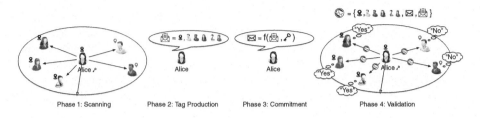

Fig. 2. The four phases an agent follows to produce a proof of her location.

Bluetooth and Wi-Fi range. After collecting the broadcasted context, nearby peers respond with their respective contexts. Similar to agent i, all nearby peers exchange their contexts to form their own list of contexts. Then agent i shares this list of contexts with his nearby peers who compare agent i's list of context with their own list of contexts to assess the validity of agent i's location. If valid, each peer responds with a digital signature certifying the validity of agent i's location. Agent i must have enough peer validations to cross the security threshold set by Orthos smart contract. In detail, agent i proves her location is as measured by her GPS or any localization method [4,6], by following the four phases of the following cryptographic protocol:

Scanning Phase: Scan for neighbours and produce $L_i = \{l_i, \mathcal{P}_i\}$, a message composed of the agent's estimated location, l_i, and her neighbors, $\mathcal{P}_i$.

Tag Production Phase: Use L_i to produce a tag $L_i^T = f(L_i(t))$ of fixed size via a pseudo-random function [15] known to every agent.

Commitment Phase: Use the secret key k_i of agent i to produce a commitment for every neighbor M_i:

$$Commt\left(L_i, L_i^T\right) \to M_i. \tag{3}$$

Verification Phase: Every neighbour receives M_i and examines whether user i is at l_i:

$$Verify\left(L_i, L_i^T, M_i\right) \to L_{ji}^V \in \{\text{yes}, \text{no}\}. \tag{4}$$

L_{ji}^V equals to "yes" if user j verifies that user i is her neighbour and "no" otherwise. User j returns "yes" if her estimated location has a difference of less than a threshold from the location of agent i.

Every user, after receiving M_i uses the public key of i to extract her location, neighbours and L_i^T. User i, by sending M_i instead of L_i makes sure that her neighbors can only answer to her claim. Misbehaving agents cannot change the location agent i claims to be in. Practically, a malicious agent can only try to produce a PoL for a location she is not currently in. By doing that, she will not be able to verify her fake location by normal agents. Via this process, user i constructs a PoL that a set of her neighbors are within a given distance:

$$\pi_i(EiQ)\left(M_i, \bigcup_{j \in \mathcal{P}_i} L_{ji}^V, \frac{1}{|\mathcal{P}_i|} \sum_{j=1}^{|\mathcal{P}_i|} 1_{\{L_{ji}^V == \text{"yes"}\}}\right) \tag{5}$$

PoL is defined as the set of messages from the neighbouring devices of a user that the user is at a specific location. Each message is signed by the neighbouring users. Figure 2 depicts the four phases of the Proof-of-Location protocol. The Orthos smart contract contains a method named `verifyLocation()` that is responsible for verifying the submitted PoLs from the mobile agents.

5.2   Orthos Protocol

A requester can add her query on the network using the `addQuery()` method by specifying the exact query (Q), query location (L), signal space (all possible signals, S), and budget (B). The requester does not need to provide personal information on the network. Once the query is added to the contract, all agents can access it. Next, we present the protocol through which agents can submit and receive a reward for their contributions. For ease of understanding, we consider an arbitrary agent i to walk through the various phases of the protocol.

Commitment Phase: Agents can access all queries of the smart contract and chose to participate in the queries related to a nearby location. Agents can submit their reports using the `submit()` method of the smart contract. Since Ethereum is a public blockchain, in order to conceal an agent's report, we require them to submit the hash of their report. For an agent i, `submit()` takes a cipher c_i, which is the commitment $(c_i = keccak256(r_i, k_i)^5$, where r_i is the reported signal and k_i is the secret key of the agent) of the reported signal, list of peers (identified by their Ethereum addresses) and a list of digital signatures by the peers validating the agent i's location. Every agent is allowed to update her report as long as the phase continues but only the latest report will be considered.

Reveal Phase: Agent i, reveals her commitment by submitting r_i and k_i using the `reveal()` method. The agent report is accepted only if her commitment matches with the reported value i.e. $c_i = keccak256(r_i, k_i)$ and if the submitted proof of location is accepted by the `verifyLocation()` method that implements the verification phase of the PoL protocol.

Scoring Phase: Once the reveal phase is over, agent i calculates the score of her contribution by calling `calcScore()`. Agent i is scored using the requester specified mechanism. For RPTSC, R_i is calculated using Eq. 1 and the final score is based on R_i, as described by Eq. 2. The score of agent i is stored on the smart contract before being normalized when all agents have been scored. Agent i gets his reward in the next phase.

Reward Distribution Phase: Once the scoring is finished, agent i adds the corresponding reward to her balance by calling `updateBalance()`. To ensure budget balancing, Orthos normalizes the scores irrespective of the payment

---

[5] Keccak is a versatile cryptographic function. Best known as a hash function, it nevertheless can also be used for authentication, encryption and pseudo-random number generation. For more information, please refer to https://keccak.team/keccak.html.

scheme and calculates the reward for each agent i by:

$$u_i = \frac{score_i}{\sum_{j \in \mathcal{A}} score_j} \times B, \tag{6}$$

where B is the total budget for the request. Agents can call `getBalance()` to get their balance and `withdraw()` to transfer it to their Ethereum accounts.

6   Performance Evaluation

We implement Orthos as a decentralized application (DApp) that is composed of Ethereum smart contracts that are deployed on Rinkeby Testnet Network[6] and an Android mobile application that is presented in Figs. 1 and 3. We measure the gas needs and the cost in USD of each implemented method of Orthos. Additionally, we recruited 27 students (18 male and 9 female) with an average age of 22 years and asked them to install Orthos and participate as mobile agents. We generated a query to ask them about the difficulty of the subject and provided four signals. We used the acquired data to measure gas costs for executing Orthos. Each query completes in about 10 mins.

Implementation. Agents are identified via their Ethereum address. For every new account, Ethereum generates a random pair of a public key and the correspondent private key. The keys are completely unrelated to the real-world identity of the agent, hence, granting an anonymous medium of participation to the agent. The Ethereum address is the last 20 bytes of the hash of the public key. Agents are encouraged to create a new Ethereum address for every new query to avoid any privacy leaks. The mobile part of Orthos is built to target mobile devices with Android SDK version 28 and supports devices with minimum SDK version 23. To connect a mobile device with the Ethereum blockchain, the device must host an Ethereum node. However, the hosting of an Ethereum node on a mobile device is energy demanding and demotivating for mobile agents. As a solution to this problem, we use the Infura API[7]. Infura is a hosted Ethereum node cluster that supports

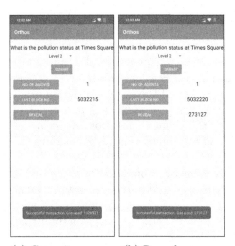

(a) Commit answer.   (b) Reveal answer.

Fig. 3. After submitting an answer, by triggering the `submit()` method, the developed application waits until the deadline to reveal the submitted answer, by calling the `reveal()` method. After that, Orthos calculates the score of each report and distributes the rewards.

---

[6] https://rinkeby.etherscan.io/.

[7] https://infura.io/docs.

JSON-RPC over HTTPS and WebSocket interfaces and allows mobile agents to perform requests and set up subscription-based connections to Ethereum blockchains. Once the connection to the Ethereum blockchain is established, we integrate wrapper functions to the mobile part of Orthos to automate the call of smart contract methods on the blockchains. We use *Web3j*[8] to generate equivalent wrapper functions of the smart contract for Java/Kotlin which we then use for the development of the mobile part.

Table 2. Gas consumption for deploying Orthos, and transact with it on Rinkeby Ethereum testnet. For converting gas to USD we used the default gas price (1 GWei) and the price of Ethereum on 13-Nov-2019. (i.e., USD = gas$\cdot 188 \cdot 10^{-9}$).

Name	Gas used	USD cost
`ContractCreation()`	2495101	0.47
`addQuery()`	442183	0.08
`submit()`	1013457	0.19
`reveal()`	74138	0.01
`verifyLocation()`	183733	0.03
`calcScore()`	6431116	1.20

Table 3. Helping methods. `getScore()` and `getBalance()` are gas-free while the gas needs of `withdraw()` and `updateBalance()` are negligible.

Name	Description
`getScore()`	Returns the score for a particular query
`getBalance()`	Returns the total balance of an agent in the protocol
`withdraw()`	Withdraws the total balance from the protocol
`updateBalance()`	Updates agents' balance after the query

Experiments. Orthos enables mobile agents to both add queries and respond to existing ones. Table 2 lists the methods that require gas to be executed while Table 3 lists additional helping methods for secondary functionalities such as payments between the query requester and the responding mobile agents. Table 2 shows that the required gas for deploying a smart contract that implements RPTSC (`ContractCreation`) is 2495101, which corresponds to less than half USD. Adding a new query for spatio-temporal data using `addQuery()` requires only 8 cents. Every participating mobile agent spends 19 USD cents for the call

---

[8] https://www.web3labs.com/web3j.

of `submit()` on the first phase of Orthos protocol, 6 USD cents during the second phase for the calls of `reveal()` and `verifyLocation()`, and 1.2 USD for the calculation of her score via the `calcScore()` on the third phase. The collection of the reward is gas-free. Note that for the cost calculation we considered the default gas price that leads to the completion of each call within 15 seconds. Lower gas prices can reduce the cost for each mobile agent but delay the collection of the data. Depending on the deadline of a query, the mobile agents are responsible to device the gas price they are willing to use for submitting their readings.

7   Design Tradeoffs

We design Orthos as an Ethereum-based framework that functions via smart contracts. Although the use of smart contracts on every component of Orthos guarantees its auditability and generalisability, it increases the cost of its operation in terms of gas. In this section we discuss the design tradeoffs for the stored data and the computational demanding components of Orthos.

Storage Requirements of Orthos. Actions performed on Orthos are recorded as transactions and get logged to the Ethereum blockchain. Anyone can access these logs and verify the operations of Orthos. There are two methods to store persistent data on the smart contract, *contract storage* and *log storage*. Data stored on the *contract storage* can be accessed by the corresponding smart contract and other smart contracts depending on the permissions provided. However, the cost of storing data on the *contract storage* is very high, and therefore only state variables and only the most crucial data required by the smart contract should be stored there. Table 4 provides cost details for *contract storage*. Orthos stores agent commitments and their reports on the *contract storage* as it needs it to verify agent reports and then use it to compute their scores. The contract also stores the agents' PoLs which are required to validate their location.

A cheaper alternative is *log storage* where data is stored on transaction logs created by triggering events[9]. For every log event, the gas price is:

$$Gas\_prince = 8 * (nBytes) + 375 * (1 + iArgs),$$

where $nBytes$ denotes the number of bytes and $iArgs$ the number of the indexed arguments. A limitation to this form of storage is that smart contracts cannot access directly the data stored on *log storage* and need additional functions for that. Another alternative is to use external storage (e.g., IPFS [2]) and store hashed of the externally stored data. Unfortunately, this increases the required setup on the agents' mobile devices.

---

[9] https://docs.soliditylang.org/en/v0.4.24/contracts.html/events.

Table 4. Contract storage costs on 13/11/2019, 1 ETH=188\$, 1 gas=10^{-9} ETH.

Storage	Gas	Cost (ETH)	Cost(USD)
256-bit word	20000	0.00002	0.177
1 MB (31250 words)	625×10^6	18.75	5531.25
1 GB (1000 MB)	625×10^9	18750	531250

Table 5. Provable fee structure.

Data source	Base price	Proof type		
		TLSNotary	Android	Ledger
URL	0.01\$	+0.04\$	+0.04\$	N/A
WolframAlpha	0.03\$	N/A	N/A	N/A
IPFS	0.01\$	N/A	N/A	N/A
Random	0.05\$	N/A	N/A	+0.0\$
Computation	0.50\$	+0.04\$	+0.04\$	N/A

Reward Calculation. It is possible to store the reports on the logs and then use third party services (*oracles*) to compute the agent reward using the logged data. In this way, each agent will save more than 50% of her participation cost. However, the requester will have to cover the fees for the oracle service provider. *Provable*[10] is one such popular oracle service provider designed to act as an untrusted intermediary. Provable is referred to as a *provable honest* service as it provides cryptographic proofs showing that the data they provide is really the one that the server gave them at a specific time. It works in the following way: first, a smart contract uses the provable API to request for a task execution off-chain, and then *Provable* performs the task off-chain and makes a callback transaction to provide the results of the task and the proof of authenticity. With each request, the contract must pay enough fee to *Provable* to execute the task and send a callback transaction. The fee consists of two parts: The gas that corresponds, using a recent exchange rate, to the USD price for the data source and the authenticity proof requested and the gas *Provable* will spend for sending the callback transaction. Table 5 provides fee details for the data source and authenticity proof.

Note that using an oracle service to compute the rewards off-chain defeats the purpose of an otherwise decentralized framework as the services centrally compute all the rewards. Hence, the rewards are computed on blockchain and stored on public storage to maintain transparency. The rewards are only associated with Ethereum addresses and therefore do not compromise privacy even though stored publicly. We allow agents to accumulate their reward as a balance

---

[10] https://provable.xyz.

on the smart contract and retrieve it whenever they want. It is a design trade-off to avoid repetitive transactions that pay agents agent for every query.

8 Conclusion

Smart cities require constant and accurate data to function properly. Existing data acquisition systems are built on centralized architectures that imply trusting third parties on providing reliable and secure services. Motivated by these challenges in robust spatio-temporal information acquisition in smart cities, we proposed *Orthos*, a blockchain-based framework that enables the deployment of information elicitation mechanisms. After introducing the necessary characteristics of data acquisition mechanisms in spontaneous localized settings and analyzing the state of the art, we concluded that RPTSC is the most suitable. Additionally, we proposed the Proof-of-Location protocol to assist Orthos on guaranteeing that agents participating in information elicitation mechanisms are at the expected locations when reporting their measurements. We used Ethereum smart contracts to develop the methods needed to support any information elicitation mechanism. To test Orthos and assess its applicability, we deployed its smart contracts on a popular Ethereum testnet and developed an Android Application to perform experiments with a live audience. In summary, Orthos assist agents in posting their queries and answer others' queries on their mobile devices at extremely very low rates. It protects agents' privacy and provides a secure and transparent platform for exchange and acquisition of information with no tampering or interference by any centralized entity.

References

1. Abraham, M., Jevitha, K.P.: Runtime verification and vulnerability testing of smart contracts. In: Singh, M., Gupta, P.K., Tyagi, V., Flusser, J., Ören, T., Kashyap, R. (eds.) ICACDS 2019. CCIS, vol. 1046, pp. 333–342. Springer, Singapore (2019). https://doi.org/10.1007/978-981-13-9942-8_32
2. Benet, J.: Ipfs-content addressed, versioned, p2p file system. arXiv preprint arXiv:1407.3561 (2014)
3. Bogner, A., Chanson, M., Meeuw, A.: A decentralised sharing app running a smart contract on the ethereum blockchain. In: Proceedings of the 6th International Conference on the Internet of Things, pp. 177–178. ACM (2016)
4. Bulusu, N., Heidemann, J., Estrin, D.: GPS-less low-cost outdoor localization for very small devices. IEEE Pers. Commun. **7**(5), 28–34 (2000)
5. Buterin, V., et al.: A next-generation smart contract and decentralized application platform. white paper (2014)
6. Čapkun, S., Hamdi, M., Hubaux, J.P.: GPS-free positioning in mobile ad hoc networks. Cluster Comput. **5**(2), 157–167 (2002)
7. Chatzopoulos, D., Gujar, S., Faltings, B., Hui, P.: Privacy preserving and cost optimal mobile crowdsensing using smart contracts on blockchain. In: 2018 IEEE 15th International Conference on Mobile Ad Hoc and Sensor Systems (MASS), pp. 442–450. IEEE Computer Society (2018)

8. Chatzopoulos, D., Gujar, S., Faltings, B., Hui, P.: Localcoin: An ad-hoc payment scheme for areas with high connectivity. CoRR abs/1708.08086 (2017)
9. ConsenSys: Mythril. https://github.com/ConsenSys/mythril (2017)
10. Dasgupta, A., Ghosh, A.: Crowdsourced judgement elicitation with endogenous proficiency. In: Proceedings of the 22nd International Conference on World Wide Web, pp. 319–330 (2013)
11. Eberhardt, J., Tai, S.: On or off the blockchain? insights on off-chaining computation and data. In: De Paoli, F., Schulte, S., Broch Johnsen, E. (eds.) ESOCC 2017. LNCS, vol. 10465, pp. 3–15. Springer, Cham (2017). https://doi.org/10.1007/978-3-319-67262-5_1
12. Ethereum: Remix. https://github.com/ethereum/remix (2016)
13. Faltings, B., Li, J.J., Jurca, R.: Incentive mechanisms for community sensing. IEEE Trans. Comput. **63**(1), 115–128 (2014)
14. Han, G., Liu, L., Chan, S., Yu, R., Yang, Y.: Hysense: a hybrid mobile crowdsensing framework for sensing opportunities compensation under dynamic coverage constraint. IEEE Commun. Mag. **55**(3), 93–99 (2017)
15. Impagliazzo, R., Levin, L.A., Luby, M.: Pseudo-random generation from one-way functions. In: Proceedings of the Twenty-First Annual ACM Symposium on Theory of Computing, pp. 12–24. ACM (1989)
16. Jurca, R., Faltings, B.: An incentive compatible reputation mechanism. In: IEEE International Conference on E-Commerce, CEC 2003, pp. 285–292. IEEE Computer Society (2003)
17. Jurca, R., Faltings, B.: Robust incentive-compatible feedback payments. In: Fasli, M., Shehory, O. (eds.) AMEC/TADA -2006. LNCS (LNAI), vol. 4452, pp. 204–218. Springer, Heidelberg (2007). https://doi.org/10.1007/978-3-540-72502-2_15
18. Lambert, N., Shoham, Y.: Truthful surveys. In: Papadimitriou, C., Zhang, S. (eds.) WINE 2008. LNCS, vol. 5385, pp. 154–165. Springer, Heidelberg (2008). https://doi.org/10.1007/978-3-540-92185-1_23
19. Luu, L., Chu, D.H., Olickel, H., Saxena, P., Hobor, A.: Making smart contracts smarter. In: Proceedings of the 2016 ACM SIGSAC Conference on Computer and Communications Security, pp. 254–269. ACM (2016)
20. Miller, N., Resnick, P., Zeckhauser, R.: Eliciting informative feedback: the peer-prediction method. Manag. Sci. **51**(9), 1359–1373 (2005)
21. Prelec, D.: A bayesian truth serum for subjective data. Science **306**(5695), 462–466 (2004)
22. Ra, M.R., Liu, B., Porta, T.L., Govindan, R.: Medusa: A programming framework for crowd-sensing applications. In: MobiSys. ACM (2012)
23. Radanovic, G., Faltings, B.: A robust Bayesian truth serum for non-binary signals. In: Proceedings of the 27th AAAI Conference on Artificial Intelligence (AAAI 2013), pp. 833–839. AAAI Press (2013)
24. Radanovic, G., Faltings, B.: Incentives for truthful information elicitation of continuous signals. In: Proceedings of the 28th AAAI Conference on Artificial Intelligence, pp. 770–776. AAAI Press (2014)
25. Radanovic, G., Faltings, B.: Incentive schemes for participatory sensing. In: Proceedings of the 2015 International Conference on Autonomous Agents and Multi-agent Systems, pp. 1081–1089. ACM (2015)
26. Radanovic, G., Faltings, B., Jurca, R.: Incentives for effort in crowdsourcing using the peer truth serum. ACM Trans. Intell. Syst. Technol. (TIST) **7**(4), 48 (2016)
27. Riley, B.: Minimum truth serums with optional predictions. In: Proceedings of the 4th Workshop on Social Computing and User Generated Content (2014)

28. Szabo, N.: Formalizing and securing relationships on public networks. First Monday **2**(9) (1997)

29. Tikhomirov, S., Voskresenskaya, E., Ivanitskiy, I., Takhaviev, R., Marchenko, E., Alexandrov, Y.: Smartcheck: static analysis of ethereum smart contracts. In: 2018 IEEE/ACM 1st International Workshop on Emerging Trends in Software Engineering for Blockchain (WETSEB), pp. 9–16. IEEE, ACM (2018)

30. Tsankov, P., Dan, A., Drachsler-Cohen, D., Gervais, A., Buenzli, F., Vechev, M.: Securify: practical security analysis of smart contracts. In: Proceedings of the 2018 ACM SIGSAC Conference on Computer and Communications Security, pp. 67–82. ACM (2018)

31. Wang, L., Zhang, D., Yan, Z., Xiong, H., Xie, B.: effsense: a novel mobile crowd-sensing framework for energy-efficient and cost-effective data uploading. IEEE Trans. Syst. Man Cybern. Syst. **45**(12), 1549–1563 (2015)

32. Witkowski, J., Parkes, D.C.: Peer prediction with private beliefs. In: Proceedings of the 1st Workshop on Social Computing and User Generated Content (2011)

33. Witkowski, J., Parkes, D.C.: Peer prediction without a common prior. In: Proceedings of the 13th ACM Conference on Electronic Commerce, pp. 964–981. ACM, ACM (2012)

34. Witkowski, J., Parkes, D.C.: A robust Bayesian truth serum for small populations. In: AAAI, vol. 12, pp. 1492–1498. AAAI Press (2012)

35. Wolberger, L., Mason, A., Capkun, S.: Platin - proof of location protocol on the blockchain (2018). https://platin.io/

36. Xu, R., Chen, Y., Blasch, E., Chen, G.: Blendcac: a smart contract enabled decentralized capability-based access control mechanism for the iot. Computers **7**(3), 39 (2018)

37. Zhang, P., Chen, Y.: Elicitability and knowledge-free elicitation with peer prediction. In: Proceedings of the 2014 International Conference on Autonomous Agents and Multi-Agent Systems, pp. 245–252. IFAAMAS/ACM (2014)

38. Zhang, Y., Kasahara, S., Shen, Y., Jiang, X., Wan, J.: Smart contract-based access control for the internet of things. IEEE Internet Things J. **6**(2), 1594–1605 (2018)

Simulating Vehicular IoT Applications by Combining a Multi-agent System and Big Data

Ryo Neyama[1]([✉])(iD), Sylvain Lefebvre[1](iD), Masanori Itoh[1], Yuji Yazawa[1,2],
Akira Yoshioka[1,2], Jun Koreishi[3], Akihisa Yokoyama[1,2], Masahiro Tanaka[2],
and Hiroko Okuyama[1,2]

[1] Toyota Motor Corporation, Toyota, Japan
{neyama,slvn-lefebvre,masanori.itoh,yazawa,yoshioka}@toyota-tokyo.tech
[2] Toyota Research Institute - Advanced Development, Inc., Toyota, Japan
[3] Sole proprietorship, Toyota, Japan
{akihisa.yokoyama,masahiro.tanaka,hiroko.okuyama}@tri-ad.global

Abstract. Describing an accurate simulation model of the driving behavior of real-world vehicles is a laborious or even impossible task, because a driver reacts to a dynamically changing environment. As multiple external factors determine driving behavior, it is usually difficult to obtain an accurate model, owing to a lack of sensors or inability to collect data. In this paper, we propose a novel technique to combine driving behavior in vehicular Internet of Things (IoT) big data with a multi-agent system. This enables correct and scalable simulation without modeling the behavior of vehicular IoT devices or the environment. We develop an extensible simulation framework, called FlowSim, that demonstrates the application of our technique for a simulation of camera-image data collection from connected cars.

1 Introduction

With the advocacy of the *CASE (Connected, Autonomous, Shared, and Electric)* vision by Daimler [4], connectivity based services for cars have been considered one of the key innovation enablers for automotive companies.

A developer of the next-generation services for connected cars may suffer from an insuperable gap between the car development cycle and the agility desired for making innovative services. For most car models, the development cycle is typically two to four years, and as frequent and very large-scale software updates have not been achieved yet for connected vehicles, the capacity to deploy and test new software features at scale remains limited.

If one has a new service idea for connected cars in their mind, they would first test it in order to determine an appropriate specification, or to verify its business feasibility before production. For instance, considering a data collection service from connected cars to the cloud, developers may want to verify which data uploading algorithm is the most efficient, how long it takes, or how much it

© Springer Nature Switzerland AG 2020
C. Baroglio et al. (Eds.): EMAS 2020, LNAI 12589, pp. 119–128, 2020.
https://doi.org/10.1007/978-3-030-66534-0_8

costs to collect a particular amount of data. Therefore, the research question is as follows: How can we verify services for millions of connected cars in an agile manner, such as in A/B testing [15]?

Multiple traffic simulation tools [13,14,16] or models [10,12] are available in the literature, however, it is difficult to provide parameters to make the simulation realistic. To this end, we need to have hypotheses that are difficult to obtain for countrywide or continent-wide simulations. Namely, in the case of the aforementioned data collection service, we need to have hypotheses on when, where, and how many vehicles drive, to collect the data on the road under the influence of external factors, such as drivers' intentions, traffic signals, and traffic congestions. One solution to this issue could be to extract the parameters from real-world data. However, obtaining data about external factors is challenging, due to the high cost of embedding multiple sensors and processors in cars.

To overcome the aforementioned limitations, we propose a simulation technique to combine collected data from IoT vehicular devices with a multi-agent system. Our study makes the following contributions:

Requirements. There are some characteristic requirements in vehicular IoT simulations for the development of new services in the real world. We touch upon all the issues and categorize them into functional and non-functional requirements (Sect. 2).

Technique and Framework. We propose a technique to process highly scalable simulations by combining vehicular IoT big data with a multi-agent system, as well as a reusable simulation framework FlowSim to allow users to apply the technique to various vehicular IoT simulations (Sect. 3).

Case Study. We apply the proposed technique to data collection for connected cars, and demonstrate some preliminary performance results, thereby demonstrating the usefulness of the technique and framework (Sect. 4).

2 Motivation

Most advanced services for connected cars rely on the collection and aggregation of large quantities of data from moving vehicles. The design and evaluation of efficient algorithms for collecting this data at scale is particulary challenging as most of the infrastructure for such services is not available yet. As an example of such challenging connected-car service, we decided to study the case of Map-Generation Data Collection.

2.1 Use Case: Map-Generation Data Collection

Automated high-definition (HD) map generation and distribution by utilizing vehicular camera images [3,7] consist in collecting images and road status information from running vehicles in order to generate up-to-date and accurate maps. As depicted in Fig. 1, a) the system collects on-board camera images of roads *(map-gen data)* from cars and stores them in a cloud-based service, b) the collected data are integrated using the service, thus generating an HD map, c) and

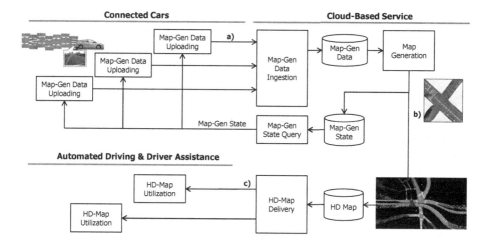

Fig. 1. Generation and Distribution of HD Maps

delivering the HD map with a road network to automated driving systems or driver assistance systems.

Balancing between the cost and quality is a vital design decision in this service. While the coverage, quantity, and quality of the collected data influence the quality of the generated HD maps and the service itself, uploading high-quality map-gen data is expensive in communication and data center operations.

We consider the use of a simulator to verify the relationship between cost and quality (coverage, more specifically) during map-gen data collection. As discussed in Sect. 1, it is challenging to provide suitable parameters to the simulator. Therefore, we use vehicle log data containing only position, speed, and time stamp information, which are easily obtainable from current car models.

Here, we assume a road network denoted by an undirected graph $G = \{V, E, I, F\}$ where V is a set of vertices (intersections), $E \subseteq \{(x,y)|x, y \in V \wedge x \neq y\}$ is a set of edges (road links), I is a pair of functions that map an edge to its unique identifier and vice versa, and F is a set of functions that map an edge to its features, such as a road link length.

We have a set of cars $O = \{o_i\}$. When a car o enters a road link with an ID l at a time stamp t, and requires d seconds to pass through the road link, we obtain a record $p_i = (o, l, t, d)$, thereby resulting in a set of records $P = \{p_i\}$, which forms the vehicle log.

Let $c_{t,o}$ be the communication cost needed to collect the data from a car o at a simulation time t, $len(\cdot), gen_t(\cdot) \in F$ the functions that, for a given road link (and time), provide the length, and determine whether an HD-map segment is generated, respectively, and $H_t = \{h_i|h_i \in E \wedge gen_t(h_i)\}$ represents the set of generated road links at t.

Our simulation goal is to evaluate two metrics, namely i) the total cost of communication in collecting the map-gen data and ii) the coverage of generated road links for the entire road network at a simulation time t_n. Formally:

$$C_n = \sum_{i=1}^{n} \sum_{j=1}^{|O|} c_{t_i, o_j} \qquad R_n = \frac{\sum_{i=1}^{|H_{t_n}|} len(h_i)}{\sum_{i=1}^{|E|} len(e_i)}$$

One can consider multiple data collection strategies, e.g. always uploading, randomly uploading, or filtering uploads by checking the status of each road link using the on-cloud service. C_n and R_n can vary depending on the data collection strategy S_m.

2.2 Requirements

In the case of map-gen data collection, we have the following requirements:

Correctness. We create a business plan based on the simulation results. Therefore, the results obtained have to be sufficiently accurate. It is difficult to manually build an accurate model for simulation, as discussed in Sect. 1.

Scalability. We create HD maps for a country or continent, and not solely for a block or city, which means that the system is required to scale up on the order of millions of cars.

Extensibility. We use various data collection strategies or simulation assumptions, e.g. communication method or in-vehicle storage size, as well as other applications, in addition to the map-gen data collection.

The *correctness* and *scalability* are in a trade-off relationship. The more we try to obtain accurate results, the greater the need to serialize task execution in the simulation, thereby rendering the system difficult to scale. In Sect. 3, we will discuss a method to balance the *correctness* and *scalability*.

3 Simulation by Combining a Multi-agent System with Vehicular IoT Big Data

3.1 Proposed Simulation Technique

To achieve both *correctness* and *scalability* in simulation, we propose a simulation technique that combines a multi-agent system and vehicle IoT big data. Figure 2 shows the simulation data pipeline, which comprises two parts:

i) Vehicular IoT big data preparation. We generate a virtual vehicle log by filtering the (real) vehicle log (P in Sect. 2.1), thus assigning real vehicles to the virtual ones. Virtual vehicle log records have one-to-one correspondence with the real vehicle log records: the system only offsets the records' time stamps and replaces the vehicle IDs. Therefore, *correctness* can be maintained without the need for modeling based on various hypotheses, as discussed in Sect. 1.

ii) Simulation by a multi-agent system. We carry out the simulation based on the bulk-synchronous parallel (BSP) model [19]. In each superstep of BSP, each agent thread runs concurrently for better *scalability*, while communicating with each other to make a right decision. This is eventually followed by a barrier

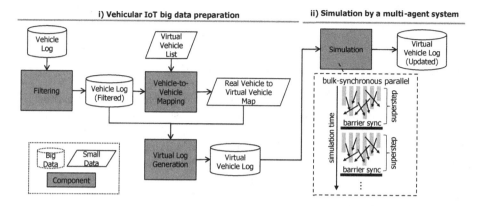

Fig. 2. Simulation Data Pipeline

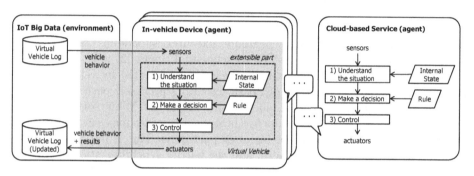

Fig. 3. Simulation by a Multi-agent System

synchronization at a point of sliced simulation time for better *correctness*. This balances the trade-offs mentioned in Sect. 2.2, according to the application's requirement.

As shown in Fig. 3, the in-vehicle device and the cloud-based service work as agents, while IoT big data works as the environment in a multi-agent system. The simulation regards the virtual vehicles' behaviors extracted from the data (p_i in Sect. 2.1) as the signals from the environment, and thereby simulation users can focus on modeling the in-vehicle device that provides the services (see the motivation in Sect. 2).

For example, in the map-gen data collection introduced in Sect. 2.1, the in-vehicle device 1) understands the characteristics of captured data (e.g. road type and map-gen data size) based on the behaviors, how long it can communicate with the cloud-based service for data uploading, and how much local storage is available. Then, 2) it ensures that there is enough free disk space to save the captured data, and exchanges request and response messages with the cloud-based service to determine whether it should upload the data on the local storage.

Finally, 3) it stores the captured data to the local storage, and uploads the data on the local storage based on the available communication time.

3.2   The FlowSim Framework

We present a framework called FlowSim that is designed and implemented by generalizing the proposed technique, and we discuss the method for achieving *extensibility*. The components specified in Fig. 2 are implemented as follows:

Vehicle-to-Vehicle Mapping. We map a set of virtual vehicles $U = \{u_j\}$ to real vehicles O to "copy" the behavior of a real vehicle o_i to one or more virtual vehicles $\{u_{j_1}, u_{j_2}, \ldots\}$, thus giving 1-to-$n$ correspondence.[1] The user can change the way virtual vehicles are generated along the simulation time and how they are mapped from a given list of real vehicles.

Virtual Log Generation. We generate a virtual vehicle log from the real vehicle log.[2] The users can modify or aggregate the vehicle log from the original one, according to the application's requirement.

Simulation. The simulation repeatedly executes supersteps (see BSP in Sect. 3.1). We implement supersteps as sequential Spark [2] jobs. The virtual vehicle log is partitioned by (virtual) vehicle ID, and sorted by vehicle ID and time. Within a superstep, a set of Spark executors processes each partition in parallel. The partitioning scheme relies on the vehicle IDs. While sorting vehicles by ID and time ensures that events are processed in order for each vehicle, this guarantee does not hold across vehicles or partitions. This is mitigated by the choice of a suitable superstep length, and the barrier synchronization after each superstep execution.

As discussed in Sect. 2.1, we intend to evaluate various data collection strategies, i.e. $S_1, S_2, \ldots$. We can implement various algorithms to trigger events, such as capturing map-gen data based on vehicle log records. Also, we can provide a new strategy to decide whether the in-vehicle device uploads map-gen data, by requesting the cloud-based service for the map-gen state. In other words, it uploads map-gen data for that road link, if and only if no HD-map segment was generated for the road link. In our implementation, we use a key-value store, Hazelcast IMDG [6], for this purpose.

We can implement our own virtual data communication module, e.g. mobile network and Wi-Fi, as well as various network bandwidth models such as a uniform bandwidth or a bandwidth based on the Poisson distribution.

Instead of gathering results for each simulated vehicle, we rely on our data pipeline to gather and generate statistical aggregates on data collection for each

---

[1] It is desirable that one real vehicle is assigned to only one virtual vehicle, from the viewpoint of *correctness*; otherwise, this can duplicate the behavior of the real vehicle in the simulation, which is unrealistic. To this end, a sufficient number of real vehicles are required, namely $|U| - |O| \ll |O|$ when $|U| > |O|$.

[2] In the system, we store the input data, intermediate data, and output data onto the Apache Hadoop [1] Distributed File System (HDFS), with two replicas. We use Apache Spark [2] to process data in a scalable way.

type of road, which helps generalizing the results. We address issues such as data ageing in the model by frequently updating input data and running the simulation again. One can connect the simulation data pipeline to external components that can use this data to update their own processes, thus closing the feedback loop between the control system and the simulation framework.

4   Case Study: Map-Gen Data Collection Simulation

4.1   Evaluation Environment

We used Scala (version 2.11.12) on top of Apache Spark 2.3.1 to develop the system. Log data and intermediate states were stored in HDFS (3.0.0) and Hazelcast IMDG (version 3.11.1), respectively. The Spark cluster spans 24 nodes (1 executor and 23 workers) over two racks and uses a single Hazelcast node. Machines are equipped with two Intel Xeon Gold 6126 24C CPUs and 384 GB of RAM along with 2.9 TiB of NVMe-SSD storage. The nodes are connected through a 100 Gb Ethernet network. Every machine runs Ubuntu 18.04 with kernel v4.15.0, and we use Docker (version 18.09.0) to deploy the software stack.

4.2   Evaluation with Map-Gen Data Collection

We applied FlowSim to the simulation of map-gen data collection and confirmed that the proposed technique and FlowSim work as expected. Table 1 summarizes the information about the input data (the real vehicle log), settings, and results of the simulation. We used the input data described in Sect. 2.1. By counting the number of collected map-gen data for each road link, we could calculate the cost C_n and the coverage R_n under each data collection strategy $S_1, S_2, \ldots$ (see Sect. 2.1).

Figure 4 shows the execution time and the speedup (the right axis) of the simulation. Despite the large input data volume, the large number of real and virtual vehicles, and the long simulation period, the simulation can run in a reasonable time (1 h 49 m 19 s). The speedup indicates how much the system could improve the latency with 23 workers vs. 1 worker, namely 23 in linear speedup. Although the system showed poor speedup (1.56 and 9.96) for i) Vehicular IoT big data preparation (i.e. Vehicle-to-Vehicle Mapping and Virtual Log Generation) mentioned in Sect. 3.1, these steps account for only a small percentage (5.5 %) of the total execution time. In contrast, the system showed excellent speedup (18.14) for ii) Simulation by a multi-agent system, which accounts for most of the execution time (94.5 %).

5   Related Work

In [9] Ahmed et al. provide a survey of existing vehicular cloud computing simulation frameworks. They highlight the need for modularity and bidirectionality to integrate mobility simulators and network simulators. While this survey notes

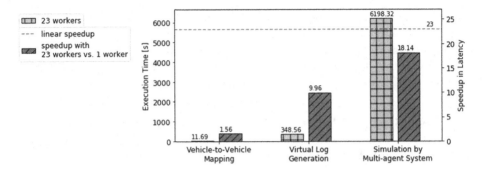

Fig. 4. System Performance for Each Simulation Step

Table 1. Map-Gen Data Collection Simulation

Item		Description
Input data	Data acquisition area	Japan
	Data acquisition period	365 d
	Data size (w/o replicas)	44.2 GB
	Number of data records	2,608,986,929
	Number of unique vehicles	414,329
Simulation settings	Number of vehicles (fixed)	1,000,000
	Simulation period	365 d
	Micro-batch interval	5 d
Simulation results	Number of captured map-gen data	
	On the vehicles	2,535,104,457
	Number of collected map-gen data	
	On the cloud-based service	29,520,776

that the majority of studies rely on the SUMO [16] mobility generator, there also exist multiple approaches for extending multi-agent mobility simulators, such as MATSim, see [14,17].

The common strategy for integrating traffic/mobility simulators and higher level agent simulation [17] or network simulation [18] is to build a software bridge between the two simulators. This relies either on log files or sockets, or the simulation software API. For example, the Veins [18] framework uses bi-directional coupling between the network simulator Omnet++ [20] and SUMO. This coupling enables authors to observe the influence of vehicle-to-vehicle communication protocols on the simulated traffic.

The main limit of these approaches is that careful synchronization is needed between the two simulators to maintain correctness and realistic simulation. We believe this can hinder the scalability of these approaches. Therefore we use a trace-based approach to generate events, which trades off flexibility for scalability.

For example, Ahlbrecht et al. [8] implemented the Jason multi-agent framework on top of Apache Spark [2], demonstrating the efficiency of this approach by running a simulation of up to one million agents on a single node. While this approach yields important performance and scalability benefits by leveraging in-memory data processing frameworks to implement multi-agent simulation, the user has to provide an accurate simulation model.

In [11] Blythe et al. built a multi-agent simulation to predict usage on the GitHub platform [5]. They modeled the behavior of agents with a graph link prediction algorithm, trained using historical usage data. Although this study highlights the need to combine large agent simulation with big data mining and analysis tools, to provide better modeling of global services, extracting the nature of the original data is challenging when we apply this approach to vehicular IoT big data.

6   Conclusions and Future Work

Traffic simulation is one of the most dependable ways to verify new services for connected cars in an agile manner. However, creating a correct behavior model for vehicles is difficult, or even impossible, when we consider countrywide or continent-wide simulation.

We classify the system requirements into correctness, scalability, and extensibility. To this end, we propose a new simulation technique that combines a multi-agent system, IoT big data, and a framework, FlowSim that allows us to run simulations for various applications. We verified the usefulness of the proposed technique and FlowSim through a case study with map-gen data collection. The system had a practical impact on design choices for the development of our connected vehicle systems.

We leave the comparison with another agent based simulation or vehicular network simulator and the application of FlowSim to other applications, such as a dynamic map platform evaluation, for future work. Although our technique is scalable and can maintain correctness, we cannot simulate an anomaly or adversarial behavior that the original data set does not contain, because we use the original data set without modification. For the same reason, the behavior of agents cannot diverge from the information contained in the data, which limits the flexibility of our approach.

References

1. Apache Hadoop. https://hadoop.apache.org/
2. Apache Spark. https://spark.apache.org/
3. Automated Mapping Platform – HD Mapping that Empowers. https://www.triad.global/areas-of-focus/automated-mapping-platform
4. CASE – Intuitive Mobility. https://www.daimler.com/innovation/case-2.html
5. GitHub (a software development platform). https://github.com/
6. Hazelcast IMDG (In-memory Data Grid). https://hazelcast.org/

7. Toyota to Display New Map Generation System at CES 2016. https://global. toyota/en/detail/10765074

8. Ahlbrecht, T., Dix, J., Fiekas, N.: Scalable multi-agent simulation based on MapReduce. In: Criado Pacheco, N., Carrascosa, C., Osman, N., Julián Inglada, V. (eds.) EUMAS/AT -2016. LNCS (LNAI), vol. 10207, pp. 364–371. Springer, Cham (2017). https://doi.org/10.1007/978-3-319-59294-7_31

9. Ahmed, B., Malik, A.W., Hafeez, T., Ahmed, N.: Services and simulation frameworks for vehicular cloud computing: a contemporary survey. EURASIP J. Wirel. Commun. Netw. **2019**(1), 4 (2019)

10. Bham, G.H., Benekohal, R.F.: A high fidelity traffic simulation model based on cellular automata and car-following concepts. Trans. Res. Part C Emerg. Technol. **12**(1), 1–32 (2004)

11. Blythe, J., et al.: Massive multi-agent data-driven simulations of the github ecosystem. In: Demazeau, Y., Matson, E., Corchado, J.M., De la Prieta, F. (eds.) Advances in Practical Applications of Survivable Agents and Multi-Agent Systems: The PAAMS Collection, pp. 3–15. Springer International Publishing, Cham (2019). https://doi.org/10.1007/978-3-030-24209-1_1

12. Burghout, W., Koutsopoulos, H.N., Andreasson, I.: A discrete-event mesoscopic traffic simulation model for hybrid traffic simulation. In: 2006 IEEE Intelligent Transportation Systems Conference, pp. 1102–1107. IEEE (2006)

13. Düntgen, C., Behr, T., Güting, R.H.: Berlinmod: a benchmark for moving object databases. VLDB J. **18**(6), 1335 (2009)

14. Horni, A., Nagel, K., Axhausen, K.W.: The Multi-agent Transport Simulation MATSim. Ubiquity Press, London (2016)

15. Kohavi, R., Longbotham, R.: Online controlled experiments and a/b testing. Encycl. Mach. Learn. Data Min. **7**(8), 922–929 (2017)

16. Lopez, P.A., et al.: Microscopic traffic simulation using sumo. In: 2018 21st International Conference on Intelligent Transportation Systems (ITSC), pp. 2575–2582. IEEE (2018)

17. Padgham, L., Nagel, K., Singh, D., Chen, Q.: Integrating bdi agents into a matsim simulation. In: Proceedings of the Twenty-First European Conference on Artificial Intelligence, pp. 681–686. ECAI'14, IOS Press, NLD (2014)

18. Sommer, C., German, R., Dressler, F.: Bidirectionally coupled network and road traffic simulation for improved ivc analysis. IEEE Trans. Mob. Comput. **10**(1), 3–15 (2010)

19. Valiant, L.G.: A bridging model for parallel computation. Commun. ACM **33**(8), 103–111 (1990)

20. Varga, A.: Discrete event simulation system. In: Proceedings of the European Simulation Multiconference (ESM'2001), pp. 1–7 (2001)

Accept a Challenge: The Multi-Agent Programming Contest
Challenging Tasks and How to Deal with Them

Tobias Ahlbrecht[1]([✉]) [iD], Jürgen Dix[1] [iD], Niklas Fiekas[1] [iD],
and Tabajara Krausburg[1,2] [iD]

[1] Department of Informatics, Clausthal University of Technology,
Clausthal-Zellerfeld, Germany
{tobias.ahlbrecht,dix,niklas.fiekas}@tu-clausthal.de
[2] School of Technology, Pontifical Catholic University of Rio Grande do Sul,
Porto Alegre, Brazil
tabajara.rodrigues@edu.pucrs.br

Abstract. The multi-agent programming contest (MAPC), is an annual attempt to motivate people to learn about and develop multi-agent systems to solve a complex challenge. We try to find scenarios, in which multi-agent systems can be suitably applied. These scenarios and the competition in general also often serve researchers as a testbed for their systems and frameworks. We analyze the results and solutions of the contest of 2019 and take a broader look at the agent technology that has been used to solve the competition's challenges since its inception in 2005, and how it has been applied.

Keywords: Multi-agent systems · Agent-oriented software engineering · Competition

1 Introduction

The Multi-Agent Programming Contest (MAPC) is annually organized to bring together people who are interested in building multi-agent systems, ranging from those who want to get a first glimpse to those who are providing agent frameworks and technology to the community. The Contest's modus operandi is to create scenarios, in the form of small games played by other software agents, where using agent technology should offer benefits over conventional programming approaches.

Everything started in 2005 as the *CLIMA Contest* and specifically focused on the evaluation of new approaches from the field of computational logics. Then, from 2007 up to 2012 it was organized as part of the ProMAS workshop, opening up to Multi-Agent Systems in general.

Over the years, the scenarios became more and more complex, maturing together with the agent technologies used to create solutions. While the MAPC,

© Springer Nature Switzerland AG 2020
C. Baroglio et al. (Eds.): EMAS 2020, LNAI 12589, pp. 129–143, 2020.
https://doi.org/10.1007/978-3-030-66534-0_9

as the name suggests, encourages the use of multi-agent frameworks or agent-oriented software engineering in general, conventional programming approaches, like procedural or object-oriented programming (e.g., using plain C or Java) were never prohibited. In its 15 years of existence, the Contest has seen a lot of varying approaches and technologies, where some have been tried once, while others are used over and over again.

In this paper, we report on the results of the MAPC 2019 together with a historical analysis focusing on the participants of the MAPC and what kinds of approaches were tried over the years (in Sect. 5, the main contribution of this paper). In another paper [1], we take a look at the other side, i.e. how the Contest itself, especially its various scenarios have evolved since 2005.

2   Related Work

The MAPC and its results have been regularly published. We point to a brief Contest overview article [2] that includes all editions up to 2014 and of course, the one that is now more up to date [1].

A number of other competitions targeting multi-agent systems exist as well, however, each one centers around a different aspect. For example, the brand-new Intention Progression Competition[1] aims to find good solutions for intention progression problems, i.e.iven an agent with specific goals in an environment, which intention to proceed with in each step.

One big competition is surely the RoboCup Rescue Simulation League[2] [25], where participants have to create agents for disaster response management. All agents have to be implemented using the Agent Development Framework. Thus, the effectiveness of agents is emphasized as opposed to the suitability of agent frameworks in the MAPC.

Then, there is the host of Trading Agent Competitions (TAC), like the still ongoing Power TAC [16], where agents have to trade in an energy market. Here, only single agents are implemented and the focus naturally lies on reasoning about trading-related problems.

Finally, the International Automated Negotiating Agents Competition[3] (ANAC) naturally deals with implementing and evaluating good negotiation strategies.

Whereas all these competitions are looking for solutions to very specific problems, we are instead trying to find problems (or rather settings) where using agent concepts is advantageous.

3   Running the Contest

In this section we give a brief overview of how we run the Contest, alternatives of doing so along with advantages and disadvantages and our plans for the future.

---

[1] https://www.intentionprogression.org/.

[2] https://rescuesim.robocup.org/competitions/agent-simulation-competition/.

[3] https://ii.tudelft.nl/nego.

3.1   Setup

The MAPC is conducted in an entirely remote fashion. First, the scenario is announced and the new software package released, usually in the beginning of the second quarter of the year. The software package contains *MASSim* (Multi-Agent System Simulation), i.e. everything that is needed to run the server side of the Contest and the same software that we run later in the year to host the matches. The teams connect remotely to the Contest server communicating via simple JSON messages over regular TCP sockets. After successful authentication, the server sends the current percepts to each connected agent and expects an action message within the next 4 s. Then, the server processes all actions (in random order) and computes the new state of the world and the cycle repeats. This setup has the advantage, that the participants are in charge of running their agents and do not need to adapt their systems to any specific infrastructure. Also, if they encounter an unexpected bug that would render their agents useless they still have a chance to fix it. On the other hand, this means that the teams generally have different working conditions in terms of available hardware and their connection to the server. For example, teams with a slower connection have less time to compute their actions.

Usually, the teams have to pass a light qualification round to ensure that they can communicate with the server and, nowadays, to show that they can solve some simple tasks in the current scenario.

During the Contest, each team plays three simulations with different parameters against each other team. A win is awarded three points and the team that scores the most points wins the MAPC.

3.2   Alternatives

The overall structure of the Contest has proven to work out fine. However, we are always looking for ways to improve the Contest. For example, the first version of *MASSim* dictated that each game had to be played by exactly two teams. In a later version, we kept the possibility to have many teams share the same environment. While we think that this is an interesting option, we are still looking for scenario features that best exploit this mechanism.

Also, we see that many competitions require that participants submit their code before the tournament, which is then run by the organizers (or their system) in a completely automated fashion. We also think that this is a tempting approach for our MAPC, as all teams would have the same prerequisites in terms of hardware and connection to the server. Additionally, it would allow us to introduce interesting new features like restricting communication between the agents, simulating a completely different level of situatedness. In the same direction, it would enable us to do away with the four seconds for deliberation and network communication and the stepwise execution of the simulation in general, going towards a more realistic setting, where new percepts can arrive at "any time" and actions take up some "real" amount of time.

Admittedly, this would require more effort from each team: They would have to make sure that their agent system runs on our infrastructure and they would have to make sure that the agents are very robust, so that they either do not crash or are able to recover and that most bugs are squashed before the Contest. Additionally, they may need some facilities to reason about time. As multi-agent systems can be very robust and fault-tolerant, we see the latter requirement as an interesting challenge, though.

4   The Multi-Agent Programming Contest 2019

The MAPC 2019 was held on 16 October 2019. Only four teams participated this time, but each team was able to hold their ground. After an initial qualification round, which only team *TRG* passed, all remaining teams were able to qualify in a subsequent round.

4.1   Scenario

The scenario of the MAPC 2019, "Agents Assemble", replaced the previous "Agents in the City" scenario after having been used in three consecutive editions.

In the new scenario, agents move in a shared 2D grid environment. Other important objects include obstacles and blocks. While the former are fixed in position and limit where the agents can go, the latter can (and have to) be attached to each of the four sides of an agent. During the course of the game, tasks are randomly generated by the environment. These tasks describe shapes that can be created by attaching different blocks to each other. The agents have to construct these shapes and deliver them to specific locations in the environment to score points.

All agents can only perceive what is in a certain radius around them. If they meet another agent, they only see its team but not which agent it is, requiring some communication effort to identify teammates.

The scenario provides actions for moving around, rotating 90 degrees, picking up and connecting blocks to each other (with the help of an additional agent), or leaving blocks and deconstructing shapes. A special action, clear, can be used to remove obstacles. If an agent is hit with a clear action, it gets temporarily disabled. However, a clear action has to be aimed at the same target cell for a number of steps and is visible to all agents in proximity.

Similar to the clear action, clear events occur at random locations throughout the simulation. They have a larger radius than the action and also scatter new obstacles around their center, realizing a more dynamic environment.

4.2   Participants and Their Approaches

Four teams, as listed in Table 1, participated in the 2019 MAPC, all of them trying an agent-based approach. We will briefly describe each team and the agent technology that was used, leading to a bigger picture in the next section, where we track the technology through the complete history of the MAPC.

Table 1. Participants of MAPC 2019

Team	Affiliation	Platform	Score
FIT BUT	Brno University of Technology, CZ	Java	15
GOAL-DTU	Technical University of Denmark, DK	GOAL	10
LFC	University of Liverpool, GB	JaCaMo	22
TRG	Carleton University, CA	Jason	5

Platforms By platform we mean the main technological "driver" of the agent system. This year, all platforms were Java-based. The team *FIT BUT* [28] directly used Java to implement their own BDI-inspired agent system. The other three teams decided to use established agent platforms: *GOAL-DTU* [15], as the name suggests, used the GOAL agent programming language[4] [12]. Finally, *LFC* [8] used JaCaMo[5] [4], a platform combining the well-known Jason agent language with CArtAgO, an environment framework, and Moise, an organizational framework, while *TRG* [29] used pure Jason[6] [5].

Tools and Development Most teams used the specific IDE for their chosen platform. *GOAL-DTU* used Eclipse for GOAL and *LFC* used Eclipse with the JaCaMo plugin. *FIT BUT* used (IntelliJ) IDEA to create their Java agents, while *TRG* used IDEA to work on both Java and AgentSpeak code. No team used any (agent-based) development methodology, like Prometheus or Tropos.

Additional Frameworks Additional AI features were, as usual, rarely implemented. Only *LFC* made use of the Fast Downward planning system [11] for path planning.

Notably, *TRG* implemented a custom tool to visualize the percepts of their agents.

Results *LFC* took the first place, followed by *FIT BUT*, *GOAL-DTU* and *TRG*. All teams won at least one simulation and the score intervals between two rankings are very evenly distributed. *LFC* and *FIT BUT* were nearly uncontested, however, *LFC* won all simulations against *FIT BUT*. Interestingly, *FIT BUT* won all simulations against *GOAL-DTU* while *GOAL-DTU* won one simulation against *LFC*. *FIT BUT* in turn lost one simulation against *TRG*. We further note that the outlier was usually the second simulation, which was configured to offer more difficult tasks (i.e. requiring bigger shapes). While no team has actually delivered one of the bigger tasks, we cannot rule out that they attempted or at least considered to do them. Also, there were fewer smaller

---

[4] https://goalapl.atlassian.net/wiki/.

[5] http://jacamo.sourceforge.net/.

[6] http://jason.sourceforge.net/wp/.

tasks, possibly benefiting teams that worked faster but less consistently. In general, the second simulations overall yielded the lowest scores, i.e. had the fewest tasks completed in comparison.

While most teams tried a straightforward approach of completing as many tasks as fast as possible, *TRG* dedicated many agents to defending the goal zones in hopes of preventing the opposing team from delivering their tasks. Unfortunately, this approach seems to have bound too many resources without having the desired effect in many cases.

5   Contestants and Their Agents

In this section, we take a deeper look at all participants of the MAPC, from 2005 up to the most recent one in 2019, what motivated them to take part, what kinds of solutions they developed, how they did it, which problems they often faced and generally what did and (mostly) did not change in the last one and a half decades.

5.1   Technologies

Over the years a number of different technologies have been used by the contestants. These technologies were used to develop agents, to abstract the environment, to design agents' interactions as a team, etc. We review past editions of the MAPC and introduce the frameworks used by the teams in those contests.

Agent Platforms Regarding the programming languages, in total, 15 different agent platforms[7] have been chosen by different teams for developing agents for the Contest. In Fig. 1a, the number of entries that used a given platform in any MAPC is shown.

Some well-known programming languages such as Java, Python, C#, and C++, that are not designed specifically for agent-oriented software engineering or logic reasoning, have been used quite frequently in the contest. This shows there exists a trade-off between feeling comfortable with a programming language and dealing with the complexity of the MAS-oriented problem designed for the MAPC. Regarding the declarative paradigm, the general logic-based Prolog and its variations were used a few times by teams that sought to represent the domain as logical facts and rules to exploit the robustness of such an approach[8]. FLUX [27] uses a symbolic representation in addition to *fluent calculus* as a reasoning mechanism to derive conclusions, but was only used by one team in the early days of the Contest. Not easy to classify, but also a regular contender, GOAL [12] is purely focused on declarative goals that an agent aims to

---

[7] Note we use the term "agent platform" to describe the primary framework or language used to implement an agent system.

[8] Not counting Prolog as part of many dedicated agent platforms.

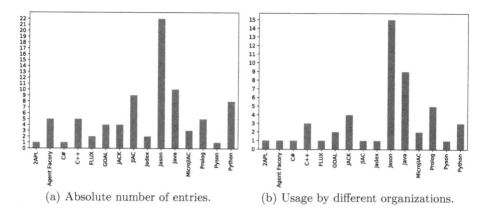

(a) Absolute number of entries.   (b) Usage by different organizations.

Fig. 1. Absolute number of entries for a given agent platform alongside its usage by different organizations in all editions of the Multi-Agent Programming Contest. For instance, Jason has been used 22 times in the MAPC by 15 involved organizations.

achieve, trying to attain a simpler deliberation cycle than most full-fledged BDI platforms.

Then, we also had programming languages (2APL [10], Jason [5], and Pyson[9]), as well as frameworks in Java (JACK [7], Agent Factory [24], and Jadex [21]) that focus on or at least support the development of BDI agents. Of these, Agent Factory is usually used with extensions that support the development of agents such as AF-APL, AF-AgentSpeak, and AF-TeleoReactive [24]. The last two agent platforms to mention are JIAC [18] and MircroJIAC [20]. Whilst MicroJIAC is a lightweight Java agent framework, JIAC provides a full set of tools to design, implement, and deploy agent systems.

Although many options are available for developing agents, one can see in Fig. 1b that the usage of them have been confined to few different organizations (e.g., universities). Few exceptions emerge to this, namely Jason and Java. This pattern may tell us that most of teams look at the MAPC as a good opportunity to try out their own agent frameworks. This clearly shows one avenue of how the MAPC is useful to the MAS community.

It is interesting to note that (sometimes implicitly) agent platforms share common principles with each other (e.g., the BDI paradigm tends to separate concerns related to beliefs, desires and intentions in an agent). Based on this observation, we partition the agent platforms into clusters. To do so, we define the following categories:

Conventional programming: in this category, we place all approaches that are not directly developed using a MAS perspective. For instance, all agents' beliefs are centralized into a single entity that decides the actions to be sent to the contest server.

Logic-based: approaches that are based on the symbolic representation of the domain and reason about states through a formal calculus mechanism that

---

[9] https://github.com/niklasf/pyson.

outputs an action to be performed. FLUX [27] is an example for such an approach.

Reactive agents: agents do not keep a state of the world. Agents perceive the environment and solely based on these observations decide the course of actions to be carried out.

Agent-based: in this category, agents do keep a state of the world to reason about the course of actions in addition to social skills to enable cooperation.

BDI agents: agent platforms that consider a sophisticated reasoning mechanism in terms of beliefs, desires, and intentions [22]. Such support is explicitly provided in some of the agent development platforms, e.g., JACK [7], JIAC [18], 2APL [10], etc.

We analyzed the team description papers along with the teams' answers to the respective MAPC survey to assign a category for each agent platform. Note that one programming language (e.g., Java) could fit into different categories, depending on how a particular team used it to implement their agents. This analysis was conducted by three researchers in which the outcomes were always double-checked (i.e., each entry was analyzed and discussed by at least two researchers). The results are depicted in Fig. 2.

We observe that the preferred approach is to develop a team of agents in accordance with agent-based paradigms, in particular, agents that maintain a state of the world being observed. This could be motivated by many reasons, for instance, teams were learning a particular MAS framework and decided to test it out in the contest (this discussion is further developed in Sect. 5.2). Moreover, at some times, programming languages based on other paradigms rather than MAS were used to provide an agent based approach. This is often due to a lack of familiarity with MAS tools or the general desire to show the qualities of a language.

Supporting Frameworks Apart from the focus on the development of agents themselves, a MAS may require additional tools and frameworks to better deal with a given domain or decrease the implementation complexity. For instance, one may want to state explicitly an organization of agents. Through the years, contest teams have used some frameworks for supporting their development and it is worth introducing some of them.

To design a team of agents, well-known methodologies such as Gaia [31], MaSE [30], Prometheus [19], and Tropos [6] are part of the contest teams' toolboxes. However, conventional approaches for software development are also part of it, for instance, the SADAAM [9] methodology provides agile techniques oriented to agent development. It is important to note that some agent frameworks already encapsulate tools for dealing with many problems related to MAS development, as in the case of JIAC [20]. For most of the teams that aimed to design a MAS organization, Moise [14] was chosen as it enables the specification of the organization in terms of its structural, functional, and normative dimensions.

The usage of these methodologies over the years is depicted in Fig. 3. One can note that frameworks for designing MAS, like GAIA, Tropos, and even

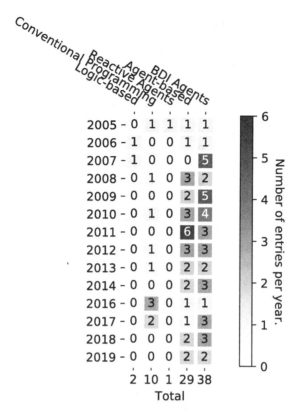

Fig. 2. Team's entries partitioned into clusters according to the chosen approach to develop their agents.

Prometheus, have lost contest teams' interest in recent years. This is particularly intriguing since the MAPC tries to avoid trivial winning solutions. It may be interesting to explore what are the new demands of MAS designers and check if current methodologies match those needs.

Apart from methodologies, we also mention some agent frameworks used by contestants. For message exchange, JADE [3] easily enables communication between distributed agents. CArtAgO [23], mainly used by Jason teams, abstracts away the environment from the agent dimension; it works as a first-class abstraction for it. In terms of quickly prototyping, one interesting approach was to use an agent-based modeling tool, NetLogo[10], to experiment with strategies to be performed in the MAPC.

Besides general MAS reasoning, we find that AI techniques are still severely underused in the MAPC. This is most likely due to the considerable learning and development effort required to get AI-related mechanisms to work well enough. For the most part, teams have tried some approaches for planning, e.g., a Fast

---

[10] https://ccl.northwestern.edu/netlogo.

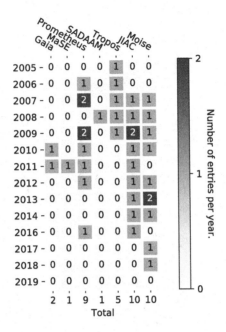

Fig. 3. Main supporting methodologies used by contest teams.

Downward planner [11], RHBP [13], a planner for ROS, or answer set programming with DLV [17].

Another important aspect of the MAPC is agent coordination. In addition to the already mentioned Moise, most attempts in this regard (aside from custom protocols) were realized through some form of auction-based mechanism, with the contract net protocol [26] being the most prominent representative.

5.2 Survey

Starting in 2011, we devised a (more or less) standardized survey that we let each attending team fill out after the Contest. It contains questions about the teams themselves, which platforms and tools they have used, how they implemented their agents and which strategies they pursued. While the agent systems do not necessarily allow us to draw conclusions about the quality of the agent platforms that were used to create them, we can at least gather some (subjective) feedback with our survey.

Motivation We always ask all participants why they participated in the Contest at all. The most frequently given reason is to learn more about multi-agent systems or some specific agent technology or platform. Often, the Contest scenario is used within some course or student project: The students have a concrete goal while it is usually their first contact with agent-oriented programming.

Nonetheless, they regularly achieve competitive results. On the other hand, we see researchers who want to evaluate their own contributions to the agent community, ranging from certain aspects of agent programming and design, to entire agent platforms. Rarely, we see people attending just because of the competition, or to test and improve their software engineering skills.

Time Spent When we look at the time invested, we note that there is no correlation to the Contest performance. Most teams within the same year spend roughly the same amount of developer hours, with few outliers. Generally, 300 h in total seems to be a sweet spot for developing an agent team for the MAPC. Usually, the time investment does not depend on the number of people involved, as we have seen various team sizes, from over 10 people to just singular developers.

Additionally, teams who are new to the Contest generally do not spend more time on their agents than teams who have participated before, even in consecutive runs of the "same" scenario.

Also, despite the scenarios getting more complex, the teams are not spending more time on average. On the contrary, the total time spent seems to be in a slight decline after all. Weirdly, in the new 2016 scenario, where teams had to implement a lot of scenario-specific functionality (and even said so), appreciably less time was spent than in the Mars scenario the year before. One reason might be, that in the Mars scenario, a solution could have been very simple and thus, a lot of time could be spent on optimization, while it was rather unclear when a solution was actually performing well before running it against other approaches. In the following scenario, the potential for optimization (of strategies for example) may have been smaller.

Size of Solutions Comparing program sizes (i.e. lines of code), we first note that conventional solutions in e.g., C++ often are at least as big as or considerably bigger than agent technology-based entries in the same year, which makes sense given that the reasoning method is already implemented for the latter.

Among agent languages, especially GOAL entries tend to be very small, while Jason/JaCaMo solutions are mostly of average size. Also, contrary to expectation, there is no clear trend as to the split between agent code (i.e. AgentSpeak) and Java code (for internal actions). Some teams keep their reasoning logic very small and leave a lot to be calculated, maybe even planned, in Java, while others do not even have half as much Java code but more than triple the amount of AgentSpeak code. While this sounds like a lot, the latter solutions (with more agent code) tend to be smaller in total.

6   Lessons Learned

Over the years, both participants and organizers contributed to building a set of lessons learned on designing and deploying MAPC (see [1] for the impacts on scenario design). When asked directly in the survey, participants reported lessons learned from the following three categories.

Practical application of agent technologies: This includes how to deal with specific technical problems. While some of the problems are unique or relate to particular platforms, recovering from errors, portability (even where participants manage their own environment) and debugging are recurring challenges. Improving multi-agent platforms in these areas motivates ongoing research. Looking back, despite these occasional issues, participants were generally happy with the platforms they used. This may be explained in part by survivorship bias or teams choosing technology that they are already (at least somewhat) familiar with. However, it also applies to participants using multi-agent technologies for the first time.

Project management: This category includes how to balance work on implementation and strategical considerations. Some participants admitted that they underestimated the time required to compete successfully or that they would have chosen a different balance with hindsight. One idea to guide participants may be to introduce milestones with varying levels of difficulty, as opposed to a singular qualification round. On the other hand, this would add organizational overhead and limit possible approaches. For example, for some methodologies or approaches it may not be possible to deliver incremental solutions. While the usage of methodologies is in decline for some years now, we prefer to keep the door open for their return.

Approaches to "solve" the scenarios: Even seemingly simple scenarios may be difficult to master. Common strategies are to decompose the problems, where multi-agent platforms and frameworks help to organize teams of agents, and to make an initial viable solution more efficient by improving task allocation, also supported by multi-agent platforms and frameworks.

7   What Is Next

In this section, we take a look at which suggestions the participating teams have made to improve the Contest since 2011, what we could already realize and what we can do in the future. We grouped all recommendations into *organization*, *setup* (how the Contest generally works on a technical level), and everything that pertains to the *scenario*. For a quick review of all the MAPC scenarios we refer the reader to [1].

Organization: Many teams have suggested more friendly matches, both after but mostly before the Contest. Of course, there is always a possibility for teams to set this up between themselves. We have never tried to institutionalize this before. Generally, teams usually try not to show too much of their strategy before the actual matches, so the usefulness is unfortunately rather limited. Also often requested is some kind of "dummy agent team", that can be played against for testing. We already had one in previous editions, though its capabilities were only very limited and thus, it was also not that useful.

The other points are mostly related to releasing information (e.g., about the scenario or the final parameters) earlier. We always try to be as early as our other responsibilities admit, but history has shown that many teams only start working months after the scenario's release, or just a few weeks before the Contest anyway. As for the parameters, we have started announcing some parameter ranges or likely parameters, or at least which parameters are fixed and which will be kept secret, since we do not want the teams to know the exact characteristics of the environment they will play in. On the other hand, teams are complaining if the parameters are set too narrow and not requiring enough flexibility.

Setup: Sometimes, a team proposed to restrict the communication between the agents. As we already noted in Sect. 3, this would only be possible if we make fundamental changes to how the Contest is conducted, i.e. run the agents locally in separate containers. This would at the same time fulfill the wish for similar prerequisites for all participants. If we actually decide to pursue this direction, we have to make sure though that we are not restricting the approaches that can be used in the MAPC, since the current versatility is one of its big advantages.

Scenario: Some teams desire more freedom for agents to decide what to do in the contest. For instance, agents could change roles during a match, or even call new agents to the round, etc. This type of feature would not come for free to the agents; they would have to pay a price for it (e.g., let some scores go or achieve a particular mission). In the 2018 contest, we implemented a feature that allowed agents to improve their skills, but it ended up underused. Regularly, after each contest, teams also ask for an increase in the number of agents, maps, and other parameters. Usually, this type of request is granted as we start a new scenario setting reasonable fair parameter values. One suggestion that has also been addressed is related to individual perceptions. It should not be possible for an agent to get an agent mate's perceptions; to do so, it must interact with others to combine local views (2019 MAPC). Another interesting feature is to provide "living" entities that are not directly controllable by teams to interact in the environment. This was first done in the *Cow Herding Scenario*, and later requested again by contestants. One request that has been long asked for is to enable cooperation between agents of different teams. This is a magnificent feature to develop and see being used, but hard to impossible to implement in competitive environments in a way that makes sense. As a last matter, two requests that seem to be conflicting among themselves:

– provide focus on a specific problem of MAS at each contest; and
– avoid to pose too specific domain problems (e.g., optimization problems).

As a general field of AI, MAS demands many problems to be addressed and the MAPC, as a steady supporter of research in it, aims to come up with problems that match the needs of researchers and can be tackled by a multitude of different approaches.

To conclude, we have seen a great number of contributors to the MAPC over the years, be it participants, organizers, supporters or friends of the Contest and we are thankful to each and everyone of them. It is always a challenging endeavor to design and run – and certainly also to participate in – the Multi-Agent Programming Contest.

References

1. Ahlbrecht, T., Dix, J., Fiekas, N., Krausburg, T.: The multi-agent programming contest: A résumé. CoRR abs/2006.02739 (2020). https://arxiv.org/abs/2006.02739
2. Ahlbrecht, T., Dix, J., Schlesinger, F.: From testing agent systems to a scalable simulation platform. In: Eiter, T., Strass, H., Truszczyński, M., Woltran, S. (eds.) Advances in Knowledge Representation, Logic Programming, and Abstract Argumentation. LNCS (LNAI), vol. 9060, pp. 47–62. Springer, Cham (2015). https://doi.org/10.1007/978-3-319-14726-0_4
3. Bellifemine, F.L., Caire, G., Greenwood, D.: Developing Multi-Agent Systems with JADE (Wiley Series in Agent Technology). John Wiley & Sons Inc., Hoboken, NJ, USA (2007)
4. Boissier, O., Bordini, R.H., Hübner, J.F., Ricci, A., Santi, A.: Multi-agent oriented programming with jaCaMo. Sci. Comput. Program. **78**(6), 747–761 (2013)
5. Bordini, R.H., Hübner, J.F., Wooldridge, M.: Programming multi-agent systems in AgentSpeak using Jason. John Wiley & Sons, Hoboken, NJ, USA (2007)
6. Bresciani, P., Perini, A., Giorgini, P., Giunchiglia, F., Mylopoulos, J.: Tropos: an agent-oriented software development methodology. Auton. Agent. Multi-Agent Syst. **8**(3), 203–236 (2004). https://doi.org/10.1023/B:AGNT.0000018806.20944.ef
7. Busetta, P., Rönnquist, R., Hodgson, A., Lucas, A.: JACK intelligent agents - components for intelligent agents in Java. AgentLink Newsl. **2**, 2–5 (1999)
8. Cardoso, R.C., Ferrando, A., Papacchini, F.: Lfc: Combining autonomous agents and automated planning in the multi-agent programming contest. arXiv preprint arXiv:2006.02736 (2020)
9. Clynch, N., Collier, R.: SADAAM: Software agent development an agile methodology. In: Proceedings of the 1st International Workshop on Languages, Methodologies and Development Tools for Multi-Agent Systems. vol. 5118. Springer, Heidelberg (2007)
10. Dastani, M., Hobo, D., Meyer, J.J.C.: Practical extensions in agent programming languages. In: Proceedings of the 6th International Joint Conference on Autonomous Agents and Multiagent Systems (AAMAS 2007), Association for Computing Machinery, New York, NY, USA (2007). https://doi.org/10.1145/1329125.1329294
11. Helmert, M.: The fast downward planning system. J. Artif. Int. Res. **26**(1), 191–246 (2006)
12. Hindriks, K.V., De Boer, F.S., Van Der Hoek, W., Meyer, J.J.C.: Agent programming with declarative goals. In: International Workshop on Agent Theories, Architectures, and Languages, pp. 228–243. Springer (2000)
13. Hrabia, C., Wypler, S., Albayrak, S.: Towards goal-driven behaviour control of multi-robot systems. In: 2017 3rd International Conference on Control, Automation and Robotics (ICCAR), pp. 166–173 (2017)
14. Hubner, J.F., Sichman, J.S., Boissier, O.: Developing organised multiagent systems using the moise+ model: Programming issues at the system and agent levels. Int. J. Agent-Oriented Softw. Eng. **1**(3/4), 370–395 (2007). https://doi.org/10.1504/IJAOSE.2007.016266

15. Jensen, A.B., Villadsen, J.: Goal-dtu: Development of distributed intelligence for the multi-agent programming contest. arXiv preprint arXiv:2006.06844 (2020)
16. Ketter, W., Collins, J., Weerdt, M.d.: The 2020 power trading agent competition. ERIM Report Series Reference (2020–002) (2020)
17. Leone, N., Faber, W.: The DLV project: a tour from theory and research to applications and market. In: Garcia de la Banda, M., Pontelli, E. (eds.) ICLP 2008. LNCS, vol. 5366, pp. 53–68. Springer, Heidelberg (2008). https://doi.org/10.1007/978-3-540-89982-2_10
18. Lützenberger, M., et al.: A mas framework for industrial applications. In: Proceedings of the 2013 International Conference on Autonomous Agents and Multi-agent Systems, pp. 1189–1190 (2013)
19. Padgham, L., Winikoff, M.: Developing Intelligent Agent Systems: A Practical Guide. John Wiley & Sons Inc., Hoboken, NJ, USA (2004)
20. Patzla, M., Tuguldur, E.O.: MicroJIAC 2.0 - the agent framework for constrained devices and beyond. Tech. rep., Technische Universität Berlin (Jul 2009). http://www.dai-labor.de/fileadmin/files/publications/microjiac_20_2009_07_02.pdf, tUB-DAI 07/09-01
21. Pokahr, A., Braubach, L., Lamersdorf, W.: Jadex: A BDI Reasoning Engine, pp. 149–174. Springer, US, Boston, MA (2005). https://doi.org/10.1007/0-387-26350-0_6
22. Rao, A.S., Georgeff, M.P.: Modeling rational agents within a BDI-architecture. In: Proceedings of the Second International Conference on Principles of Knowledge Representation and Reasoning (KR 1991), 473–484 (1991)
23. Ricci, A., Piunti, M., Viroli, M., Omicini, A.: Environment programming in CArtAgO. In: El Fallah Seghrouchni, A., Dix, J., Dastani, M., Bordini, R.H. (eds.) Multi-Agent Programming, pp. 259–288. Springer, Boston, MA (2009). https://doi.org/10.1007/978-0-387-89299-3_8
24. Russell, S., Jordan, H., O'Hare, G.M.P., Collier, R.W.: Agent factory: a framework for prototyping logic-based AOP languages. In: Klügl, F., Ossowski, S. (eds.) Multiagent System Technologies, pp. 125–136. Springer, Berlin Heidelberg (2011)
25. Skinner, C., Ramchurn, S.: The RoboCup rescue simulation platform. In: Proceedings of the 9th International Conference on Autonomous Agents and Multiagent Systems: vol. 1 , pp. 1647–1648 (2010)
26. Smith, R.G.: The contract net protocol: high-level communication and control in a distributed problem solver. IEEE Trans. Comput. **12**, 1104–1113 (1980)
27. Thielscher, M.: Flux: a logic programming method for reasoning agents. Theory Pract. Log. Program. **5**(4–5), 533–565 (2005). https://doi.org/10.1017/S1471068405002358
28. Uhlir, V., Zboril, F., Vidensky, F.: Multi-agent programming contest 2019 fit but team solution. arXiv preprint arXiv:2006.09718 (2020)
29. Vezina, M., Esfandiari, B.: The requirement gatherers' approach to the 2019 multi-agent programming contest scenario. arXiv preprint arXiv:2006.02816 (2020)
30. Wood, M., Systems, M., Science, B.: Multiagent systems engineering: A methodology for analysis and design of multiagent systems (02 2001)
31. Wooldridge, M., Jennings, N.R., Kinny, D.: The Gaia methodology for agent-oriented analysis and design. J. Auton. Agent. Multi-Agent Syst. **3**, 285–312 (2000)

The Intention Progression Competition

Simon Castle-Green, Alexi Dewfall, and Brian Logan[(✉)][iD]

University of Nottingham, Nottingham NG8 1BB, UK
{simon.castle-green,brian.logan}@nottingham.ac.uk
academia@aksan.dev

1 Introduction

In this extended abstract, we briefly recall the background, aims and format of the Intention Progression Competition, describe the format and generation of the test problems used to evaluate entries, and outline the architecture of the competition software. We conclude by briefly describing the history and current status of the 2020 Intention Progression Competition. For more details on the background and aims of the competition, we refer the reader to [5].

A key problem for an autonomous agent with multiple, possibly conflicting, goals is 'what to do next'—which plan should be selected to achieve each of the agent's goals, and which step of these plans should the agent execute next. Poor choice of plans and/or the order in which actions are executed can give rise to conflicts that may result in a failure to achieve one or more goals. The problem of 'what to do next' combines both means-ends reasoning and action scheduling, and was termed the *intention progression problem* (IPP) in [5]. The intention progression problem has been an active area of research since at least the 1990s, e.g., [1] and many approaches have been proposed (see [5] for a brief survey). However research in this area suffers from fragmentation, and a lack of common terminology, data structures and enabling tools.

The *Intention Progression Competition* (IPC)[1] was proposed in a Blue Skies paper at AAMAS 2017 [5] as a means of incentivising research around the IPP. The IPC was inspired by competitions such as the International Planning Competition,[2] in that submissions take the form of executable code and are evaluated on a set of (unseen) benchmark intention progression problems. However, unlike the planning competition, a key feature of the IPP is the dynamic nature of the agent's environment and the goals to be achieved, and in this respect the IPC has similarities with the Multi-Agent Programming Contest.[3]

Competition entries take the form of a *solver* for intention progression problems. Each solver is evaluated on a set of unseen intention progression problems. Each IPP instance specifies a set of goals to be achieved, the plans (agent program) available to achieve them, and the initial state of the agent's environment.

The first edition of the Intention Progression Competition is supported by the University of Nottingham School of Computer Science.

[1] www.intentionprogression.org.
[2] www.icaps-conference.org.
[3] www.multiagentcontest.org.

C. Baroglio et al. (Eds.): EMAS 2020, LNAI 12589, pp. 144–151, 2020.
https://doi.org/10.1007/978-3-030-66534-0_10

Some goals in a problem instance are given initially, while others are only given after a specified delay.

The solver forms a part of a simple agent that operates in a simulated environment. The agent and simulated environment are provided as part of the competition, and are the same for all entries. In a run of the competition, the agent is initialised with an IPP instance. At each tick (deliberation cycle) in the run, the agent asks the solver which intention to progress next. The solver must return the next basic action in one of the agent's currently active plans. The agent then returns the selected action to the environment for execution. If the preconditions of the action hold in the current environment state, the environment is updated with the action's postconditions and the updated state is returned to the agent. The environment is dynamic: in addition to applying the postconditions of the action, the environment may change spontaneously. This cycle repeats until all the goals in the IPP instance have been achieved, or a timeout is reached.

In the remainder of this abstract, we briefly motivate the framing of the IPP in terms of goal-plan trees, describe the problem domains used for the evaluation of entries and outline the architecture of the IPC competition software, before giving the current status of the competition.

2 Goal-Plan Trees

In [5] the IPP is formalised in terms of Belief-Desire-Intention (BDI) agents. BDI agents are characterised by having a library of pre-defined plans that are used to achieve the agent's goals. Each plan consists of steps which are either basic actions or sub-goals. Each sub-goal is in turn achieved by some other plan. This relationship is naturally represented as a tree structure termed a *goal-plan tree* (GPT) [1,7,8]. The root of a GPT is a top-level goal (goal-node), and its children are the plans that can be used to achieve the goal (plan-nodes). Usually there are several alternative plans to achieve a goal: hence, the child plan-nodes are viewed as '*OR*' nodes. By contrast, plan execution involves performing all the steps in the plan: hence, the children of a plan-node are viewed as '*AND*' nodes. The adoption of goal-plan trees for the IPC was motivated by their wide use in the BDI agent research community, and their similarity to Hierarchical Task Network (HTN) planning [2], in particular recent work on 'HTN-Acting' [3,6] which combines HTN planning with plan execution. It was hoped that the use of a familiar format would foster cross-fertilisation between these two communities.

In the IPC, the program of a BDI agent is represented by a forest of goal-plan trees. The root of each tree represents a top-level goal the agent is able to achieve. An IPP instance consists of a forest of GPTs, a set of top-level goals, and a specification of the initial state of the agent's environment. For the first edition of the IPC, IPP instances are encoded in an XML format and generated by the tool GenGPT.[4] GenGPT is capable of generating forests of goal-plan

---

[4] GenGPT is available from www.intentionprogression.org.

trees for both synthetic and 'real-world' problem domains of varying degrees of complexity, giving intention progression problem instances of differing levels of difficulty.

A variety of synthetic and 'real world' problem instances of increasing levels of difficulty are provided as part of the competition resources. These test instances are similar to the (unseen) problem instances used to evaluate competition entries, and are intended to facilitate the development and testing of competition entries. The problem instances were calibrated using scheduling approaches commonly found in BDI agent programming languages and platforms, including 'round robin' (RR), 'first in first out' (FIFO), and the MCTS-based scheduler presented in [8].[5] The low difficulty problems are easy to solve with simple techniques such as FIFO, and are provided primarily for basic testing and debugging of entries. The high difficulty problems are designed to be challenging for state of the art approaches such as MCTS-based scheduling. We anticipate that it will be necessary to increase the difficulty level of the most challenging problem instances in future editions of the competition.

2.1   Synthetic Domain

The goal-plan trees for the synthetic domain are derived from abstract BDI programs that have similar structure to 'real world' BDI programs, however the goal, plan and action names are arbitrary, and the literals defining the environment are not a model of any particular environment.

Each forest of synthetic trees are defined by six parameters: the depth of each goal-plan tree, the number of subgoals in each non-leaf plan (leaf plans contain only action nodes), the number of plans to achieve a goal, the number of actions in each plan, the number of environment variables that may appear in the tree as pre- and postconditions, and the number of goal-plan trees in the forest. The trees are generated such that: (a) each plan is well formed (the plan can be successfully executed in some environment), and (b) taken individually, each goal-plan tree is executable (there is at least one way to achieve the top-level goal in all (static) environments). By varying the number of environment variables, we can vary the likelihood of actions and plans in different goal-plan trees having the same pre- and postconditions, and hence the probability of both positive and negative interactions between goal-plan trees. This, together with variations in the dynamism of the environment, allows the performance of each IPP solver to be evaluated under different conditions.

2.2   'Real World' Domains

In addition to the synthetic domain, entries will be evaluated on instances of intention progression problems in two 'real world' domains: the Miconic-N domain and the Logistics domain. The goal-plan trees for these domains are derived from simple BDI programs loosely based on common examples from the

---

[5] We are grateful to Yuan Yao for assistance in calibrating the test problem instances.

BDI literature. As with the synthetic domain, each real-world domain is defined by a set of parameters, and a variety of problem instances of increasing difficulty are provided for each domain as part of the competition resources.

Miconic-N Domain. The Miconic-N Domain defines a set of simple 'elevator world' problems, in which the goals of the agent involve moving people from one floor of a building to another. Unlike traditional elevators, the Miconic-N elevator allows passengers to enter their destination floor when calling the elevator using a n-digit keypad installed in each elevator lobby (where n is the number of floors in the building). The specification is based on the description of the Miconic-10 domain in [8], which in turn is based on the HTN formulation in [4]. In the scenario, a single Miconic-N elevator is controlled by the agent. For simplicity, there are no restrictions on the number of people the elevator can carry. The top-level goals are of the form 'move passenger i from floor j to floor k'. A subset of the goals in a problem instance are given to the agent initially and the remaining goals are given over the course of the run. The environment is deterministic, i.e., it changes only when the agent performs an action and actions are guaranteed to succeed if their preconditions are true. The environment is parameterised by the number of floors and the number of possible passengers. The environment state is specified by propositions for each possible position (floor) of the elevator and of each passenger, as well as propositions for each passenger being in the elevator.

Logistics Domain. The Logistics Domain defines a set of simplified logistics problems in which the goals of the agent involve delivering packages from one location to another. The agent controls a vehicle which can carry a limited number of packages at any given time. Locations are arranged in a 'ring' with each location directly connected to two adjacent locations by 'roads'. In addition, there are a number of randomly generated 'chordal roads' connecting non-adjacent locations. The chordal roads effectively provide a set of 'shortcuts' that may or may not be available at a particular point in a run. The top-level goals are of the form 'transport package i to location j'. A subset of the goals in the evaluation set are given to the agent initially and the remaining goals are given over the course of the run. The environment is non-deterministic. To reflect traffic jams, road closures etc., the chordal roads may or may not be traversable at any given point in a run (controlled by the environment simulator), while the ring is always traversable (so packages can always be delivered). Actions are guaranteed to succeed if their preconditions are true. The environment is parameterised by the number of locations and the number of possible packages. The environment state is specified by propositions for each possible location of the vehicle and of each package, as well as propositions for each package being in the vehicle and the number of packages currently carried.

3   Software Architecture

The IPC software stack consists of three components and is shown in Fig. 1. The Environment Simulator represents the agent's environment. The BDI Interface represents a BDI agent that receives goals and percepts from the environment and returns actions to achieve the goals. These two components are provided, and together form the competition framework. The third component, the IPP Solver, is the competition entry, and decides which action should be returned by the agent at the current cycle. The components communicate via sockets, allowing entries to be developed and tested on a single machine, and for the Environment Simulator to be run remotely during the competition itself.

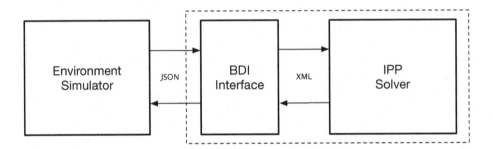

Fig. 1. The IPC software architecture.

3.1   Environment Simulator

Each run of the competition consists of three phases: an initialisation phase, an active phase, and a completed phase. In the *initialisation* phase, the Environment Simulator sends to the BDI interface: the forest of goal-plan trees to be used for the current intention progression problem instance, the initial state of the environment, and the initial set of goals to be achieved. In the *active* phase, the Environment Simulator accepts action requests from the BDI Interface. If the preconditions of the requested action hold in the current environment, the simulator updates the environment state to reflect the postconditions of the action and any exogenous changes representing the actions of other agents etc. If the preconditions of the requested action do not hold in the current environment, the action request is discarded. The (possibly updated) environment state is returned to the BDI Interface, together with any additional goals the agent should achieve. The random seed used to control spontaneous environment changes and goal generation forms part of the problem instance, ensuring that the same updates/new goals occur at the same point in a run for all entries. When all the top-level goals in the problem instance have been achieved or a timeout is reached, the run enters the completed phase. In the *completed* phase, the simulator sends the interface the log of all actions performed during the run, before closing the connection.

The simulator communicates with the BDI Interface via messages in JSON format.

3.2 BDI Interface

The BDI Interface represents a BDI agent that receives goals and percepts from the environment and performs actions to achieve the goals. The BDI Interface handles communication between the Environment Simulator and IPP Solver. At each cycle in the active phase, the IPP Solver sends the interface the action to be performed by the agent at this cycle. The interface forwards the action to the simulator, and returns the simulator's response to the action to the solver. The response contains:

- the state of the environment following execution of the action;
- the current list of goals and which of these have been achieved; and
- session information including the current session state (initialisation, active or completed) and the time remaining

The interface communicates with the IPP Solver via XML messages.

The role of the BDI Interface is to simplify development of solvers and the running of the competition. It translates XML commands to and responses from the simulator into and from JSON format (with some basic syntax checking on the input side) so the solver doesn't have to do this. It also logs the time of each command from the solver and response from the simulator, so that the elapsed time taken by a solver can be computed. (Currently, this is only for information, but future competitions may wish to include elapsed time in scoring.)

3.3 IPP Solver

The IPP Solver is a stand-alone program that decides which of the agent's intentions to progress at this cycle. Following initialisation, the solver enters a cycle of reading the current environment state and goals to be achieved, and choosing an action to perform. The solver must return the next basic action in a plan for one of the current top-level goals. If execution has reached a subgoal in a plan, this involves choosing an appropriate plan for the subgoal and returning the first action of that plan. The solver then returns the selected action to the BDI Interface which forwards it to the Environment Simulator for execution. The cycle repeats until the run enters the completed phase.

Implementing the decision making of the solver is the key challenge of the IPC.

4 The 2020 Intention Progression Competition

We conclude by briefly describing the history and current status of the 2020 Intention Progression Competition.

Following the formation of an international Steering Committee to advise on the rules of the competition and how it should be run, the first edition of the Intention Progression Competition was announced at EMAS 2019. Participants were asked to register at the IPC website.[6] Registrations opened in July/August 2019, and 22 teams registered for the competition. Following registration, participants received access to the entrants' portal on the IPC website containing the competition resources. Each participant was also allocated a dedicated virtual machine for the purposes of testing their entry against the BDI Interface and Environment Simulator. (Entries could be developed and tested on the participant's own computer, but we required that the final code was submitted via the participant's dedicated VM for evaluation on the unseen benchmark IPP problems.) The final version of the competition platform including the competition website, resources and software were released in September 2019. Work continued on calibrating the test and unseen evaluation problems in late 2019, and a revised set of test problem instances was released in January 2020. Final entries were due in late March/April 2020, with winners to be announced at EMAS/AAMAS 2020 in Auckland, New Zealand.

In mid March, it became clear that many teams would be unable to participate due to the Covid-19 pandemic, and on the 21st of March we took the difficult decision to postpone the competition. The first Intention Progression Competition will now be held at a later date. If circumstances allow, our provisional target is EMAS/AAMAS 2021.

We would like to thank all the teams who registered for IPC 2020 for their support, and we hope that they will be able to participate when the competition takes place in future.

References

1. Clement, B.J., Durfee, E.H.: Theory for coordinating concurrent hierarchical planning agents using summary information. In: Hendler, J., Subramanian, D. (eds.) Proceedings of the Sixteenth National Conference on Artificial Intelligence and Eleventh Conference on Innovative Applications of Artificial Intelligence, 18–22 July 1999, Orlando, Florida, USA, pp. 495–502. AAAI Press/The MIT Press (1999)
2. Clement, B.J., Durfee, E.H., Barrett, A.C.: Abstract reasoning for planning and coordination. J. Artif. Intell. Res. **28**, 453–515 (2007). https://doi.org/10.1613/jair.2158
3. Ghallab, M., Nau, D., Traverso, P.: Automated Planning and Acting. Cambridge University Press, New York (2016)
4. Koehler, J., Schuster, K.: Elevator control as a planning problem. In: Chien, S., Kambhampati, S., Knoblock, C.A. (eds.) Proceedings of the Fifth International Conference on Artificial Intelligence Planning Systems, Breckenridge, CO, USA, pp. 331–338. AAAI, April 2000

---

[6] Registrations for the first IPC are still open at www.intentionprogression.org.

5. Logan, B., Thangarajah, J., Yorke-Smith, N.: Progressing intention progresson: A call for a goal-plan tree contest. In: Das, S., Durfee, E., Larson, K., Winikoff, M. (eds.) Proceedings of the 16th International Conference on Autonomous Agents and Multiagent Systems (AAMAS 2017), Sao Paulo, Brazil, pp. 768–772. IFAAMAS, May 2017)

6. de Silva, L.: HTN acting: a formalism and an algorithm. In: André, E., Koenig, S., Dastani, M., Sukthankar, G. (eds.) Proceedings of the 17th International Conference on Autonomous Agents and MultiAgent Systems, AAMAS 2018, Stockholm, Sweden, Richland, SC, USA,10–15 July 2018, pp. 363–371. International Foundation for Autonomous Agents and Multiagent Systems/ACM (2018). http://dl.acm.org/citation.cfm?id=3237441

7. Thangarajah, J., Padgham, L., Winikoff, M.: Detecting and avoiding interference between goals in intelligent agents. In: Proceedings of IJCAI 2003, pp. 721–726 (2003)

8. Yao, Y., Logan, B.: Action-level intention selection for BDI agents. In: Thangarajah, J., Tuyls, K., Jonker, C., Marsella, S. (eds.) Proceedings of the 15th International Conference on Autonomous Agents and Multiagent Systems (AAMAS 2016), Singapore, pp. 1227–1235. IFAAMAS, May 2016

Author Index

Ahlbrecht, Tobias   129

Baldoni, Matteo   61
Baroglio, Cristina   61
Boissier, Olivier   42
Bordini, Rafael H.   42

Castle-Green, Simon   144
Chatzopoulos, Dimitris   100
Chopra, Amit K.   78
Christie V, Samuel H.   78
Collenette, Joe   87
Collier, Rem W.   1
Croatti, Angelo   42

Dastani, Mehdi   21
Dewfall, Alexi   144
Dignum, Frank   21
Dix, Jürgen   129

Faltings, Boi   100
Fiekas, Niklas   129

Gujar, Sujit   100

Hübner, Jomi F.   42
Hui, Pan   100

Itoh, Masanori   119

Kifetew, Fitsum   21
Koreishi, Jun   119
Krausburg, Tabajara   129

Lefebvre, Sylvain   119
Lillis, David   1
Logan, Brian   87, 144

Micalizio, Roberto   61
Moti, Moin Hussain   100

Neyama, Ryo   119

O'Hare, Gregory M. P.   1
O'Neill, Eoin   1
Okuyama, Hiroko   119

Prada, Rui   21
Prasetya, I. S. W. B.   21

Ricci, Alessandro   42

Tanaka, Masahiro   119

Vos, Tanja E. J.   21

Yazawa, Yuji   119
Yokoyama, Akihisa   119
Yoshioka, Akira   119

Printed in the United States
By Bookmasters